Correct English Usage

Correct English Usage

P.N. Parashar

Commonwealth

Correct English Usage

Edition : 2024

ISBN 81-7169-739-9

Published by :

COMMONWEALTH PUBLISHERS
4831/24, Prahlad Street,
Ansari Road, Darya Ganj,
New Delhi - 110002
Ph. : 23275511, 23257835
e-mail : campusbooks@hotmail.com

Typesetting by :

Arnav Computers
Delhi - 110051

Printed at :
Efficient Offset Printers
New Delhi

PREFACE

English has become an international language by now. Even in the English speaking world, there are many types of speaking English language. American English has adopted many spelling deviations from the British English and has its own character. But the Indian English is very close to British English in pronounciation spelling grammar and accent. The new Indian English literature has many similarities with the British literature.

In Indian Universities, Colleges, Schools and in the army and governmental organisations, the standard English is mainly on the British pattern. This book has preferred on the British lines.

We are grateful to the Indian Institute of foreign languages, Hyderabad, the British Council in India and the Ministry of Human Resource Development, Government of India for the research work done in the area of English Teaching, which has been very helpful in preparing this book. The author is grateful to Shri Ajay, Verma the dynamic publisher for bringing out this type of book for Indian students, teachers and the general public.

Author

Contents

1

Basic Principles

Experience is the best of all schools. Certainly no one learns so thoroughly, and few learn so rapidly, in any other. And experience need not be a dear school, if it is competently organised and is conducted by a capable teacher who illuminates each situation in prospect and in retrospect. School and college curriculums should consist of experiences. The school of experience is the only one, which will develop the flexibility and power of self-direction requisite for successful living in our age of swift industrial, social, and economic change. To inculcate authoritarian beliefs, fixed rules of conduct, unreasoned and therefore stubborn attitudes, is to set our youth in futile and fatal conflict with the forces of modern life. By meeting situations, modifying conditions and adapting themselves to the unchangeable, our boys and girls will learn to live in a dynamic and evolving world. Today, more, than ever, the curriculum should consist of experiences.

The ideal curriculum consists of well-selected experiences - The first step in constructing it is to survey life, noting what experiences most people have and what desirable possible experiences they miss. From this display the curriculum builder must select typical examples, distributed as well as possible throughout its entire range.

It is true some kinds of experiences cannot well be imported into the school - marriage, for example, and such experiences as grief, wrong-doing, and the suffering of injustice which we would eliminate if we could from life as well as from the school. Such experiences, which for one reason or another our young people cannot or should not have in actuality but which they must be prepared to have later, we should offer indirectly through literature.

The programme just presented constitutes, of course, the entire school curriculum, in which each department participates when and as it can. The place of English in this programme is obvious : to provide the communication (speaking, writing, listening, and reading) necessary to the conduct of social activities, and to provide indirect (vicarious) experiences where direct experiences are impossible or undesirable. Perhaps no other subject gains so much as does English from the integration of the school with everyday life.

In schools, which have not yet adopted an integrated experience curriculum, the course of study in English must consist of more limited, though still genuine, experiences. (Because in most schools each subject is studied in practically complete isolation from the others, this pattern curriculum in English is designed to suit that condition. It will also fit, without major change, into an "activity" programme).

An effective programme in school English must make provision for carrying the literary and linguistic activities beyond the confines of the English classroom.

1. Since the quality of the reading and of the speaking and writing determine, to some extent, the pupils, progress in other subjects improvement of the English arts must be sought in all the studies and activities throughout the school day.

In the elementary school this is not difficult, since generally the teacher has the same children most of the day and can readily correlate the reading and language activities with the work of the other subjects. A reasonable general plan for this is : first, to concentrate in the English period on the opening up of new ideas about language, discussion of principles and technical details, and practice for skills; and second, in the other subjects to apply and illustrate.

In the secondary school the problem of correlation is more difficult. Perhaps the most useful concept is to regard efficiency in the English arts not as an English department objective but as an institutional objective. All the teachers of all the subjects should be, to some extent, teachers of English, Science teachers who require students to keep notebooks, history teachers who expect "outside" reading and oral and written reports, mathematics teachers who depend upon pupils' reciting and demonstrating; all teachers who cause pupils to employ reading and language, must assume some responsibility for the quality of the reading and the language.

But it is unwise for the English department to attempt to force upon the other departments any plan of cooperation, no matter how well formulated. The principal of the school, together with the representatives of all the departments and probably with the English teachers carrying the major burden of the work and responsibility, must devise and guide a programme of correlation and cooperation. Such a plan is in use in many schools of the United States; it is quite indispensable in a successful high-school English programme.

2. Most of the formal and informal groupings and activities in the co-curricular life of the school necessitate the use of many types of language and reading. The parties and "social" affairs, the clubs and organizations (and not merely the specifically "English Clubs"), the school and class enterprises, the assembly programmes, the school paper and magazine, the library and reading room - all the rich, varied life characteristics of the modern American school - place the children in situations wherein language and reading must be employed and wherein their effective employment is socially motivated and socially rewarded.

The teacher of English can ask for observations and for class discussions of the language activities in these out-of-class situations and she can gradually educate her pupils to regard their English activities in these situations as illustration, demonstration, and extension of the work of the English class. She can also utilise the class as a tryout situation, where the pupils may present, for example, readings or speeches they are to make on some school programme, or "stories" they are writing for the school paper, and may profit by class discussion and criticism. A resourceful English teacher will find and utilise many such opportunities for trying the work of her class with the language and reading situations throughout the co-curricular life of the school.

3. The pupils of the elementary and high school are also frequently engaged in personal and community enterprises which

involve them in language situations. If the English teacher can contrive means of "following" them out into these situations and connecting up the school work in English with the actual scenes in which English is employed, she will widen her classroom to community dimensions. This can be done in much the same way as is indicated above. The pupils can be led to take note of their own and others' uses of language and to report successful and unsuccessful examples. Pupils who are, for example, on a Young People's Society programme in their church or at a Father and Son banquet may try out and improve their talk or their reading in the English class.

The programme of experiences must be well balanced—Accordingly this pattern curriculum presents each major field of English sub-divided into "experience strands" and asks each teacher to lead his class each year through at least one unit in each strand.

Since the principal, objective of creating expression in school is the individual pupil's joyous realisation of the values of his own experiences, *creative expression* is put on the same footing as communication or literature, as a *major phase of every pupil's work* every year.

In daily living, *techniques are essential* - as instruments; consequently, in school life techniques should receive adequate attention - as instruments. Some study of principles and even practice exercises are needed, but such academic procedures must be kept in their proper place as accessories to the life experiences. (In simpler societies, where children might participate in the serious employments of their elders, it was perhaps sufficient for the school to give formal training, because out-of-school experiences supplied both motive for and application of school subject-matter. That day has long since passed, and in too many instances neither motive for nor application of school "study" or "drill" remains. The school of today and tomorrow seeks to bring outside activities within its walls and to step out with its students to participate in many community activities. In connection with these activities it finds the best occasions for teaching the information, ideas, and skills which obsess the old-fashioned pedagogue).

These technical and factual matters are incorporated in the units as *enabling* objectives. They are not to be left to chance, nor are they to be taught separately as valuable in themselves. They should be incidental, but not accidental.

Moreover, *techniques are to be cumulative.* A skill or fact learned in one unit of a strand is to be employed whenever it applies in all subsequent units of that strand. Techniques of general application are collected at the end of each strand, with the suggestion that by the time the strand is completed they should have become habitual.

The term subject-matter, as traditionally used, is here avoided, though the three paragraphs just preceding this provide most adequately for the reality which that term represents. Subject - matter is merely the collected and organised, too frequently also desicated, solutions to problems which the race has met and mastered. This social heritage is priceless, but preoccupation with its transmission makes the teacher a formalist and drillmaster, and by inhibiting or distorting the normal development of the pupils develops a static or retrograde civilisation. Pupil's use of subject - matter to solve their own problems is at once the most economical way for them to assimilate it and the indispensable condition of developing their own capacities.

The programme of experiences must be orderly - In order that the pupil may gain the confidence and the clarity of mind that come from success, his experiences must be arranged in a carefully graded order of social and intellectual difficulty. No experience unit should require too many new techniques, or any technique, which is beyond the maturity of the pupils. The various committees have graded the units in this pattern curriculum very carefully, but local circumstances may call for a changed order.

Because of the great variation in ability of different classes even within a single school, specific units cannot wisely be allocated to definite grades. The samples of a year's work are not intended to suggest that the supervisor should prescribe such a collection of units for any year. The teacher and pupils must remain free to proceed as rapidly or as slowly as their situation and ability may require.

Experiences must be adopted to the needs and capacities of individual learners - The classification of pupils according to their abilities or achievements - not necessarily according to intelligence quotients, and certainly without any labelling of sections at "fast" or "slow", "bright" or "dull" - is highly desirable as a partial solution of the problem of adaptation. Strong classes may move more rapidly through the curriculum, and may engage in some of the "optional experiences" listed; weak classes may repeat or prolong certain experiences which are particularly important. And even where grouping is not intentionally practiced, classes differ widely in breadth and speed of learning. Accordingly, definite allocation of units to specific grades is abandoned and the teacher is directed to take each class where she finds it in each strand and to proceed with it as far as time and ability permit.

Adaptation, however, includes other elements besides acceleration and retardation. In each unit there appear opportunities for leadership, for reaching out into other subject-matter and other activities; and for some pupils there is need to simpler materials to use in experience of the same general nature. The curriculum, besides discussing this problem in general, should offer in every expanded unit suggestions both for enrichment and simplification. The adaptation sections or columns of the expanded units in this document illustrate this principle.

Measurement of the growth resulting from the experiences in the curriculum is desirable. Occasionally such measurement may be helpful in determining whether an individual should go with his class on to new experiences or should report those he has just had. Chiefly, however, these measures are needed to help the teacher evaluate his own procedures and the curriculum maker his choice of experiences. Incidentally, until satisfactory measures are devised and applied, the standing dispute between the advocates of the experience curriculum and the traditionalists who cling to formal subject matter and methods of instruction cannot be conclusively decided. Such measures must cover something more than progress in the mechanics of compositions and the incidents in and facts about literature; they must measure composition power, social spirit and poise, perception of beauty, and habitual choice of worthy literature. The use of such dynamic, if vague, tests of growth as are included at the bottom of each expanded unit in this pattern curriculum is preferable to entire dependence upon standard tests in mechanics of composition, reading, and literary knowledge.

A curriculum in English is necessarily multifarious in content and complex in statement. Imperfections in its construction are inevitable and confusions in its interpretation are to be expected. The guiding idea for both builder and user is the conception of the curriculum as body of *guided experiences parallelling present and future out-of-school experiences.* Everything in these outlines is to be read in the light of that conception. Everything in the classroom should be done in the light of the same conception.

Reference

1. In the proverb about experience as a dear school, the word *experience* evidently refers to *meeting real situations*, with all that may be involved. The proverb assumes that the experience includes a more or less free decision, action, and taking consequences. It implies that the natural consequences of an act, when they are recognised as such, will cause learning. *To learn* obviously means *to modify* one's *future behaviour*, in psychological parlance, to acquire changed tendencies to act. The words *experience* and *learn* are used much in this report, always with the these proverbial, everyday meanings.

2

Integration

The term's *correlation* and *integration* are used loosely to cover all sorts of attempts to establish connections between the various subjects of school and college study. More strictly, correlation, fusion, and integration form a series of progressive intensity.

Correlation may be so slight as casual attention to related materials in other subjects, for example, noting while reading the spirited, polished, superficial verse of the Cavalier Poets the ideals and social graces of the cavalier as studied in history. Correlation becomes a bit more intense when it is planned in advance to make the materials of one subject interpret the problems or topics of another.

Fusion designates the combination of two subjects, usually under the same instructor or instructors; supposedly the partners are equal, but usually one dominates and uses the other. One of the most common fusions is the blending of literature and history, the history, which has the more definite outline, usually dominating. Fusion may extend to the combination of a whole group of subjects, for example, literature, music, dancing, architecture, plastic arts, and graphic arts. Such courses are organised by common principles, common themes, or other common elements of the subjects included.

Integration is the unification of all study (and other experience). It comes about, for the most part, not through conscious combining of different subjects or activities but through the initiation of vital activities which reach out into various fields and absorb subject content as the roots of a tree absorb food from the soil - without regard to fences on the surface. Complete integration has not yet been achieved anywhere, and may not be desirable. The closest approaches to complete integration are some of the progressive-school units in which such a purpose as the provision of milk and other needs for the children of an indigent family dominates the work of a group for weeks, subject-matter divisions being ignored and any material used whenever it serves the group purpose.

The value of any attempt at correlation seems to vary directly in proportion to (1) its naturalness, (2) its intensity, (3) its range, and (4) the breadth and soundness of the teacher's culture. The teacher's culture is perhaps the most essential of these four factors because the others are largely dependent upon it. For the rest, it is axiomatic that such natural connections as that between Puritan traditions and the punishment of Hester Prynne are both more fruitful and more lasting than such far fetched associations as that of the details of duck's foot with "The Ugly Duckling". It should be self-evident that the more numerous the connections which are established between subjects the better, and also that the greater the number of subjects connected the more the correlation will contribute to a perception of the general pattern and significance of life. Probably all *sound* correlation's, discoveries of *live* connections, are worth all they cost.

Nevertheless, most correlation and fusion programmes are only weak palliatives of the disease, which they set out to cure. That disease is a mild form of dissociated personality, producing at one extreme the absent-minded professor of the cartoons and at the other the self-praised "practical" man of fixed ideas and narrow sympathies. The cause of the malady is the artificial separation of one subject from another, and even more potently, the divorce of all school study and drill from dynamic experience. Educator say that the purpose of all education is to prepare pupils for successful future living by rich present living - and then, too often, proceed to offer them *only intellectual* activity, chiefly *re*-thinking of other men's thoughts.

Truly rich living, any *real* living, includes much more than such purely intellectual activity or (and) the practice of technical skills. Normal living is a composite of dynamic experiences in which the will, the feelings, memory, and reason are all exercised as a single organism. Such typical life experiences as running an errand for mother, organising a baseball team, giving a party, producing a play, conducting an election campaign or a community drive, all have other elements quite as prominent as the intellectual. It is chiefly of such materials that the warp of life is composed. Unaccompanied by the woof of intellectual activities such as fact learning, reflection, and acquisition of needed skills, these activities may remain separate strings, lacking the beauty and greater usefulness, which a well-woven fabric might have. So there is need for school! On the other hand the academic exercises in spelling, using effective detail in narrative, noting the effect of the similes in *Sohrab and Rustum* are, if not interwoven with these emotional, volitional threads of life, just so much woof without any warp, sure to fall to pieces the moment our grasp is relaxed. *The school must manage a functional combination of the dynamic experiences of active life and the intellectual activities, which have been teacher's chief concern.*

Some experimental schools attempts to unite dynamic experience and academic study by bringing the dynamic experiences into school and then adding directly to them such study of facts, such reflective consideration, such mastery of techniques as will (1) make them proceed more smoothly' and (2) reveal their inner nature and their place in the general scheme of the universe. This programme requires within the school a miniature world of work and play which shall include all the essentially different common types of experience. It offers *as the activities proceed* facts and skills useful in carrying them on, and whenever opportunity appears stimulates the pupils to reflect upon the values of their activities and the relation of these activities to others. For example, in the conduct of the school store, there may be offered information about salesmanship, exercises for the development of distinct or pleasing speech, stimulation to consider the service stores render to society. The advantage of this programme is that it brings the whole composite of willing, thinking, and feeling directly under school control, and thus makes proportion and organisation possible. Serious disadvantages of this programme are the waste of resources and precious time in duplicating experiences already obtained outside the school; the impossibility of transplanting some kinds of experience into the school room; our lack of knowledge as to which experiences should be brought into the school; and the inability of most teachers to organise and administer such units.

A contrasting programme relies upon extra-school hours for the dynamic experiences and tries to offer, as opportunely as possible. Information, technical procedures, and stimulation to reflection. Under this programme, the relation of school to life outside is not exactly that of an experimental laboratory to a factory, nor exactly that of a workshop to a theatre, nor exactly that of a recreational center to a big industrial plant; but it has something of all these and of additional service relationships. The first snag this plan strikes is the fact that out of school the pupils frequently do not have the same experience at the same times, if at all, and that consequently the school work must be more completely individualised than our present teaching techniques make possible. For example, all the pupils may have to carry messages from their mothers to neighbours, sooner or later, but not on the same day so that schoolwork can be connected with it. All must at some time begin to use the telephone, but this experience may be years earlier for some than for others. The second difficulty is similar namely, that in some underprivileged communities the extra-school experiences are so stunted and warped that even if saturated with academic activities they would still furnish a very inadequate education. There is, moreover, very great danger that the teacher may begin to examine out-of-school work and play to find possible motivations for the subject-matter he has already planned to teach, instead of considering what so-called subject-matter is needed to facilitate and interpret the work and play.

The basic aim or principle of the two programmes is identical; to use the *intellectual activities* to *facilitate* and *interpret dynamic experience*. Since it is only in devices that they differ, there need be no hesitation in adopting an eclectic policy and using both so far as they will serve.

Because of its economy and because of the greater certainty of vitality in it, the programme of using the pupil's extra-school experiences should be followed so far as pupils have the same of similar experiences at the same time and so far as these common experiences are of sufficient variety.

Experiences which can be guided and illuminated satisfactorily only if all the pupils have then simultaneously must be provided by the school, and so must those essential experiences normal to the pupil's capacity but not brought about by their environment. A constantly growing proportion of American schools are persistently experimenting and advancing in this direction.

A school programme *centering upon pupil's dynamic experiences* of work and play, of joy and sorrow, will put an end to the dissociation of the practical from the theoretical elements of personality and prevent the splitting up of intellectual life into mutually repellent fragments. It will provide the opportunity to see (and live) life as a whole.

3

Selecting and Providing Literature Experiences

The literature curriculum should consist of experiences with and through stories, poems, plays, essays, and books of information or discussion addressed to the general reader.

Usual extra-school experiences *with* literature include choosing what to read, actual reading, and voluntary discussion of what has been read. Experience *through* literature are imagining the sights, sounds, and social situations, which the author has described, and feeling the emotions which accompany them. If these are the literature activities in which our pupils are and will be engaged, our duty is to help them to do these as well as possible. And doubtless our best procedure is to let them have these experiences now under such guidance as will lead to the best performance.

Experiences *Through* Literature

The experiences through literature are the ultimate objective. The author's sensory and social experiences, his imaginings, and his feelings are what he has tried to put into his writing, and they are what the reader wishes to get. To A.E. Housman the sight of cherry trees in bloom (and the feelings aroused) seemed worth sharing with us, and he put them into "Loveliest of Trees". Robert Louis Stevenson's reflections upon funeral customs and common attitudes toward death seemed to him to have intrinsic value, and he gave them to us in "Aes Triplex". Tennyson's daydreams of Arthur and his knights, suffused with an ethical glow entirely foreign to the original stories of the pagan king, he poured into the *Idylls* for us to dream again at our pleasure. The intrinsic worth of such experiences is the only valid reason for the reading of literature.

The number and variety of experiences thus embodied are limitless. Which shall we choose for our literature curriculum?

Present Value to Pupils - First, the pupil should be given experiences that have intrinsic worth for *him, now.* No matter how much the story may thrill us sophisticated adults who make and teach the courses, no matter how much the play may inspire us or the poem charm us, if it is beyond the intellectual and emotional range of the our pupils, we are worse than wasting time to attempt to impose it upon them. To take an extreme example, Shelley's "Serenade" would be wholly out of place in a fifth grade, not because the words are strange or the sentences difficult, but because the pupils *cannot enter into the experience* the poem offers. Very few of us would ever be guilty of such an egregious misplacement, but in less obvious cases we frequently make mistakes and then insist upon continuing them because the oration is so enlightening, the verse so beautiful, the character in the story so interesting - to us. To argue that even though the pupils do not like it it is good for them is to lose sight of the fact that their lack of pleasure is conclusive evidence of their failure to get the experience adequately.

More studies of the suitability of our usual literature prescriptions are needed and more accurate methods of investigation than the customary informal questionnaire. Moreover, many selections now used with doubtful success need to be tried at different grade levels. For example, the charming but generally disliked "Ancient Mariner" should be tried both below and above its present locus in the junior high school, where fantasy is relatively unpopular. And many works not now extensively used in school deserve a trial. The titles listed in the outlines, which follow, have been selected chiefly on the basis of the personal observation of members of the literature committees and checked against the meagre objective studies available.

To repeat, the pupil should be given experiences that have intrinsic value for *him, now.* But not all pupils in a class, or all classes even of the same grade in the same school, are ready for the same experiences. The course in literature, perhaps more than any other, must be flexible so that the teacher may choose material to suit the personalities and the social situation in each class. Types of experience rather than specific titles should furnish the outline of the curriculum. Much of the classwork as well as the "home" reading in literature must be entirely individual, each pupil reading material of his own choice from a wide range of offerings.

One word of caution : the limitation of offerings in the literature curriculum to those selections which pupils enjoy must not be allowed to exclude those works whose worth pupils realise *after reading them* under the guidance of their (competent) teachers. To allow the aversion caused by someone's dispraise of a book to shut off a child or a class from an important indirect experience which might easily be theirs is clearly foolish. To yield supinely to child *whim*, however aroused, is cowardice. Only when repeated skillful presentations have failed to bring appreciation should we discard a selection, which it seems to, us ought to be valuable for children. Thus, though Burke's *Conciliation* seems to have definitely failed in most classrooms. *Alice in Wonderland* has succeeded too often to be abandoned just because some boys think they will not like a book about a girl. Unless local circumstances or the teacher's inability to handle the particular selection interfere, pupils should have an opportunity to become acquainted with Alice. In the individualized parts of the classwork and in home reading it is usually best not to attempt to override child whim but to seek some way around it.

Fortunately, it is possible to keep within the bounds of pupil capacity and taste and yet to have an abundance of material available. There is still opportunity, even necessity, for us to select and organise into a programme these experiences through literature. What shall the selective and organising principles be ?

Undesirable Elements - First, whatever is harmful to the child or youth must be excluded : the false and such horror and sex experiences as the immature cannot sustain without shock and warping of their natures. The false includes sentimentality, glamorous presentation of evildoing, inconsistent characterisation, misrepresentation of moral causes and effects, and contravention of natural laws unless these are, as in fairy stories, tacitly suspended. The horrible, practically always fantastic, apparently affects children with steady nerves very little, but in every group there are a few hypersensitive who really suffer and are damaged. Since most of the horror stories seem to have little value beyond excitement, they may well be omitted. In matters of sex the literature class need not be prudish; such works as "Guinevere" and *The Scarlet Letter* no longer embarrass high school pupils. On the other hand, Galsworthy wisely remarked that presentation of the physical side of sex is inartistic because it always results in overemphasis. Few teachers are in danger of offering their pupils reading matter that is dangerous on this score.

Wide Variety - Secondly, the variety and range of experiences *through* literature should be as wide as possible. The easy physical conditions of modern life, the great emotional strain of it, and the new psychology have led to a revival of the old ideal of a rounded development of personality. Since the value of literature, beyond the immediate one of pleasure, is in the enlargement of the individual by means of indirect experience, the more directions the enlargement takes the more valuable the literature will prove.

The corollary of this second principle is that the inculcation of knowledge or of ethical ideals, the posing of social problems, the cultivation of the power to perceive beauty, or the mere provision of an escape from trying actuality are, all of them, too narrow objectives. Good literature performs each of these services, at times; each of these values is uppermost in some selection. But an *adequate* literature programme must be designed to produce *all* of these results, and others, in just proportion. Most good literature produces more than one of these effects at the same time. The literature committees therefore prefer not to adopt any of these objectives singly even for a year or a semester; they fear the narrowing of the vicarious experience through any approach for a specific purpose, especially through search for a specific value which the author did not feel as dominant in his original experience. The strands and units of which they have built their course are based rather on varieties of experience than upon effects the experiences are to produce. If vividly and thoughtfully lived, these experiences will produce the maximum of total enrichment, intellectual, esthetic, and moral.

Experiences *with* Literature

But experiences *through* literature presuppose experiences *with* literature. Indeed, it is the latter with which the teacher, after the literature has been selected, is chiefly concerned, because it is the experiences *with* literature which are subject to direct manipulation.

Freedom to Choose - An experience which our pupils should have very frequently is choosing for themselves what they will read. Prescription must be lessened or loosened in classroom reading and practically abolished in outside or "home" reading. For the graduate never to have read a sentimental, improbable, or badly written book is a misfortune. We should let the boys and girls make choices between good and poor books while we are still at hand to help them establish standards. This choice of reading material includes, at its best, finding materials to read, accumulating a list of "liked" authors, consulting classified book lists prepared by experts, and perusing such critical magazines as the *Saturday Review of Literature*.

Freedom in choosing what to read should be accompanied by freedom to choose whether to read or not, for the reading habit cannot be economically developed through compulsion. The school does best not to require any particular amount of leisure reading but to so surround the pupils with reading stimulation's and opportunities that they will become accustomed to occupying free time with books and magazines, perhaps even to "making" time for following up their reading interests. There is abundant evidence that pupils will read more, now and hereafter, under stimulation and guidance than under specific requirements.

Both Individual and Group Reading - Unquestionably, silent reading of material adapted as well as possible to the individual reader should be the commonest experience with literature. Much of this must be, pending the development of new teaching techniques, a group activity, in order that the teacher may economically provide the needed coaching : anticipatory suggestions of ways of getting the most out of a given selection, stimulation and assistance in using the dictionary and other necessary references, and guidance in reflection after the reading is completed. Moreover, the compulsion to read certain selection or books exposes many young people to kinds of literature that they could probably never be brought to sample voluntarily but which they like when they have experienced the flavour. A large part of the class reading, however, may be quite individual, with choice limited only by the supply of books available and the individual's knowledge of where to find what he wants.

Limited Discussion - Discussion normally follows the reading of most pieces of literature. If, however, discussion is too much prolonged or is a spiritless question-and-answer rehearsal of the "fact" just read, it may be positively harmful. So conducted, it casts a pall over the literature itself and makes book talk seem so pedantic an activity that all normal young people wish to shun it. Most young people need not understand all the words and allusions or see *all* the detailed beauties which make so many works jewelled cloths of gold to the teacher, and the attempt to make them do so is practically certain to dull their sense of proportion and kill their pleasure. Nor need the teacher hesitate to offer a simple explanation of a difficulty or to point out directly a bit of artistry. Commonsense and courage curtail discussion and allow pupils to use for further reading the time thus saved. Incidentally such cessation of group activity makes possible conference with individuals who need stimulation or guidance.

As does ordinary social discussion of literature among cultivated adults, classroom talk should centre upon main events and impression, upon the larger aspects of character and upon the theme if there is any. It may touch briefly upon some matter of literary artistry, but should rarely tarry long upon such a subject; brief comment accompanied by citation or oral reading is the most common, because the most satisfactory, treatment of esthetic elements. The class should be a rather informal literary club in which the teacher is simply the most experienced member.

Oral Reading - Reading aloud is an experience with literature no longer very common outside the schoolroom. Important when books were scare, it is now employed chiefly for the enjoyment of poetry and tidbits of narrative. No literary club, much less a family circle, would think of listening to a relay reading of a work which the members had just finished reading silently. The use of oral reading in the literature class should be confined to (1) citation and (2) prepared reading of passages or works notable for melody or dramatic quality.

Literary Types - Experiences *with* literature vary also with the form of the selections read - short story, novel, drama, narrative poetry, lyric poetry, and essay. Each of these forms presents difficulties, which the reader must learn to surmount, and therefore the curriculum must provide experiences with all of them. Fortunately there are some content units which are naturally composed almost entirely of single literary types. By taking advantage of these and artificially creating a few additional such formally homogenous units it is possible to introduce the mastery of the peculiar difficulties of each form as techniques or enabling objectives. This plan is recommended and is illustrated in this pattern curriculum.

Special Units

The general rule that the strands of this outline are based upon content, that is, experiences *through* literature, has two apparent exceptions.

Systemaic Studies - First, there are included some special units - "Getting Acquainted with a Literary Type" in the tenth grade, "Getting Acquainted with an Author" in the eleventh grade, and "Getting Acquainted with the Literature of a Period" in the twelfth—which are quite long and held together by other characteristics than similarity of content. These approaches to literature are firmly established in colleges, and to prevent too sharp a break between the work of secondary schools and higher institution it seems desirable to introduce these large units anticipatory of college methods.

Discussion of Photoplays and Radio Programmes - The second and more important exception to the content organisation is the presentation of strands of radio and photoplay units. The fact that these experiences do not come through books has too long prevented recognition of the fact that they are essentially literary and caused schools to neglect them. Partly to make sure that they receive adequate attention, and partly because of the extreme differences in the nature of the experiences *with* literature that they offer they have been given separate treatment.

Procedures with these new materials are still entirely experimental and tentative. Some suggestions appear in the units themselves. The most important principle for the teacher to keep in mind is that the objective is to bring the pupils to *like batter* photoplays and broadcasts and not merely to enable them to predict with accuracy which ones the teacher will approve. To this emotional approval they must be *led*; they cannot be driven or jerked to it. Leading is to be accomplished through the stimulation and guidance of honest, frank discussion by the pupils, with a minimum of expression of teacher opinion, and that never dogmatic or didactic. The teacher must not be discouraged if native incapacity, bad social and esthetic backgrounds and the low level of commercial offerings prevent full and immediate success of the attempt to cultivate the taste of the mass of young people. Like the fight for health, the struggle for culture must be systematic and persistent.

4

Literature Experiences, Kindergarten - Grades 6

A. Enjoying Action and Suspense

1. Primary Objective : To enjoy nursery tales in which suspense is the chief attraction told or read by the teacher.

   Enabling Objectives : To maintain attention to the end of the story. To imagine clearly the overhanging danger, without too far forgetting that it is only make-believe. To understand clearly the escape or the capture. To enjoy the parallel incidents.

   Typical Materials : "Peter Rabbit", "The Little Red Hen and the Fox", "The Gingerbread Man", "Little Red Riding-Hood", "The Wolf and the Seven Kids", "The Billy-Goats Gruff", "The Three Little Pigs", "The Three Bears".

2. *Primary Objective* : To hear with enjoyment adventures composed of too many incidents or of incidents too intricate for the youngest school children.

   Enabling Objectives : To hold the incidents of the plot in mind to the end of the story. To appreciate the "sympathetic" central characters. To see what produces the happy outcome.

   Typical Materials : "Snow-White and the Seven Dwarfs", "Snow-White and Rose-Red", "Scrapefoot", "The Alligator and the Jackal", "The Little Gray Pony" (Lindsay), "Fulfilled", "The Fisherman and the Genie", "The Fisherman and His Wife", "Raggylug" (Seton), "The Jackal and the Camel", "The Monkey and the

Crocodile", "The Lad Who Went to the North Wind", "Jack and Giant-Killer", "Jack and the Beanstalk."

3. *Primary Objective* : To live through the trials and ultimate triumph of the youngest child and other similarly unfortunate characters.

   Enabling Objectives : To read the stories in easy versions for oneself. To see the Cinderella motif so often present. To learn to expect three incidents.

   Typical Materials : "Cinderella", "Boots and His Brothers", "The Princess on the Glass Hill", "Cap o' Rushes" (Rushie Coat, King Thrusbeard, Katie Woodencloak, Allerleirah), "Puss in Boots", "The Golden [Black] Bird", "Beauty and the Beast", "The Twelve Months", "Hansel and Gretel", "Nix Naught Nothing".

4. *Primary Objective* : To enjoy simple stories of physical adventure in familiar or primitive settings.

   Enabling Objectives : To imagine the scenes vividly enough to feel the muscle and skin sensations of the heroes or heroines. To follow the chain of incidents, now somewhat longer than in Unit 4.

   Typical Materials : Three Little Ojibways (March), Runaway Papoose (Moore), Sinopah, the Indian Boy (Schultz), Red Ben (Lippincott), The Secret Cave (Everson), "The Big Bear" (Major), Floating Island (Parish), Toby Tyler (Kahler), Robin Hood (Tappan).

5. *Primary Objective* : To enjoy stories of lively action in far countries.

   Enabling Objectives : To read description with more care than in ordinary stories. To enjoy the "differentness" of the background. To see, in some measure, how the surroundings affect characters and their actions.

   Typical Materials : Kari, the Elephant and Gay Neck (Mukerji), The Jungle Book and the Second Jungle Book (Kipling), Wild Life Under the Equator (Du Chaillu), David Goes Voyaging (Putnam), The Adventures of Billy Topsail (Duncan), A Boy Scout with Byrd (Siple), Juan and Juanita (Baylor), Swiss Family Robinson (Wyss), The Willow Whistle (Meigs).

6. *Primary Objective* : To enjoy action stories laid in earlier times, usually with historical intention.

   Enabling Objectives : To build up, as rapidly as the author makes possible, the appropriate atmosphere. To see people and actions as through the eyes of their contemporaries, with their more limited knowledge and their different ethical and social standards. To judge a story, *after* reading, for its consistency and probable truth to the time it represents. To realize that the standards of the past do not apply to our affairs.

   Typical Materials : Theras and His Town (Snedeker), Two Children of Tyre (Kent), Otto of the Silver Hand, Merry Adventures of Robin Hood (Pyle), The Story of Rolf, The Viking's Bow (French), The Treasure of Carcassone (Robida), King Arthur and His Noble Knights (MacLeod), The Prince and the Pauper (Clemens), The Colonial Twins, The American Twins of the Revolution (Perkins), Captain Madeline (Du Bois), A Boy at Gettysburg (Singmaster), Young Trailers (Altsheler), Hitty (Field).

B. Enjoying Humor of Various Kinds

1. *Primary Objective* : To have fun with queer-sounding jingles.

   Enabling Objectives : To become sensitive to queer sounds in rhymes and stories. To learn the rhymes well enough to repeat them rapidly. To stress the queer sounds in repeating the rhymes.

   Typical Materials : Rhymes in traditional stories, such as "Little Pig, Little Pig, Will you let me come in", "fee, fie, fo, fum", "Lambikin, Lambikin", and "My daughter ha' ate five pies today". Such counting-out rhymes, as "Intry, mintery, cutery, corn", Ibbity bibbity, sibbity, sab", "Engine, Engine Number Nine", and "Eeny, meeny, miney, mo." "A Faroggie Would A-Wooing Go." "Oom-pah, Boom-pah" and "Betwixt and Between", from Lofting's Porridge Poetry. "Timothy Twigs and

Timothy Twogs" from Richards' Tirra Lirra. "Peter Piper", "The House That Jack Built", "The Old Woman and the Six pence".

2. *Primary Objective* : To enjoy newspaper comics, and other similar material. To develop some discrimination between the good and the poor.

   Enabling Objectives : To know the conventions of the comic, strip, especially the placement of the dialogue. To recognise the thoroughly lifelike and the very unnatural in the behaviour of the comic characters. To distinguish the really clever idea from the mere slapstick. To prefer the artistic distortion to the crude and hideous in drawing and the raw in colour.

   Typical Materials :The "funny pages" in dailies the children have in their homes and can bring to school - perhaps one day old. Comic pictures from John Martin's Magazine, and the Child's World. Some culled *by the teacher* from Life and Judge. Imagined illustrations for such stories told by the teacher as "The Golden Goose" (Grimm) or "The Magic Fiddle" (Grimm).

3. *Primary Objective* : To enjoy simpleton stories.

   Enabling Objectives : To see what the characters in the story ought but do not do. To take their foolish behaviour as funny rather than disgusting - i.e., to take the stories in their author's spirit.

   Typical Materials : "Epaminondas" (S.C. Bryant), "The Three Sillies", "The Wise Men of Gotham", "Clever Elsie", "Hans in Luck", "The Husband Who Was to Mind the House", "Master of All Masters", "Mr. Vinegar".

4. *Primary Objective* : To sharpen the wits on riddles and similar witticisms - not plays on words.

   Enabling Objectives : To get an understanding of what a riddle is by examining a number of them - both questions and answers. To see that the answer is always true but unexpected. To see that the fewer the acceptable answers the better the riddle.

Typical Materials : Riddles in many school readers. John Martin's Joke Book. Humor columns in newspapers and children's magazines. The Book of Riddles. What-is-wrong-here? And What-is-missing here? Pictures in papers and magazines.

5. *Primary Objective* : To enjoy the nonsense of Edward Lear and similar writers : situations, pictures, words.

   Enabling Objectives : To imagine vividly the persons and actions of the poem or story. To allow queer coined words to suggest pictures and ideas. To see the ideas in the pictures.

   Typical Materials : Edward Lear : Nonsense Botany, Nonsense Alphabet, Limericks, "The Quangle Wangle's Hat", "The Duck and the Kangaroo", "The Table and the Chair", "The Owl and Pussy Cat", "The Jumblies". Hugh Lofting; Porridge Poetry, "Linoleum and Petroleum", and "Vera Virginia". Lewis Carroll : "You Are Old, Father William", "The Walrus and the Carpenter". A.A. Milne : "The King's Breakfast". O.W. Holmes : "Ballad of the Oysterman". Short Stories for Short People (Aspinwall).

6. *Primary Objective* : To enjoy comic alliteration and alteration of words especially when it exaggerates.

   Enabling Objectives : To recognise the alliteration and its intentional abuse. To recognise (subconsciously) the original form of altered words. To be on the alert for queer names or for chances to transmogrify serious words.

   Typical Materials : "Tale of the Film-Flam" (Field), "The Dinkey Bird" (Field), "Elephantony" (Richards), "Geographi" (Richards), "The Jabberwocky" (Carroll), Rootabaga Stories (Sandburg), "Strictly Germproof" (Guiterman), "Disobedience" (Milne), the child's code-language called Pig Latin.

7. *Primary Objective* : To enjoy the reading and writing of parodies and limericks.

   Enabling Objectives : To know the originals parodied. To sense the difference in spirit but the parallel in form between the originals and the parodies. To feel (rather than scan) the rhythm of a poem to be parodied. To note the rhythm and rhyme scheme of limericks and the varieties of humour in their content : puns, indirect statement, "physical" humour.

Typical Materials : "How Doth the Little Crocodile", The Mock Turtle's Song", and "The Photographing of Father" (Carroll), Norsk Nightengale (Kirk), A Nonsense Anthology (Wells), Book of American Limericks (Wells), Complete Limerick Book (Reed), Limericks (Lear).

8. ***Primary Objective*** : To enjoy tales of exaggeration.

Enabling Objectives : To recognise the hugeness of the exaggeration and its playful character.

Typical Materials : Paul Bunyan (Stevens), Paul Bunyan and His Great Blue Ox (Wadsworth), Adventures of Baron Munchausen (Raspe), Tales of Laughter (Wiggin-Smith), Tall Tale Club (Thomas), Tall Tales of the Kentucky Mountains (Mackaye), "Sunrise in His Pocket" from Davy Crockett (Rourke), Cervantes' Don Quixote retold by Judge Parry.

9. ***Primary Objective*** : To enjoy humorous stories in which the fun arises as much from the characters as from the situations.

Enabling Objectives : To perceive the characters as others see them. To realise the inconsistency of a character or the incongruity of character and situation.

Typical Materials : The Peterkin Papers (Hale), Tome Sawyer (Clemens), Helen's Babies (Habberton), Alice in Wonderland (Carroll).

10. ***Primary Objective*** : To comprehend and appreciate ironical stories.

Enabling Objectives : To catch the usual signals of irony the choice of improbable or impossible details slightlymock-heroic language, and playful proper names. To see the weakness of the person or institution satirised.

Typical Materials : "The Princess and the Pea", and "The Emperor's New Clothes" (Anderson), "The Pelican Chorus" (Lear), "Why the Big Game Between the Hot Grounders and the Grand Standers Was a Hot Game" (Sandburg).

C. Enjoying the World of the Senses

1. *Primary Objective* : To enjoy handling books and looking at the pictures in them.

   Enabling Objectives : To begin at the front and to tune the leaves in order one at a time. To look at the left-hand page before the right-hand. To expect a story. To see whether the succession of pictures tells a story. To notice colour, lifelikeness, and humor in individual pictures.

   Typical Materials : "Mother Goose, Little Black Sambo (Banner-man), Peter Rabbit (Potter), The Happy Hour Books - Chicken Little and Little Half Chick, Humpty Dumpty, The Three Little Pigs - Golden Goose Book (Brooke), Social Science Readers (8 volumes), The Farmer in the Dell (Hader), The First Picture Book (M.S. Martin), The A.B.C. Book (Falls), Clever Bill (Nicholson), Angus and the Ducks (Flack), Ask Mr. Bear (Flack), The Picture Book of Animals (Lord), Peggy and Peter (Towsley), Johnny Crow's Garden (Brooke), Hey Diddle Diddle (Caldecott), Mother Hubbard, Her Picture Book (Crane), Billy's Farm Friends (Dobbs).

2. *Primary Objective* : To enjoy the physical response to rhythm and rhyme.

   Enabling Objectives : To respond to rhythm by tapping or by bodily movement. To identify rhyming words as they occur.

   Typical Materials : Mother Goose, "Hoppity" (Milne), "The Swing" (Stevenson), "Sleep, Baby, Sleep", "Three Little Kittens", Finger Plays (Poulsson), "The Rain", and "The Cow" (Stevenson), Pinafore Palace (Wiggin), "John" (Midline), "Mix a Pancake" (Rossetti).

3. *Primary Objective* : To enjoy picture books with text.

Enabling Objectives : To realise that pictures and text will tell the same story. To repeat or read the stories or key expressions in them while turning the pages. To imagine the incidents clearly enough to "feel" the story.

Typical Materials : Most of those listed under *A*. Also : Come, Lads and Lasses (Caldecott), Good Times on the Farm (Dietz), Open Door First Reader (Neal-Storm).

4. ***Primary Objective*** : To read aloud for playmates or for mother or others of one's family simple picture books with easy stories.

Enabling Objectives : To be thoroughly familiar with the stories. To recognise many of the individual words. To relive and retell the story rather than to pronounce the words.

Typical Materials : Most of the books listed under *A* and *C*. Also : Clean Peter and the Children of Grubbylea (Adelberg), A.B.C. for Everybody (Sewell), A Riddle Book (Dootson), At the Zoo (Lewis), A Week with Andy (Pitman-Dearborn), Busy Carpenters (Tippett), I Go Fishing (Tippett), I Live in a City (Tippett), Open Door Second Reader (Neal-Storm), How the Animals Came Out of the Ark (Smith), The Chicken World (Smith), Captain John Smith and Pocahontas (Smith), Pelle's New Suit (Beskow), The Cock, the Mouse and the Little Red Hen (Lefevre; illustrated by Sarg).

5. ***Primary Objective*** : To enjoy illustrated stories and books.

Enabling Objectives : To enjoy pictures that make the story real. To find in the story the part the picture refers to. To clarify ideas through pictures. To enjoy the fanciful and imaginative pictures as well as photographs.

Typical Materials : Johnny Goes to the Fair (Lenski), Happy All Day Through (Bowman), Animal Picture Tales from Russia (Carrick), Millions of Cats (Gag), Tinka, Minka, and Linka (McNeer), Bluebonnets for Lucinda (Sayers), Skyscraperi (Naumburg, Lambert, Mitchell), Poppy-Seed Cakes (Clarke), When We Were Very Young (Milne), Pied Piper of Hamlin (illustrated by Hope Dunlap), Ola (d'Aulaire), Peppi the Duck (Wells).

6. ***Primary Objective*** : To enjoy experiences in books that emphasise touch, taste, sight, smell and hearing.

   Enabling Objectives : To connect experiences in books with those of real life. To watch for sights, sounds, smells, tastes, and touch of things not known before.

   Typical Materials : De la Mare : "Poor Henry", "Someone", "Tartary", "The Barber's", "Bread and Cherries", "The Rainbow". Also : "Bed in Summer" and "The Land of Counterpane" (Stevenson), "The Moon's the North Wind's Cooky" and "Dirge for a Righteous Kitten" (Lindasy), "The Sugar Plum Tree" (Field), "Animal Crackers" (Morley), "Rain in the Night" (Burr), "Sea Shell" (Lowell), "Christmas Morning" (Roberts), "Sand between the Toes" (Milne), "Daisies" (Sherman), "Starts" (Teasdale), "The Wind in a Frolic" (Howitt), "A Boy's Song" (Hogg), "Hansel and Gretel", "Nail Soup", The Magic Squirrel (Grishina), "All the World Is Colour" (Pierce and Jermaine L'hardy), Wonders of the Jungle (Ghosh), Eskimo Twins and Dutch Twins (Perkins).

7. ***Primary Objective*** : To enjoy traditional singing-games and some of the simpler ballads.

   Enabling Objectives : To fit the action to the music and words. To feel the rhythm with the muscles as well as the ear and voice. To "let loose" and play heartily. To search for similar material in old song books. To collect such material from parents and other adults.

   Typical Materials : "Farmer in the Dell", "London Bridge Is Falling Down", "Tisket-Tasket", "Bingo", "Skip to My Lou", "Pig in the Parlour", "Wash the Ladies' Dishes", "King William was King James' Son", "Clementine," "The Animal Fair", "Oh Dear, What can the Matter be?" "Bullfrog on the Bank", "King of the Cannibal Islands", "Coche-lunk-che-lunk-a-lay-lee", American Songbag (Sandburg), Heart Songs (Joe Chappell), Sing It Yourself (Dorothy Gordon), British Singing Games (Gomme).

8. ***Primary Objective*** : To enjoy poems in which rhyme, alliteration, repetitions are pronounced.

Enabling Objectives : To recognise the recurrence of rhyme in a poem. To perceive "patterns" made by length of lines, number of lines, and rhyme scheme. To notice repetition and refrain. To recognise and enjoy alliteration.

Typical Materials : "If I Were King" and "Sneezles" (Milne), "What is Pink?" (Rossetti), "Silver" and "The Bees' Song" (De La Mare), "The Potatoes' Dance" (Lindsay), "Mr. And Mrs. Spikky Sparrow" (Lear), "Robinson Crusoe's Story" (Carryl), "The Wind" (Stevenson), "The Song Sparrow" (Van Dyke), "The Rain Song" (Loveman), "Windy Nights" (Stevenson), "Robert of Lincoln" (Bryant).

9. ***Primary Objective*** : To enjoy hearing and reading dialect poems and stories.

Enabling Objectives : To recognise different types of dialect as Negro, cowboy, Italian, French, Norwegian, etc. To know that dialect is suitable for stories and verse but not for use in real life. To know that America has a body of folklore as well as other countries, much of it in song and story.

Typical Materials : "Get Up and Bar the Door" (old ballad), "Whoopee Ti Yi Yo" (Lomax, collector), "Lullaby" (Dunbar), "Da Leetla Boy" (Daly), "Leetle Bateese" (Drummond), "Yim" (Kirk), "The Mountain Whippoorwill" (Banet), A Book of Ballads (Stempel), The American Songbag (Sandburg), "Brer Rabbit and the Wonderful Tar Baby" (Harris).

10. ***Primary Objective*** : To enjoy poems and stories in which word music or/and sensory imagery is especially important elements.

Enabling Objectives : To hear the poems mentally while reading silently. To take time to realise the imagery - calling up colours, for example, in the verbal pictures.

Typical Materials : "The Grasshopper" (Lindsay), "Morning" (Dickinson), "Velvet Shoes" (Wylie), "Fog" (Sandburg), "Faery Song" (Keats), "I Meant to Do My Work Today" (Le Gallienne), "The House with Nobody in It" (Kilmer),

Poems by a Little Girl (Conkling), The Wind in the Willows (Grahame), Tales from Silver Lands (Finger), "September" and "October" (Jackson), "A Comparison" (Farrar), Little Boy Lost (Hudson), "How They Broke Away to Go to the Rootabaga Country" and "The White Horse Girl and the Blue Wind Boy" (Sandburg), "Old Pipes and the Dryad" and "The Clocks of Rondaine" (Stockton), Hari, the Jungle Lad (Mukerji), "The Blue Bird" (Howitt), "Tartary" (De la Mare).

D. Exploring the Social World

1. *Primary Objective* : To enjoy vicariously happy relations with pets and other animals.

   Enabling Objectives : To image the appearance and the voices of the animals, familiar or strange. To keep attention on the action to the end of each incident.

   Typical Materials : "Shopping" (Milne), "The Begging Deer" (Rowe), "The Friendly Cow" (Stevenson), "The Turtle" (Lindsay), "The Goldfish" (Aldis), "The Elephant" (Wynne), "The Worm" (Roberts), "Puppy and I" and "The Little Black Hen" (Milne), "The Animal Store" and "Little Dog Toby" (Field), "Midget and Bridget" (Hader), "I Love Little Pussy" (Taylor), Prancing Pat (Orton), Dick and Tom (Van Doren), Our Pets (Nida), Skags the Milk Horse (Huber), Cinder the Cat (Huber), Baby Animals (Troxell and Dunn).

2. *Primary Objective* : To enter imaginatively into the feeling and actions of other children, especially children in different surroundings.

   Enabling Objectives : To perceive the different circumstances under which they live. To see ways in which they think and act as the reader does. To approach the stories in an interested, sympathetic attitude rather than in one of amused superiority.

   Typical Materials : "Foreign Children" (Stevenson), "A Child's Prayer" (Thompson), "Susanna's Auction" (Boutet de Monvel), Little Pear (Lattimore), Little Eagle (Deming), Dutch twins Primer (Perkins), Little World-Children

(Scantlebury), Rabbit Lantern (Rowe), Miki (Petersham), Peter Pocket (Justus), Little Black Eyes (Kent), Children of Many Lands (Perdue), The Little House in the Woods (Hunt), The Little Swiss Woodcaver (Brandeis).

3. ***Primary Objective*** : To enjoy simple books about trains, ships, airplanes, radio, et cetera.

   Enabling Objectives : To recognise the unusual and therefore interesting features of each mode of travel. To see some of the practical as well as the picturesque phases of transportation.

   Typical Materials : "The Airplane" (Wynne), "The Dirigible" (Bergengren), "The Railway Train" (Dickinson), "The Ship of Rio" (de la Mare), "Taxis" (Field), "Wings of Lead" (Crane), Story About Boats and Engine's story (Read), The Story of the Ship (Grant), Wide Road Ahead (Lent), Picture Book of Travel (Hader), Picture Book of Ships (Gimmage), Little Black-nose (Swift), Clear Track Ahead (Lent), 10,000 Miles with a Dog Sled (Stuck), A Train, A Boat, and an Island (Kuh), Story Book of Transportation (Petersham), America Travels (Dalgliesh), I go a Travelling (Tippett), Full Steam Ahead (Lent).

4. ***Primary Objective*** : To witness sympathetically the trials and privations of others.

   Enabling Objectives : To see the difficulties against which they struggle. To imagine how it would feel to be in the same circumstances. To perceive something of the motives for their actions. To apply ethical standards but not those of etiquette.

   Typical Materials : "A Little Song of Life" (Reese), "Why the Chimes Rang" (Alden), "The Happy Prince" (Wilde), "The Boys and Frogs" (Aesop), Little Lost Pup (Guiterman), A Dog of Flanders (de la Ramee), Moufflou (de la Ramee), The Birds' Christmas Carol (Wiggin), Just Across the Street (Field), Children of the Moor (Fitinghoff), Susie Sugarbeet. (Ashmun), Waterless Mountain (Armer), Black Beauty (Sewell), "The Little Match Girl" (Andersen).

5. ***Primary Objective*** : To enjoy the intellectual experience of fables.

Enabling Objectives : To recognise the similarity between these imaginative stories and the illustrative anecdotes told by public speakers. To see that the charm of the fable lies chiefly in the effectiveness with which it illustrates an idea. To regard the morals of fables as bits of worldly wisdom, frequently without any colouring of good or bad.

Typical Materials : " The Fables of Aesop, as collected by Joseph Jacobs, or as retold in rhyme by Oliver Herford, especially: The Cat, the Monky and the Chestnuts, The Boy Who Cried Wolf, The Ass in the Lion's Skin. The Wind and the Sun, The Dog and His Image, The Dog in the Manger, The Milkmaid and Her Pail, The Crow and the Pitcher, The Hare and the Tortoise, The Lion and the Mouse. Some of Lincoln's stories of comparison.

6. ***Primary Objective*** : To witness with admiration acts of bravery and heroism.

Enabling Objectives : To distinugish courage from fool - hardiness. To know that there are other kinds of courage than the physical variety. To recognise traits of character that makes a man or woman heroic.

Typical Materials : "Boy Who Conquered Himself" (Forbes) is Citizenship Through Story-telling, "Columbus" (Wynne), "St. Christopher" (Tabb), "Barbara Frietchie" (Whittier), "Jin Bludso" (Hay), "The Good Joan" (Reese), "Vita Lampadail or "The Torch of Life" (Newbolt), "Little Hero of Haarlem, "Bravery of Elizabeth Jane" in Short Stories from American History (Blaisdell), Grace Darling, "Daniel in the Lion's Den" (Bible), "Landing of the Pilgrims" (Hemans), "David and Goliath" (Bible), "Quest of the Four-Leafed Clover" (Laboulaye), "St. George and the Dragon" in Heroic Legends (Herbertson), The Story of Nancy Hanks (Phillips), When They Were Girl (Moore), America First (Evans), Overland in a Covered Wagon (Miller), Reindeer of the

Waves (Harshaw), Joan of Arc (Boute de Monvel), Go! Champions of Light (Olcott), Nuvat the Braw (Doone), Scarlet Fringe (Fernald and Slocombe), Pueblo Boy (Cannon), Christopher Columbus (Potter).

7. ***Primary Objective*** : To follow up in books some special interest or hobby.

Enabling Objectives : To understand the explanations of activities. To know where in the library the "activity" books are. To stick to one activity long enough to know enough about it to be really interested.

Typical Materials : The Young Stamp Collector's Own Book (Butler), Playing With Clay (Wheeler), 200 Tricks You can Do (Thurston), Model Boat Building for Boys (Cavileer), Model Airplanes and How to Fly Them (Allen), Making Things for Fun (A. Frederick Collins), The Secrets of Baseball (Charnley), Prove It Yourself (Gordon), Patty Pans (La Ganke), Stories Postage Stamps Tell (Rothschild), Cork Ships and How to Make Them (Adams), Your Workshop (Plimpton), Homemade Games (Hall), Working with Electricity (Keelor), A Hundred Things a Girl Can Make (Show), Toy-making in School and Home (Polkinghorne), Boy Birdhouse Architecture (Baxter), All About Pets (Bianco), Box Book (Showalter), The Boy Showman and Entertainer (Rose).

E. Enjoying Fantasy and Whimsy

1. ***Primary Objective*** : To relive (traditional) tales of animals that talk and have human qualities.

Enabling Objectives : To listen long enough at once to follow a story to the end. To know the visual appearance and general character of the animals in the stories.

Typical Materials : "The Three Bears", "The Three Pigs", "Little Black Sambo", "Red Riding Hood", "The Pancake" or "Wee Bannock" or "Gingerbread Man", The Little Red Hen stories, Squirrel Nukin and Benjamin Bunny (Porter), Millions of Cats (Gag), Bojabi Tree (Rickert), "Dame Wiggins of Lee" (Ruskin), "Why Pigs Have Curly Tails" and "Lamb That Went to Fairyland" in Rainbow Cat (Fyleman), "Chicken Licken", "Titty Mouse and Tatty Mouse."

2. *Primary Objective* : To enjoy, without believing, *pour quoi* stories.

   Enabling Objectives : To follow the plot well enough to see the appropriateness of the reward, the punishment, to the outcome of the action, in the story. To read or listen in the make-believe rather than the matter-of-fact attitudes. To feel the whimsical charm of the explanation of natural facts.

   Typical Materials : "Why the Bear Has a Stumpy Tail", "Why the Sea Is Salt", "Why the Robin Has a Red Breast", "Where from Woodpecker Got His Red Head", Nature Myths from Man Lands (Holbrook), "The First Umbrella" (Herford), "Why All Men Love the Moon" (How the Sun, the Moon and the Wind Went Out to Dinner), Why-so Stories (Rich), How and Why Stories (for retelling) (Branner), Indian Nature Myth (Cowles).

3. *Primary Objective* : To become friendly and intimate with fairies, elves, and goblins.

   Enabling Objectives : To maintain the natural child believer in these charming characters. To visualise both natural and supernatural characters. To keep track of the situation of the principal character.

   Typical Materials : " Cinderella", "Elves and the Shoemaker" "Tom Tit Tot" or "Rumpelstiltskin", "Toads and Diamonds", Sally Gabble and the Fairies (Potter), "Pan and the Magic pencil" in The Rainbow Cat (Fyleman), Mospa the Fairy (Ingelow Books of Elves and Fairies [source book] (Olcott), "Thumbs lina" (Andersen), Patsy and the Leprechauns (Baker and Baker), Lost Merbaby (Baker), "The Three Wishes", Adventures of a Browine (Craik), Lost Village (Bancroft).

4. *Primary Objective* : To escape from the everyday into the make believe of the old folk-tales.

   Enabling Objectives : To imagine with reasonable distinctness the characters and events of the stories. To expect characters and events in sets of three. To catch promptly, the mood of the story : adventure, wonder, humours, satin or moralising.

Typical Materials : "East o' the Sun and West o' the Moon, Fair Ring (Wiggin and Smith), Household Stories (Grimm, edited by Crane), Fairy Tales from the Far North (Asbjornsen), English Fairy tales (Jacobs), English Fairy Tales (Steel), Myths of the Red Children (Wilson), Wigwam Evenings (Eastman), Donegal Fairy Stories (MacManus), Chimney Corner Fairy Tales (Hutchinson).

5. ***Primary Objective*** : To enjoy and understand literary stories with a dominant supernatural element.

Enabling Objectives : To recognise (Perhaps unconsciously) from the title, illustrations, style, and opening descriptions that certain natural laws are temporarily suspended. To continue to expect psychological consistency in the characters. To think of the point of each story in the concrete rather than in generalisations or morals - *e.g.*, "God thought the heart of the Happy Prince a precious object", not "We ought to be kind and generous to the poor".

Typical Materials : "The Happy Prince" (Wilde), "Why the Chimes Rang" (Alden), "Knights of the Silver Shield" (Alden), "The Khan of the Silver Crown", "The Miraculous Pitcher" (Hawthrone), "Prince Harweda" (Harrison), "The King of the Golden River" (Ruskin), "The First Christmas Tree" (Van Dyke), "Billy Barnicoat" (MacDonald).

6. ***Primary Objective*** : To enjoy traditional wonder-stories.

Enabling Objectives : To realise how remarkable the events are, and yet to maintain 'poetic faith'. To adopt the serious mood of the original story-teller.

Typical Materials : " The Arabian Nights, Ulysses Among The Phaeacians, The Boy Who Knew What the Birds Said (Colum), Tangle-Coated Horse and other Tales (Young), Wonder Smith and His Son (Young), The Hound of Culain (Page), The Sampo (Baldwin),

Tanglewood Tales and Wonder Book (Hawthorne), Wonder Tales from Wagner (Chapin), Golden Porch (Hutchinson), Tales of Wonder (Wiggin and Smith, New World Fairy Book (Kennedy).

7. *Primary Objective* : To experience fantasy whose motive is beauty.

Enabling Objectives : To centre attention upon the images rather than upon character or plot. To see colours as well as outlines. To choose deliberately if not spontaneously,harmonious, rich, colors and pleasing shapes.

Typical Materials : "How They Broke Away to Go to The Rootabaga Country" (Sandburg), "The Ancient Mariner" (Coleridge), "Velvet Shoes" (Wylie), "A Song of Robin Hood" (Noyes), "Solitaire" (Lowell), "Chinese Nightingale" (Lindsay), The Three Mullah Mulgars (De la Mare), Cat Who Went to Heaven (Coatsworth), The Knock at the Door (Coatsworth), Little White Goat (Lathrop).

Special Unit : Sifting the Radio Programes

1. *Primary Objective* : To get from radio as rich and as lasting pleasures and benefit as is possible.

Enabling Objectives : To be acquainted with some of the better programes suited to one's own age. To feel something of the beauty, freshness, cleverness, or truth that distinguishes these from less excellent programes. To be amused by the improbabilities and exaggerated delivery of the melodramatic programes.

Activities :

1. Listing (perhaps anonymously) programes heard habitually and other recent programes remembered vividly, for tabulation of class taste.

2. Discussion of such questions as :

   a. What is your favourite programes? Why?

   b. Do you like the so-called children's programes? Mention some that you still listen to or that you have in the past listened to with pleasure. Are there some programes that even an adult would enjoy?

c. Are there some children's programes that it would be better for a younger brother or sister not to listen to? What are some of the defects of the programes you mention?

d. Are stories and plays the only interesting prögrames on the air? What are some others, which you like?

e. What is meant by "radio manners"? Does the radio even cause quarrels in homes? Is it a discourtesy to radio artists to converse while their programe is being given?

3. Writing five rules for judging radio programes. Would everybody lay down the same rules? Is it desirable that they should?

4. Making a rough schedule of the proportions of leisure time to be allotted to different amusements : out-door sports, radio, music, hobbies, readings, indoor games and parties.

Materials : Radio programes, radio news and articles in newspapers.

Adaptation : Superior pupils : Comparing radio stories with good stories they have read. Presenting mock broadcasts, both serious (music, story-telling, playlets, poetry reading) and burlèsque (take-offs of the melodramatic). Slower pupils : Listening to programes agreed upon and rating them according to the rules formulated by the class.

Appraisal of growth : Does a second anonymous listing of programes habitually heard show improvement?

5

Literature Experiences Grades 7 - 12

A. Enjoying Action

1. *Primary Objective* : To enjoy animal stories, both short and book-length.

   Enabling Objectives : To enter sympathetically into the world of the animals. To keep clearly in mind the changing situation of the actors in the story. To discount some what the emotional sensitivity given to the animals by most of the writers.

   Typical Materials : Trail of the Sandhill Stag, Wild Animals I Have Known, Biography of a Gizzely, etc. (Seton); Watchers of the Trail, Haunters of the Silences, etc. (C. G. D. Roberts); Kari the Elephant, Gay-Neck, etc. (Mukerji); Call of the Wild, White Fang (Jack London); Lad (Terhune); Baldy of Nome (Darling); Dogs of Boytown (Dyer); Stickeen (Muir); The Story of Scotch (Mills); Jungle Book (especially "Rikki-Tikki-Tavi") Second Jungle Book (Kipling); "Reynard The Fox" (Masefield); Smoky (James).

2. *Primary Objective* : To engage vicariously in human adventure in easy settings within simple plots.

   Enabling Objectives : To sense clearly which persons and circumstances are favourable to the hero. To image vividly the critical situations. To keep the chain of incidents in mind, at least until the reading is finished.

   Typical Materials : Hans Brinker (Dodge); Captains Couragecus (Kipling); Tom Sawyer (Clemens); Cudjo's

Cave (Trowbridge); Toby Tyler (Otis); Merrylips (Dix); Jim Davis (Masefield); Adventures of Billy Topsail (Duncan); Swiss Family Robinson (Wyss); Robinson Crusoe (Defoe); Adril on an Icepan (Grenfell); Cadet Days (King); Little Shepherd of Kingdom Come (Fox); Treasure Island (Stevenson); Trumpeter of Krakow (Kelley). Such short stories as : "Gallegher" (R. H. Davis); "The Maelstrom" (Poe); "The Pit and the Pendulum" (Poe); "The Skeleton in Armor" (Longfellow); "Betty's Ride : A Tale of the Revolution" (Canby).

3. *Primary Objective* : To enjoy rapidly moving comedies of situation.

Enabling Objectives : To lay aside the serious mood and its expectations of adventure of theme. To imagine the situations vividly enough to realise their ludicrousness.

Typical Materials : What Happened to Inger Johanne (Zwilgmeyer); Anne of Green Gables (Montgomery); Rebecca of Sunnybrook Farm (Wiggin); The Casting Away of Mrs. Lecks and Mrs. Aleshine (Stockton); Tales from the Travels of Baron Munchausen (Raspe); Don Quixote (Cervantes). Such short stories as "Ransom of Red Chief" (O. Henry); "Goliath" (Aldrich); "My Double and How He Undid Me" (Hale); "The Arrest of Lieutenant Golightly" (Kipling); "The Priest and the Mulberry Tree", "The Diverting History of John Gilpin" (Cowper); "The Jumping Frog of Calaveras Country (Clemens); such play as Spreading The News (Lady Gregory); A Comedy of Errors (Shakespeare); Twelfth Night (Shakespeare); A Midsummer Night's Dream (Shakespeare); Robin Hood (Cheswick).

4. *Primary Objective* : To enjoy hero stories.

Enabling Objectives : To sympathise with the hero; to realise the seriousness of his difficulties; to see how far his success is due to his own foresight, courage, and resourcefulness.

Typical Materials : The Spy (Cooper); Daniel Boone (S.E.White); Boy's Life of Colonel Lawrence (Thomas);

Skyward (Byrd); Amundsen (Partridge); David Livingston (Finger); Girl in White Armor (Paine); Tom Brown's Schooldays (Hughes); Around the World in Eight Days (Post and Gatty); Chara Barton (Eple:). Short stories : "The First Christmas Tree" (Van Dyke); "Horatius" (Macaulay); "The Freshman Full-Back", "The Operator".

5. *Primary Objective* : To witness the action of myths and legends.

   Enabling Objectives : To exercise "poetic faith" (suspension of disbelief); to know the important gods and their characters; to become familiar with the chief heroes in the epic or cycle of legends read. *Optional, for strong students* : To realise that the myths were once serious explanations of the natural phenomena; to understand the collection of legends about major heroes.

   Typical Materials : Odyssey, Iliad, Kalevala, Song of Roland Children of Odin (Colum) or Story of Siegfried (Baldwin); A Wonder Book (Hawthorne); Tanglewood Tales (Hawthorne), Sham-Nameh, Mahabharata; Morte d'Arthur, Beowulf, Aeneid Song of Hiawatha (Longfellow); Greek Heroes (Kingsley); Myths Every Child Should Know (Mabie); Myths and Thir Meanings (Herzberg).

6. ***Primary Objective*** : To enjoy adventures which are more interesting because their backgrounds are so different from our own environment.

   Enabling Objectives : To visualise clothing, weapons, houses and other details of the background. To note peculiarities of speech and social customs, if there are any. To catch some of the attitudes and ways of thinking which are different from ours.

   Typical Materials : Talisman, Ivanhoe, Quentin Durwood, Kenil-Worth (Scott); Typee, Omoo (Melville); Three Musketeers, Count of Monte Cristo, etc. (Dumas; Last of the Mohicans Deerslayer, etc. (Cooper); Ben Hur (Wallace); Quo Vadis (Sienkewicz); Last Days of Pompeii

(Lytton); Egyptian Princess (Ebers); Scaramouche, etc. (Sabatini); Men of Iron, Otta of the Silver Hand (Pyle; Tale of Two Cities (Dickens); Richard Carvel, Crossing, Crisis (Churchill); Hugh Wyme (Mitchell); Life on the Mississippi, Roughing It, etc. (Clemens); Alice of Old Vincennes (Thompson); Kidnapped, etc. (Stevenson).

B. Exploring the Physical World

1. ***Primary Objective*** : To enjoy travel at home.

   Enabling Objectives : To see the new landscapes, different costumes, strange customs. To compare these with ones own, and to find so far as can be done readily the reasons for the likeness and difference. To note the ideas and feelings aroused in the travelers whose accounts one is reading. To recall these vicarious experiences either just for pleasure or as materials of thinking and illustration.

   Typical Materials : Lisbeth Longfrock (Aanrud); Travels at Home From Mark Twain (Chubb); Whale Hunting with Camera and Gun (Andrews): When I Was a Boy in Belgium (Jonckheere); Ten Thousand Miles in a Dog Sled (Stuck); Egypt (Holmes); China (Holems); Adrift on an Ice-pan (Grenfell); African Adventure Stories (Loring); Boots and Saddles (Custer); Boy Scout with Byrd (Siple); Boy Scouts' Book of True Adventure; Boy's-Eye View of the Arctic (Rawson); Buccaneers and Pirates of Our Coast (Stockton); By Dog Sled for Byrd, 1600) Miles Across Antarctic Ice (O"Brien); Child's Geography of the World (Hillyer); Conquest of the Poles (Judd); David Goes Voyaging (Putnam); Girls In Africa (Best); Great Moments in Exploration (Lansing); Hobnails and Heather (Lisle); Hunters of the Great North (Stefansson); Igloo (Walden); Japan, Korea and Formosa (Tietjens); Jungle Peace (Beebe); Land of the Long Night (Du Chaillu); Lion (Johnson); Marco Polo, Junior (Harry A. Franck); My Life with the Eskimos (Stefansson); Sailing Alone Around the World (Slocum); Story-Book Europe (Peck).

2. ***Primary Objective*** : To observe life under varied physical conditions.

Enabling Objectives : To imagine vividly what the people do. To compare life in one places with life in others, and especially with our own. To see universal human nature behind diverse customs. To understand the physical conditions as clearly as possible. To see the connection between conditions and ways of living.

Typical Materials : My Summer in a Garden (Warner); Jungle Peace (Beebe); Kindred of the Wild (Roberts); On the Trail of Ancient Man (Andrews); Early Men of Science (Nida and Nida); Our Physical World (Downing); When I Was a Girl in Italy (Ambrosi), A Boy in Servia (Davies); Far Away and Long Ago (Hudson); Country of the Dwarfs (Du Chaillu); Deric in Mesa Verde (Nusbaum); Pony Tracks (Remington); Man, the Miracle Maker (Van Loon).

3. *Primary Objective* : To participate vicariously in some of man's uses of nature to promote his own welfare.

Enabling Objectives : To understand the essential nature of each invention or discovery. To understand as much as is told of the steps by which the invention or discovery came about. To see something of the social significance of each. To sympathise with the elation of the inventor or discoverer.

Typical Materials : First Days of Man (Kummer); Great Inventors and Their Inventions (Bachman); Thinkers and Doers (Darrow); Young Folk's Book of Inventions (Bridges); The Technical World (magazine); Boys Book of Remarkable Machinery (Hawks); Chats on Science (Slosson); Conquests of Invention (Parkman); Marvels of Modern Mechanics (Wilkins); Everyday Mysteries (Abbot); Microbe Hunters (de Kruif); How It Works (Williams).

4. *Primary Objective* : To live with the scientists of yesterday and today.

Enabling Objectives : To catch something of the scientist's devotion to truth. To realise the fascination of investigation and the thrill of discovery. To know the personalities and achievements of at least a few great scientists or inventors. To note the increasing speed with which our world is modified.

Typical Materials : Early Men of Science (Nida); Galapagos (Beebe); Arcturus Adventure (Beebe); Boy With Edison (Simonds); From Immigrant to Inventor (Pupin); Magician of Science (Hammond); Heroes of Civilisation (Cottler and Jaffe); Masters of Science and Invention (Darrow); Pioneers of Science (Lodge).

5. ***Primary Objective*** : To participate in scientific speculation concerning the origin of man and of the world.

Enabling Objectives : To understand the theory of evolution. To know the difference between a theory and the objective facts from which it is deduced. To have some understanding of the amount and character of the evidence supporting the doctrine of evolution. To consider the evidence and the conclusion with an open mind, independent of the authority of teachers or others. To understand the theories of the formation of the solar system. To understand that the study of cosmic rays and of inter-molecular physics may change these theories.

Typical Materials : First chapters of Outline of History (Wells); Evolution (Kellogg); This Mysterious Universe (Jeans); Story of Mankind (Van Loon); Outline of Science (Thomson); Evolution for John Doe (Ward).

6. ***Primary Objective*** : To trace some phase of man's social and intellectual evolution or to witness a dramatic succession of still pictures of advancing civilisation.

Enabling Objectives : To accept sweeping statements with caution, tentatively. To explain present observations and experience by means of these historical developments. To use present observations and all one's knowledge to check the reliability of what is read. To make upon the basis of historical tendencies modest guesses concerning future developments.

Typical Materials : Child's History of Art (Hillyer and Huey); Story of Mankind (Van Loon); Child's History of World (Hillyer); Short History (Wells); The Story of Science (Thomsons); The Story of Philosophy (Durant).

C. Exploring the Social World

1. *Primary Objective* : To make our lives richer by recapitulating some of the experiences of our predecessors.

   Enabling Objectives : To experience vicariously the early world of man; to compare present-day life and thought with those of the people of other ages.

   Typical Materials : In The Light of Myth (Baker); Tale of Indian Heroes, Being Stories of The Mahabharata and the Ramayana (Steel); Story of the Cid (Wilson); Children of Odin (Colum); Book of King Arthur and His Noble Knights (Macleod); Wonder Book of Old Romance (Darton); Orpheus and His Lute (Hutchinson).

2. *Primary Objective* : To participate vicariously in the mental growth of our ancestors.

   Enabling Objectives : To gain an understanding of the mental growth of various peoples through an acquaintance with their literature; to realise how the results of social and scientific progress affect our lives today; to understand present-day social institutions in the light of the continuous contributions of the past; to participate with peoples of other times by experiencing vicariously their social, cultural, and economic expansion.

   Typical Materials : Old English Ballads, Beowulf, Story of Roland; Boy of the Lost Crusade (Echols); Early Men of Science (Nida and Nida); Up from Slavery (Washington); "Ulysses" (Tennyson); "Elegy Written in a Country Churchyard" (Gray); "Lincoln, the Man of the People" (Markham); Golden Tales of Our America (Becker); One Hundred Narrative Poems (Teter).

3. *Primary Objective* : To participate in man's desire to know more about his fellow men.

Enabling Objectives : To understand various peoples and institutions; to share in the problems and difficulties inherent in building up amiable relationships.

Typical Materials : Messer Marco Polo (Byrne); Story of Mankind (Van Loon); Saint Joan (Shaw); Heroes from Hakluyt (Finger); Story of King Arthur and his Noble Knights (MacLeod); The Virginian (Wister); This Interlocking World (McSkimmon and Della Chiesa); Oil for the Lamps of China (Hobart); The Good Earth (Buck).

4. *Primary Objective* : To enjoy travel and explorers and pioneers.

   Enabling Objectives : To experience the reasons for exploration and piosneerings; to experience the hardships and privations felt by these intrepid men; to understand the effects of the desire to expand on world relationships.

   Typical Materials : American Poetry (De Mille); The Spy (Cooper); Prisoners of Hope (Johnston); A Mirror for Witches (Forbes); Life on the Mississippi (Twain); Autobiography of Benjamin Franklin; The Fortunes of Nigel (Scott); Letters of an American Farmer (Crevecoeur); The Hawkeye, etc. (Quick).

5. *Primary Objective* : To observe man's industrial expansion.

   Enabling Objectives : To compare industry as it was before our time with our own industrial age; to participate vicariously with men and women who worked and are working under conditions both good and bad; to analyse our present economic system, and to compare it with systems of other days.

   Typical Materials : Silas Marner (Eliot); David (Copperfield (Dickens); The Last of the Mohicans (Cooper); The Slave Ship (Johnston); The Luck of Roaring Camp (Harte); Roughing It (Twain); Two Years Before the Mast (Dana); A Son of the Middle Border (Garland); The Oregon Trail (Parkman); The Crossing (Churchill); Seven Iron Men (de Kruif).

6. *Primary Objective* : To observe the effects of widening trade horizons on our daily lives.

   Enabling Objectives : To see how new frontiers and new customs were the direct result of the desire of man to increase his trading area; to catch some idea of the need for invention, investigation, and discovery; to note the organisation of big business and the resulting efficiency and economy which it implies.

   Typical Materials : I Hear America Singing (Whitman); Modern Pioneers (Cohen and Scarlett); Pete of the Steel Mills (Hall); Making of an American (Riis); Our Foreign Born Citizens (Beard); "The Thinker" (Braley); Andrew Carnegie's Own Story (Brochhausen); At School in the Promised Land (Antin); Greatness Passing By (Neibuhr); The Pit and The Octopus (Norris); The Harbor (Poole); I Went to Pit College (Gilfillan).

7. *Primary Objective* : To realise our heritage of works of art and our opportunities for enjoying them.

   Enabling Objectives : To understand that scientific and mechanical advances have given man more leisure in which to enjoy the arts; to experience music, the drama and other branches of the arts.

   Typical Materials : (Selections that indicate the struggle for existence; compare these stories to the actual leisure that is to be found today); A Goldsmith of Florence (Gibson); Sticks and Stones (Mumford); Animals in Great Sculpture (Richter); Playing with Clay (Wheeler); "Andrea Del Sarto" (Browning); Dauber (Masefield); "The Rime of The Ancient Mariner" (Coleridge); "The Barrel Organ" (Noyes); First Steps in the Enjoyment of Pictures (Oliver); In Our Convent Days (Repplier).

D. Studying Human Nature

1. *Primary Objective* : To enjoy suspense in stories and plays in which the characters are sharply individualised or etched against a background of events; that is, in stories and plays in which the characterisation challenges interest as mush as, possibly more than, the incidents do.

The reader is interested because certain incidents happen to certain characters rather than in the fact that certain incidents do occur (with the characters somewhat like puppets or stock characters).

Enabling Objectives : To follow the story easily enough to have attention to spare for character : to image all characters clearly, especially faces and facial expressions, bodily poses and characteristic tricks of manner and voices; to be aware of continuing tendencies in action - *e.g.*, generosity, caution, duplicity, wit, talkativeness, stupidity.

Typical Materials : Captain Courageous (Kipling); Tom Sawyer (Clemens); Huckleberry Finn (Clemens); Ivanhoe (Scott); Treasure Island (Stevenson); Kidnapped (Stevenson); Sea Wolf (London); Robinson Crusoe (Defoe); "Gallegher" (Davis); Little Women (Alcott); Hoosier Schoolmaster (Eggleston); Count of Monte Cristo (Dumas); Ben Hur (Wallace); Last Days of Pompeii (Lytton); Monsieur Pierre Patelin (play), The Man Who Married a Dumb Wife (France).

2. *Primary Objective* : To read appreciatively prose and verse narratives, which show clearly the motives of the characters and the effect of events upon their feelings.

   Enabling Objectives : To note the author's explanation of motives and feelings; to note what the characters say and do as indicative of their feelings.

   Typical Materials : "Sohrab And Rustum" (Arnold); "Christmas Carol" (Dickens); "Wee Willie Winkie" (Kipling); My Antomia (Cather); O. Henry's stories; Man Without a Country (Hale); Red Badge of Courage (Crane); Dark Frigate (Hawes); Scaramouche (Sabatini).

3. *Primary Objective* : To enjoy stories in which static character depiction is central.

   Enabling Objectives : To be in a receptive mood for impressions; to be willing to read unhurriedly, with a sort of detachment that enables the reader to have perspective on the characters.

Typical Materials : "The Cricket on the Hearth" (Dickens); "The White Heron" (Jewett); The Vicar of Wakefiled (Goldsmith); Alice Adams (Tarkington); Colonel Carter of Cartersvile (Smith); "The Revolt of Mother" (Freeman); The Casting Away of Mrs. Lecks and Mrs. Aleshine (Stockton); Tommy and Grizel (Barrie); Miss Lulu Bett (Gale).

4. ***Primary Objective*** : To enjoy plays in which suspense and character interest are both strong.

Enabling Objectives : To interpret action in terms of cause and effect; to relate action to motive; to see the logical relationship between character and action.

Typical Materials : "Spreading the News" (Gregory); "Rising of the Moon" (Gregory); The Rivals (Sheridan); Julius Caesar (Shakespeare); Twelfth Night (Shakespeare); The Emperor Jones (O'Neill).

5. ***Primary Objective*** : To enjoy studies of character change.

Enabling Objectives : To be sensitive to change; to be aware of differences; to note the evidences of change over a period of time.

Typical Materials : Silas Marner (Eliot); Macbeth (Shakespeare); Romola (Eliot); The Light That Failed (Kipling); The Rise of Silas Lapham (Howells); So Big (Ferber); Cimarron (Ferber); Dr. Jekyll and Mr. Hyde (Stevenson); Lord Jim (Conrad); Good-bye, Mr. Chips (James Hilton); Justice (Galsworthy); John Ferguson (St. John G. Ervine); Clayhanger (Bannett); Hilda Lessways (Bennett); Jude The Obscure (Hardy); The Return of the Native (Hardy); Ethan Frome (Wharton); The Cathedral (Hugh Walpole); Broome Stages (Clemence Dane); The Forsyte Saga (Galsworthy); Jalna (de la Roche).

6. *Primary Objective* : To recognise the constant universal elements in human nature.

Enabling Objectives : To read fiction, narrative poetry and plays with understanding and imagination so that former times and situations are recreated.

Typical Materials : Kristin Lavransdatter (Undset); The Return of the Native (Hardy); The Ring and the Book (Browning); A Tale of two Cities (Dickens); The Farm (Bromfield); Prester John (Buchan); Hamlet (Shakespeare); The House of the Seven Gables (Hawthorne); The Odyssey, the Iliad, The Song of Roland, Don Quixote.

7. *Primary Objective* : To comprehend human nature from what people say about themselves (literature of the confessional type); essays, letters, journals, autobiographies, lyric poetry.

Enabling Objectives : To know the salient characteristics of each literary type listed above in order that the reader may find the personal message without misunderstanding.

Typical Materials : Adventures in Friendship (Hugh Black); Old Lamps For New (E.V. Lucas); Points of Friction (Agnes Repplier); Letters of a Woman Homesteader (Elinor Pruitt Stewart); Far Away and Long Ago (Hudson); Lone Cowboy (James); My Garden of Memory (Wiggin); Print of My Remembrance (Augustus Thomas); Up the Years from Bloomsbury (Arliss); Letters of Charles Lamb, Letters of Rober Louis Stevenson, Letters of William James, The Education of Henry Adams; The Great Lover (Brooke); "I Hear America Singing" (Whitman); "Patterns" (Amy Lowel); "Il Penseroso" (Milton); "Ode on a Grecian Urn" (Keats); Personal Record (Joseph Conrad); Song of the Middle Border (Garland).

E. Sharing Lyric Emotion

Note : There are more units here than most schools can use. It is assumed that each faculty - not each teacher - will decide which ones to omit. The balance of fun and seriousness, of passions and technique, ought not to be seriously disturbed.

The lists of typical materials could be considerably extended, but they are long enough to make clear the nature of each unit and to call up in the mind of the enthusiastic teacher of poetry other selections of the same sort. Though a few of the traditional pieces, which are believed not to appeal strongly to adolescents have been omitted, most of the poems generally used in the better schools are included.

The use of some poems in two or more units is quite conscious. Any great poem has more than one facet, and some could be placed appropriately in half a dozen of the more or less artificial units which it seems necessary to construct in order to arrange a satisfactory balance of literature experiences. Moreover, teachers are coming to realise that pupils in school may enjoy returning to a good poem a month or a year later, just as we all do in our private reading.

In this section quotation marks around the titles are omitted for the sake of simplicity.

1. ***Primary Objective*** : To enjoy poems of delight in physical nature and in bodily activity.

   Enabling Objectives : To approach each poem with an expectation of pleasure. To recall, when possible, personal experiences parallel to the one the poet has presented. To image vividly the sights, sounds, odors, and other sensations.

   Typical Materials : A Vagabond Song (Carman); The Humble Bee (Emerson); The Barefoot Boy (Whittier); Trees (Kilmer); Going A-Nutting (Stedman); The Corn Song (Whittier); Autumn (J.S. Untermeyer); When the Frost Is on the Punkin (Riley); Rain in Summer (Longfellow); The Snow Storm (Emerson); To the Dandelion (J.R. Lowell); November Night (Crapsey); Fog (Sandburg); The Daffodils (Wordsworth); October's Bright Blue Weather (H.H. Jackson); Bicycling Song (Beeching); Swimmers (L. Untermeyer); I Keep Wondering (H. Conkling); The Hundred-Yard Dash (W. Lindsey); Skating (from Prelude, Book I, Wordsworth).

2. *Primary Objective* : To enjoy poems of the merely ludicrous.

   Enabling Objectives : To expect no serious point or idea. To imagine the persons, objects, and situations clearly enough to feel the incongruity which makes the fun. To note ridiculous coined words, intentionally inflated language, or dialect.

Typical Materials : The Plaint of the Camel (Carryl); The Owl and The Pussy Cat (Lear); Mia Carlotta (Daly); Godfrey Gordon Gustavus Gore (Rands); The Cremation of Sam McGee (Service); De Fust Banjo (Rusell); Father William (Carroll); The Yarn of the Nancy Bell (Gilbert); Strictly Germproof (Guiterman); Etiquette (Guiterman); The Height of the Ridiculous (Holmes); The Walrus and the Carpenter (Carroll); Smells, Jr. (Morley); Limericks.

3. *Primary Objective* : To enjoy poem in which rhythm or (and) onomatopoeia are prominent.

Enabling Objectives : To read such verse aloud with abandon to the swing. To enjoy the variations in the timing and stress dictated by the meaning. To feel the appropriateness of the different movements to the feelings expressed. To enjoy onomatopoetic words.

Typical Materials : The Brook (Tennyson); The Apple Orchard in the Spring (Martin); The Song of the Chattahoochee (Lanier); How They Brought the Good News From Ghent to Aix (Browning); The Seal's Lullaby (Kipling). Such contrasting pairs as America the Beautiful (Bates) and America for Me (Van Dyke); The Rainy Day (Longfellow) and Joy of the Hills (Markham); The Cloud (Shelley) and How the Water Comes Down at Ladore (Southey).

4. *Primary Objective* : To share in expressions of friendship, tenderness for pets, friends, family.

Enabling Objectives : To approach the poems naturally, without the conventional early-adolescent fear of sentiment. To read with restraint rather than sentimentality or ironical exaggeration. To think of one's own while using the names of the poet's choice.

Typical Materials : My Dog (Bangs); At the Crossroads (Hovey); Sweet and Low (Tennyson); Day Is Done (Longfellow); Pitty-pat and Tippy-toe (Field); Da Leetla Boy (Daly); To a Mouse (Burns); A Mile with Me (Van

Dyke); The Education of Nature (Wordsworth); Grace Before Sleep (Teasdale); Auld Lang Syne (Burns).

5. ***Primary Objective*** : To participate in expressions of simple religious belief and consolation.

   Enabling Objectives : To accept, at least temporarily, the poets' conceptions of infinite power and goodness. To see the objects mentioned as examples or types of large groups.

   Typical Materials : Chartless (Dickinson); To a Waterfowl (Bryant); The Spacious Firmament on High (Addison); The Sandpiper (Thaxter); Sandalphon (Longfellow); The Eternal Goodness (Whittier); A Boy's Prayer (Hogg); Christmas Carols; The First Snow Fall (Lowell); The Old Clock on the Stairs (Longfellow); The Lamb (Blake).

6. ***Primary Objective*** : To enjoy poems in which vivid (and fresh?) sensory images are especially prominent.

   Enabling Objectives : To recognise the images as themselves a source of pleasure. To take time to clarify, complete, and savor the images. To discriminate to some extent the fresh from the trite, the vivid from the vague. To note tactile and kinaesthetic and olfactory as well as visual and auditory images.

   Typical Materials : " Velvet Shoes (Wylie); Red Slippers (A. Lowell); Smells (Morley); The Raven (Poe); There's Nothing Like the Rose (Rossetti); Boats Sail on the River (Rossetti); Tampa Robins (Lanier); The Great Lover (Brooks); Ballade Catalogue of Lovely Things (Le Gallienne); God's World (Millay); How the Water Comes Down at Ladore (Southey); The Common Street (Cone); Cargoes (Masefield).

7. ***Primary Objective*** : To share in artistic expressions of general altruism and similar moral sentiments or impulses.

   Enabling Objectives : To approach each poem either in a mood of aspiration or in one of readiness for what the poet proposes. To note incidentally and without losing touch with the poet's thought and feeling such graces of expression as rhythm, imagery, and fresh diction.

Typical Materials : Duty (Emerson): Outwitted (Markham); Forbearance (Emerson); The Chambered Nautilus (Holmes); Prayers of Steel (Sandburg); The Fool's Prayer (Sill); Psalm of Life (Longfellow); The Builders (Longfellow); The House By The Side of The Road (Foss); Abou Ben Adhem (Hunt); Voluntaries Days (Emerson); If (Kipling); L'Envoi (Kipling); Dedication (Masefield).

8. ***Primary Objective*** : To share in worthy expressions of patriotism.

Enabling Objectives : To yield to the intoxication of the rhythm (probably by reading aloud). To recall the incidents or actions alluded to. To realize the social significance of our government and institutions.

Typical Materials : The Concord Hymn (Emerson); The Flat Goes By (Bennett); America for Me (Van Dyke); The American Flag (Drake); The Name of Old Glory (Riley); A Farmer Remembers Lincoln (Bynner); Lincoln, the Man of the People (Markham); O Captain! My Captain! (Whitman); Lincoln excerpt from Commemoration Ode (Lowell); Anne Rutledge (Masters); Pioneers! O Pioneers! (Whitman); The Blue and the Gray (Finch); Prayer During Battle (Hagedorn).

9. ***Primary Objective*** : To enjoy poems in which suggestion is predominant.

Enabling Objectives : To read first in the mood of surrender to the poet's leading. To reread with mind alerts to the associations and implications of words or phrases including those of the title. To supply ideas necessary to unify apparently unrelated statements or actions.

Typical Materials : Opportunity (Still); Blades of Grass (Crane); Sight (Gibson); Hills (Guiterman); Boats Sail on the River (Rossetti); Little Boy Blue (Field); The Junk Man (Sandburg); The Wayfarer (Crane); The Donkey (Chesterton); Four Little Foxes (Sarett).

10. ***Primary Objective*** : To enjoy poems of subtle humour or of humour mingled with other emotions or accompanied by didactic purpose.

Enabling Objectives : To see the serious purposes or the alternations of tenderness without allowing them to quench one's amusement.

Typical Materials : Miniver Cheevy (Robinson); The last Leaf (Holmes); Learners (Weaver); Mia Carlotta (Daly); Parodies; My Aunt (Holmes); Dorlon's Home-Walk (Guiterman); Tact (Guiterman).

11. ***Primary Objective*** : To share delight in intellectual experiences or poetic contemplation.

Enabling Objectives : To expect some significance beyond story or image. To avoid prejudice against reflection as a stuffy occupation of older people.

Typical Materials : On First Looking into Chapman's Homer, Ode to a Nightingale (Keats); Stopping By a Wood on a Snowy Evening (Frost); Flower in the Crannied Wall (Tennyson); My Heart Leaps Up (Wordsworth); Renascence (Millay); Il Penseroso (Milton); Ode on a Grecian Urn (Keats); Thoughts Facing Death (Keats); The Mermaid Tavern (Keats); Ode on The Poets (Keats); Dover Beach (Arnold); My Mother's Words (Branch); There is no Frigate Like a Book (Dickinson); Elegy Written in a Country Churchyard (Gray); The Rhodora (Emerson); Each and All (Emerson); Pierrot (Teasdale); Euclid Alone Has Looked on Beauty Bare (Millais); Good-Bye, Proud World (Emerson).

12. ***Primary Objective*** : To delight in poems with more intricate or more varied music, including free verse.

Enabling Objectives : To note the principle upon which lines are divided in free verse. To listen for the slightly irregular beat of the accents and to disregard meters and scansion. To note recurring cadences and other elements of pattern.

Typical Materials : Sea Fever (Masefiled); The Barrel Organ (Noyes); The Bells (Poe); The Congo, Santa Fe Trail (Lindsay); Little Things (Johns); I Hear America Singing (Whitman); On His Blindness (Milton); Ozymandias (Shelley); Patterns (A. Lowell); The King's Breakfast (amusing, intentional misdivision of lines, by Milne); Cinquains (Crapsey); Fog (Sandburg); Chicago (Sandburg); Pioneers! O Pioneers! (Whitman).

13. ***Primary Objective*** : To enjoy poems in which much of the charm is due to elaborate, exotic, or fanciful imagery.

Enabling Objectives : To give oneself time to fill out the exotic picture, recalling objects and pictures, which furnish material to the imagination. To reread in order to weld the details of an elaborate image into one whole.

Typical Materials : The Marshes of Glynn (Lanier); Birches (Frost); To a Skylark (Shelley); The Debutante (Carryl); May is Building Her House (Le Gallienne); Solitaire (A. Lowell); Chinoiserie (A. Lowell); Images (Aldington); The Rhodora (Emerson); Barter (Teasdale); Say Not the Struggle Naught Availeth (Clough); The Eagle (Tennyson).

14. ***Primary Objective*** : To enjoy poetic expressions of romantic love.

Enabling Objectives : To regard love as serious and not mere sport. To sympathise with both despondent and the happy lover.

Typical Materials : Remember Me When I Am Come Away (Rossetti); I Shall Not Care (Teasdale); The Bugle Song (Tennyson); School Days (Whittier); John Anderson, My Jo (Burns); My Love Is Like a Red Rose (Burns); Drink to Me Only with Thine Eyes (Johnson); When Malindy Sings (Dunbar); My Heart Is Like A Singing Bird (Rossetti); Song (D. Burnet); She Walks in Beauty Like the Night (Byron); Sonnet XXIX, "When in disgrace with fortune" (Shakespeare); Sonnet CXVI, "Let me not to the marriage of true minds" (Shakespeare); When I Was One-and-Twenty (Housman).

15. ***Primary Objective*** : To find satisfaction in expressions of troubled religious belief or of stoicism.

Enabling Objectives : To know something of the problems that trouble thoughtful people's belief in revealed religion. To realise the thrill of fighting the universe without dependence upon supernatural aid. To see the encouragements to belief which even the less credulous find.

Typical Materials : Thanatopsis (Bryant); A Parting Guest (Riley); Cool Tombs (Sandburg); The Tiger (Blake); Poems XXVII, LXV, XCVI, In Memoriam (Tennyson); Crossing the Bar (Tennyson); Invictus (Henley); Dover Beach (Arnold); Marshes of Glynn (Lanier); Up Hill (Rossetti).

16. ***Primary Objective*** : To join in poetic protests against social wrongs.

Enabling Objectives : To know enough of the world to understand what the protests are about.

Typical Materials : The Man with the Hoe (Markham); Song of the Shirt (Hood); Factory Children (E. Browning); Clean Curtains (Sandburg); Fifth Avenue (Sandburg); On a Soldier Fallen in the Philippines (Moody); A Man's a Man (Burns); The Walker (Giovannitti); Abraham Lincoln Walks at Midnight (Lindsay); After Blenheim (Southey); Grass (Sandburg); As Toilsome I Wandered Virginia's Woods (Whitman).

17. ***Primary Objective*** : To share in lyric expression of human **brotherhood, transcending sectional and national boundaries.**

Enabling Objectives : To concentrate on the individuals without regard to race or nationality.

Typical Materials : Scum o' the Earth (Schauffer); Gunga Din (Kipling); A Man's a Man (Burns); The Ballad of the East and the West (Kipling); The House by the Side of the Road (Foss); A.E.F. (Sandburg).

18. *Primary Objective* : To enjoy poems in which suggestion is either the chief charm or the chief means conveying the central impression.

Enabling Objectives : To examine with reasonable care figurative expressions and allusions. To take into account the known attitudes and temperament of the author. To yield to the mood of the poem, seeking a clue to meaning through feeling.

Typical Materials : Eldorado (Poe); Mending Wall (Frost); Caliban in the Coal Mines (Untermeyer); The Wayfarer (Crane); Richard Cory (Rohinson); Fire and Ice (Frost); I Saw a Man (Crane); When Lilacs Last in the Dooryard Bloomed (Whitman); The World Is Too Much with Us (Wordsworth); L'Allegro (Milton); Exit (Fletcher); Mermorabilia (Browning); The Patriot (Browning).

F. Giving Fancy Rein

1. ***Primary Objective*** : To enjoy humorous fantasy in which exaggeration is a principal element.

   Enabling Objectives : To enter into the jocular mood. To realise the ridiculousness of the events and yet to "suspend disbelief."

   Typical Materials : Paul Bunyan (Stevens, Shephard or Bowman); Alice in Wonderland (Caroll); Adventures of Baron Munchausen; They yarn of the Nancy Belle (Gilbert); The Height of the Ridiculous (Holmes); Rootbaga Stories (Sandburg); Wizard of Oz (Baum); Tall Stories of the Southwest.

2. ***Primary Objective*** : To enjoy relatively simple fantasies, which are vehicles for ideas.

   Enabling Objectives : To accept the suspension of certain physical laws but not of psychological or moral ones. To take intellectual pleasure in the ideas and not to think of them as burdens upon the stories.

   Typical Materials : "The Nightingale"(Anderson); Dr. Jekyll and Mr. Hyde (Stevenson); "The Happy Prince" (Wilde); "Great Stone Face" (Hawthorne); "Demon of the Matted Hair" from Jataka Tales; "The Knights of the Silver Shield" (Adden); "King Robert of Sicily" (Longfellow); "The Boy and the Angel" (Longfellow).

3. ***Primary Objective*** : To enjoy relatively simple fantastic plays.

Enabling Objectives : To visualise the settings and the characters. To imagine the action implied by the dialogue or indicated by the stage directions.

Typical Materials : A Midsummer Night's Dream (Shakespeare); "The Golden Doom" (Dunsany); "A Night at an Inn" (Dunsany); "The Blue Bird" (Maeterlinck); "Crossings" (de la Mare); "Toad of Toad Hall" (A.A. Milne); "Golden Apple" (Lady Gregory).

4. *Primary Objective* : To enjoy fantasies in which the usual story interests, suspense, characters, humour, and theme are fairly well balanced.

Enabling Objectives : To get from context or dictionary the meaning of unusual words. To be alert to plot, character humour, and theme in combination.

Typical Materials : "The Devil and Tom Walker" (Irving); "Rip Van Winkle" (Irving); "Legend of Sleepy Hollow" (Irving); "Dr. Heidegger's Experiment" (Hawthorne); "The Birthmark" (Hawthorne); Gulliver's Travels (Swift); The Story of Sindbad; Ulysses Among The Phaeacians (Bryant Or Palmer translation).

5. *Primary Objective* : To enjoy allegories.

Enabling Objectives : To see the story as a story and as a symbol at the same time (or in rapid alternation). To refrain from finding symbolism in every detail.

Typical Materials : Pilgrim's Progress (Bunyan); "Kathleen Ni Houlihan" (Yeats); "The Vision of Mirza" (Addison); Idylls of the King (Tennyson). "The Ancient Mariner" (Coleridge), though not strictly an allegory may well be used here.

6. *Primary Objective* : To become acquainted with the more important myths, especially Greek and Norse.

Enabling Objectives : To see in these fantastic stories naïve explanations of natural phenomena; to see the psychological subtlety of the Greek myths and the romantic ruggedness of the Norse; to distinguish between myth, legend and fairy-or folk-tale.

Typical Materials : Collections such as : Myths and Their Meaning (Herzberg); Classic Myths in English Poetry (Gayley); The Age of Fable (Bulfinch); The Children of Odin (Colum); In the Light of Myth (Baker). Interpretive discussions such as Myth, Ritual and Religion (Lang); Myths and Myth Makers (Lang).

7. ***Primary Objective*** : To read epic poems with satisfaction.

   Enabling Objectives : To know something of the intellectual and social life of the time and place in which the epic was composed. To know the religious beliefs of the composer. To know in advance the general outline of the story.

   Typical Materials : Iliad, Odyssey (Bryant, Palmer, or Bates translation) : Paradise Lost, Book I at least (Milton); Divine Comedy (Dante). For comparison : Faerie Queene (Spenser); John Brown's Body (Benet); Idylls of the King (Tennyson); Robin Hood ballads; Tristram or other of Robinson's Book-length narratives.

8. ***Primary Objective*** : To enjoy more difficult fantasies, which are primarily intellectual.

   Enabling Objectives : To recall the information assumed by the authors. To be sensitive to both atmosphere and slight specific hints as clues to the theme of each work.

   Typical Materials : Frankenstein (Shelley); R. U. R. (Capek); The Adding Machine (Rice); Death Takes a Holiday (Walter Ferris); Houseboat on the Styx (Bangs); Green Pastures (Connelly) or Ole Man Adam and His Children (Bradford).

9. ***Primary Objective*** : To enjoy poetic fantasies, in which beauty and mysticism predominate.

   Enabling Objectives : To yield to the moods aroused by the sensory images, their associations, and the language cadences.

   Typical Materials : Kubla Khan" (Coleridge); "Christabel" (Coleridge); "La Belle Dame Sans Merci" (Keats); "Isle of Innisfree" (Yeats); Crock of Gold (Stephens); Tempest

(Shakespeare); "Land of Heart's Desire" (Yeats); "Gods of the Mountain" (Dunsany); "The Lady of Shalott" (Tennyson).

G. Solving Puzzles

1. *Primary Objective* : To read simple mystery stories more as puzzles than as adventures.

   Enabling Objectives : To discover as quickly as possible what the mystery to be solved is. To keep in mind *while reading* all the "facts" so far revealed. To review the evidence at stopping points in the story. At the end to consider what clues one has failed to catch. To judge the reasonableness of the conclusion.

   Typical Materials : "The Gold Bug" (Poe); Mystery Tales for Boys and Girls (Smith); Boy Scouts Year Book of Mystery Stories (Mathiews); Adventures of Sherlock Holmes (Conan Doyle); The Jinx Ship (Pease); The Pool of Stars (Meigs); Blair's Attic (Lincoln); The New Curiosity Shop (Capbell); The Secret of the Empty Room (Seam); The Glacier Mystery (Smith); The Black Wolf Pack (Beard); The Secret of Hallam House (Baker); Mystery of the World's End (Bamberger); The Front Page Mystery (Graham).

2. *Primary Objective* : To play a game of intellectual tag with the authors of clever mystery stories, especially short ones.

   Enabling Objectives : To regard the characters in the story as chess pawns or checker men rather than as objects of human sympathy. To observe all clues, to note significant repetitions. To reject too obvious clues. To note at the end how the point of view from which the story is told enables the author to mislead the reader, either by concealing real clues or by adding misleading ones.

   Typical Materials : "The Purloined Letter" (Poe); The Fourth Man (Russell); "The Paradise of Thieves" (Chesterton); "The Adventures of The Mazarin Stone" (Doyle); Christabel Crystal (Wells); Miss Hinch (Harrison); The Thief (Rohlfs); The Parson (Steen) The Crime of Sylvester

Bonnard (France); Master of the Mill (Post). Also collections Such as Chesterton's The Innocence of Father Brown; Post's Uncle Abner, Master of Mysteries Doyle's Adventures of Sherlock Holmes.

3. *Primary Objective* : To play tag with the authors of intricate or subtle mystery stories, chiefly those of book length.

Enabling Objectives : To keep in mind the relation to the events of the story-teller, puzzle-solver, or some other (possible chief) actor in the plot, or omniscient author. To consider the point of view of the puzzle-solver, *e.g.*, that of a police officer. To note also the solver's personal cleverness and limitations. To become reasonably familiar with the types of plot and of concealment used by some of the better prolific writers of mystery stories.

Typical Materials : Trent's Last Case (Bentley); A Certain Dr. Thorndyke (Freeman); The Bishop Murder Case (Van Dine); The Mystery at the Blue Villa (Post); Tutt and Mr. Tutt (Train); Wheels within Wheels (Wells); The Strangler Fig (Strange); Moonstone (Collins); John Silence (Algernon Blackwood); Gray Room (Phillpotts); Circular Staircase (Rinehart); Mystery of Edwin Drood (Dickens). Short Stories by Poe, Post, Chesterton, Conan Doyle, etc., for comparison.

H. Listening to Radio Broadcasts

Note : Within an astonishingly short time - hardly more than a decade - the American people have acquired a new folkway : listening to the radio. The number of hours of time each day when the radio is "on" in American homes, places of business, offices, and school must reach figures of astronomical vastness. Now even more and more people listen in, one hopes with vague attention, while driving automobiles; soon one may expect to see people walking our streets with minute radio sets hung from their hats and going full blast as they step along. To multitudes radio offers great, and often wholesome, enjoyment.

Young people have the habit even more than those of an older generation. The radio to them is as commonplace as the weather, and its marvels are as much a matter of course as those of the telephone or the electric light or the photoplay. Many of them have the radio performing constantly during waking and sometimes working hours. The beat of a jazz band accompanies, agreeably for them, the study of Julius Caesar, the probing of a geometrical problem, or a translation from Victor Hugo. Radio, like the motion-picture theatre, provides models for thinking and feeling; it determines life attitudes, ambitions, and intonations of the voice. As an influence it throws the schools far into the shade; that influence, we should never forget, is frequently highly commendable as well as, sometimes, very bad.

Censorship, except of a very discreet sort, is much less valuable than the establishment of a critical attitude, in which the good will be properly praised and the bad perceived and, perhaps, avoided. Radio programes, aside from their implications for ethics, citizenship, vocational guidance and the like, are an *art*, and to the extent that standards can be established for an art, it may be possible to show young people how to distinguish excellence from trash. Naturally, all criteria that are set up must be labelled as tentative, temporary, variable. Dogmatism must be at all costs avoided; free discussion must be encouraged. But experience in other fields has shown the possibility of worthwhile endeavour in this. English teachers who believe that their students can be taught to like good poetry, good books, good speech need not hesitate to believe that some improvement will ensue if an attempt is made to have pupils follow Rabbi Ben Ezra in his prizing of an occasional doubt regarding radio programes.

The units which follow cover only that part of the radio material which clearly belongs to the field of literature : dramatic sketches, monologues, general culture addresses, criticism, and readings of poetry. The elements of appreciation of such materials are largely the same as those usually cultivated in literature classes and teachers apparently find this the easiest place to begin. Study listening or works listening and listening comparable to recreational reading of travel, history, and science have been given new importance by broadcast lectures and political speeches. Training in the arts of work listening and of recreational listening to factual material should certainly be given at the secondary level - as soon as satisfactory procedures for giving such training can be developed. Meantime a beginning should be made with literary listening.

Admiration is an art to be learned - Goethe

Objectives :

1. In direct relation to the English classrooms :
   - (*a*) *Esthetic and Literary* - To correlate literature experiences in radio programes with those present in the work in English.
   - (*b*) *Expressional* - To utilise opportunities for critical discussion and writing, as part of the training in expression given in English.
   - (*c*) *Expressional* - To compose sketches, addresses, interviews, and the like as if for radio broadcasting and the actual use of these wherever possible, a straining in writing and delivery - all from carefully selected models.
   - (*d*) *Linguistic* - To make use of opportunities for the study of language, as occurring, (*i*) in radio discussion of usage and related topics, and (*ii*) in a study of the technique of broadcasting and the diction of announcers and speakers, in order to raise standards of speech and improve spoken English.
   - (*e*) *Literary and Linguistic* - To increase appreciation of the spoken word and to stress the aural values of verse as given over the air.
2. In general education :
   - (*a*) *Civic* - To give young people help in making worthy use of leisure time.
   - (*b*) *Civic* - To establish standards of taste to be used in judging radio programes such standards to be differentiated to suit different kinds of programes.
   - (*c*) *Civic* - To develop ability to follow and to examine critically the lectures, discussions, and advertising statements of radio programes, as a means of creating intelligent skepticism and the power to resist propaganda.

(*d*) *Esthetic* - To increase desirable character ideals and attitudes, as a reflex of radio programes.

(*e*) *Esthetic* - To increase appreciation of the art of radio. (Corollary : Definite programe tuning.)

(*f*) *Informational* - To provide general information ("collateral listening"). (Corollary : Correlation with history, civics, economics, science, art, music, foreign languages, etc.).

1. *Primary Objective* : To get from broadcast stories and play - lets as rich and as lasting pleasure as is possible.

   Enabling Objectives : To be acquainted with some of the better programes of this nature. To note individual voices, and imagine the character behind them. To know some of the qualities of good stories and plays - plausibility if not truth, clear characterization, rapid movement, appropriate language and delivery. To have in mind examples of these excellence to serve as touchstones in judging other broadcasts. To appreciate pleasing voices and clear but natural articulation.

2. *Primary Objective* : To find and enjoy the best broadcast comics and continued sketches.

   Enabling Objectives : To recognise freshness and cleverness. To recognize coarseness invoice or content. To recognise consistency of characterisation in continued broadcasts. To see the common human weaknesses or follies which are satirised.

3. *Primary Objective* : To listen appreciatively and critically to some informational broadcasts as news summaries, stories of important public occasions, and travelogues.

   Enabling Objectives : To know enough about the recent events or the region described to understand clearly the information offered. To use the same constructive imagination employed in reading history or travel books. To recognise colouring of the news or other information, by knowing the political bias of the speaker and by noting the attitude revealed in the language, especially the adjectives, used.

4. *Primary Objective* : To listen discriminatingly to debates and speeches on public questions.

   Enabling Objectives : To perceive clearly the point under debate or discussion. To know whether the speaker is generally - not by his partisans only - considered honest in his statement of facts. To recognise the unstated assumptions the speakers make. To have some ideals of logic in reaching conclusions from facts.

5. *Primary Objective* : To find and enjoy satisfying sermons, lectures, and other up-lift broadcasts.

   Enabling Objectives : To be interested in ethical and intellectual problems. To distinguish between genuine sentiment and insincerity or sentimentality. To recognise that main points and structure of an address. To remember and use strikingly effective statements of illustrations.

I. Enjoying Photoplays

Note : This strand might appropriately be called "Discussing Photoplays", since actual attendance does not take place during classtime or as assigned homework. This phase of the literature work is much like the independent reading, consisting of class discussion which it is hoped may guide individual voluntary action in leisure time. It differs from the guidance of reading in the very few pupils need to be stimulated to use more of their leisure for this purpose; the problem is almost wholly that of elevating taste.

Any recommendation of specific units in the consideration of the photoplay must be entirely tentative. School experience in this field is still too meagre to permit any definite conclusions about the organisation of the study. Moreover, the photoplay itself an evolving so rapidly that procedures and especially examples probably would be obsolete before they could be put into type.

A further difficulty in organisation arises from the fact that the sequence of photoplays at any neighbourhood theatre rarely lends itself to any building of units. In many places, however, it is possible to centre the photoplay discussions of a year upon certain types of productions, letting the subject rest between the appearances of examples of this type. This organisation seems as the present moment to be desirable where it is possible. Its units might be something like these :

1. *Primary Objective* : To enjoy fully the better short comedies.

   Enabling Objectives : To enjoy fresh fun (fresh at least in presentation) more than stale tricks or jokes. To enjoy in photographed comedies (as distinguished from animated cartoons) plausibility and naturalness. To enjoy facial expression. To realise the characters sufficiently to feel any character comedy which is present. In animated cartoons to recognise the compatibility of characters, setting and incidents. To enjoy beauty in colouring and design - when present. (Most teachers would like to add, "To dislike the *risqué*", but discussion of such elements is likely to call attention to what had not been noticed, or at least emphasise and familiarise what should be ignored.)

2. *Primary Objective* : To enjoy the better "Westerns" and other adventure stories.

   Enabling Objectives : To keep the incidents and the character relationships straight. To distinguish between the probable and the impossible. To sympathise with the right side. To recognise good riding, good horses, natural make-up and acting.

3. *Primary Objective* : To enjoy discriminatingly light romance.

   Enabling Objectives : To be alert to plot cues. To recognise admirable qualities in hero or heroine. To recognise good singing, and natural, vigorous acting.

4. *Primary Objective* : To see newsreels with the same interest and critical attitude with which one reads the newspapers.

   Enabling Objectives : To know enough of current events to place each episode in its political, social, scientific or economic setting. To be alert to bias in selection or presentation of incidents. To take an attitude of study, looking for significance, toward industrial, political, and military scenes. To take a relaxed, appreciative attitude toward "human interest" and picturesque presentations.

5. *Primary Objective* : To enjoy the better musical comedies.

   Enabling Objectives : To prefer clever plots to stale of flimsy ones. To prefer clean, fresh jokes to dirty or stale ones. To appreciate stage pictures beauty in costumes or cast (invite an art teacher). To appreciate graceful, significant dancing (invite a physical-education teacher.) To enjoy good music : melodies, harmonies, voices, and orchestral performance (invite the music teacher).

6. *Primary Objective* : To enjoy the occasional real dramas presented on the screen.

   Enabling Objectives : To see clearly the opposing forces, and the object of contention. To see the psychological or social significance of the contest. To be alert to find acting, including telling gestures and intonations. To judge the truth of the dramatist's depiction of this slice of life.

Alternative Units

Based upon progress in discrimination between good and poor photoplay, instead of upon the content of the photoplay experiences.

1. *Primary Objective* : To correct one's estimate of photoplays recently seen by discussing their merits and faults with classmates and teacher.

   Enabling Objectives : To be frank in expressing one's own opinion. To consider with genuine fairness the opinions of others. To be aware of suspense, humour, clever bits of acting, probability (or improbability), realism in settings, clearness of characterisation.

2. *Primary Objective* : To become informed about photoplay techniques, writers, producers, directors, actors, and critics.

   Enabling Objectives : To know which magazines and newspapers have reliable photoplay information. To know what must be done to make a play of a story. To know in what ways the screen is more limited than the stage, in what ways more free. To note by copyright date or other evidence whether a book or article deals with the present or past.

3. ***Primary Objective*** : To set up standards for evaluating photoplays.

Enabling Objectives : To carry over standards of content development from literature study. To carry over from art study standards of pictorial effect. To carry over from physical education standards of grace in posture and movement. To carry over from public speaking or dramatics standards of vocal expression. To carry over from music standards of musical composition and execution.

J. Special Units

Note : The following units are a sort of preparation for college methods of studying literature. They also provide new approaches, which may awaken the interest of some pupils who were not aroused by the less formally organised experiences with literature. Each of these special units requires from two to four times as much time as a typical unit of this curriculum.

1. *Getting Acquainted with a Literary Type*

Primary Objective : To get more intelligent enjoyment from short stories.

Enabling Objectives : To recognise the limitation of the short story to a single mood, a single plot, and a simple (though possible important) theme. To recognise early in the reading of a story the type to which it belongs - *alias*, the author's purpose - and to read accordingly. To apply, informally or even subconsciously, such criteria of excellence as intellectual or emotional value of the main impression, truth of characters, plausibility of plot, dramatic intensity, appropriateness of style. To know where to find good short stories for future reading.

Appraisal : Do the pupils read more than they did? Do they choose stories of better quality? Has insight as revealed by class discussion improved during the unit? Are pupils more responsive to delicate, subtle effects? Do the pupils

Activities	*Materials*	*Adaptation*
Informal discussion of the pupils' favourite stories and changing reading tastes. Making a list of stories that members of the class have read more than once, and trying to discover their appeal. Looking over and commenting upon a list of good short stories. Rereading critically some of the stories, applying standards of merit. Making an annotated list of good short stories. Reporting to the class especially excellent stories discovered by independent reading. Comparing the short story with the one-act play. Writing original stories, using first-hand settings and types of character. Comparing several stories by the same author, to find any common characteristics.	Poe, Hawthorne, Irving, O. Henry, W.W. Jacobs, Maupassant, Merimee, Tolstoy, Galsworthy, Kipling, D.W. Steel, Lardner, Cable, Hartle, Bierce, Cobb, Doyle, Tarkington, Stevenson, Ben Ames Williams. Collection of stories by types, by countries, by subjects, by historical development of the form.	*For the slow or underprivileged* : Simple stories in which all essential incidents and motives are stated explicitly and the use of unusual or abstract works is minimised. More class reading and discussion. Dramatisation or illustration in graphic or plastic form. *For the gifted* : Elliptical, enigmatic stories. Stories which raise deeper ethical and social questions. Stories in which the diction is too difficult for most pupils. Dialect stories. Comparing prose stories with such tales in verse as "Enoch Arden," "The Falcom of Ser Federigo" or any of Chaucer in F. E. Hill's translation. Reading stories in class (*i*) to discover the different kinds, (*ii*) to note the technique : introduction, setting, plot, characters, atmosphere, single impression, compression, style. Reading critical theory of the form, *e.g.*, Poe's. Studying the history of the short story. Looking up in *Who's Who* or elsewhere biographies of favourite story writers. Examining magazines to see what quality of stories each offers.

know a reasonable number of the masters of the short story? Do the pupils have lists of stories or of authors they hope to read?

2. *Getting Acquainted with an Author*

1. *Primary Objective* : To know and value justly the work and personality of Charles Dickens.

Enabling Objectives : To know first hand as much as possible of Dickens' writing. To suspend criticism while reading the novels and short stories. To form independently some critical opinions concering Dickens' merits, considering the vividness, fundamental soundness, detailed accuracy of his characterisation; the unity and plausibility of his plots; the range and vividness of his backgrounds; the naturalness of his dialogue; the emotional force of his work. To know and weight standard critical estimates of Dickens. To see through the author;s eyes the social and economic conditions of his time and country. To know from other sources something of these social and economic conditions. To perceive something of the interaction between Dickens and the England of his day. To realise to what a large extent it is true that "to know Dickens is to know London and to know London is to know Dickens". To realise to what extent Dickens pictorialised an entire nation. To realize the abiding character of his portraiture in spite of its intense localisation. To see the England of his day as he saw it and our own day as a Dickens might see it.

Activites :

(*a*) *Oral Reading* : Good audience reading of some short unit by teacher or pupil, to be followed by individual oral readings to groups, readers sometimes to be selected by try-outs, in cooperation wherever possible with oral expression departments. Taking advantage of radio programes, motion pictures, and professional dramatic readings of plays.

(*b*) Individual silent reading (sometimes in class).

(*c*) Making a display of books, magazines, pictures with the cooperation of Dickens' lovers in the community. Giving short talks on sections of the display contributed, such as the illustrations.

(*d*) *Group undertaking* : making a Dicken's map of England by putting into an outline map places associated with his life, such as homes, haunts, memorials. Oral reports by individuals on items contributed, such as old English inns visited by Dickens.

(*e*) Becoming familiar with the chief facts in his life, especially his boyhood. Consulting and giving reports from standard biographies as well as from recent books and periodicals.

(*f*) Making lists of well - known Dickens characters with their tags.

(*g*) Making as a class report on "Dickens, the Humanitarian, listing causes he advocated and evils he attacked.

(*h*) Class symposium on "Dickens as a Humorist", with voluntary contributions of a humorous scene, character, or expression.

(*i*) Studying A tale of Two Cities. Classroom reading and discussion with teacher contributions until background is established and action started. Rapid individual reading class discussion from any one of such points of view as the following :

i. Its picture of Revolution, compared with other.

ii. Its balance of emphasis upon character, background, and plots.

iii. Its difference from other works of Dickens.

(*j*) Summing up individual reading by pupils in the form of class reports on typical scenes, customs, characters, or incidents.

Materials :

(*a*) *Typical Selection* : Parts of the Christmas Carol David Copperfield, Nicholas Nickleby, Pickwick Papers, a Tale of Two Cities, Oliver Twist.

(*b*) The novels, especially David Copperfield, Oliver Twist Nicholas Nickleby, Little Dorrit, Hard Times, Old Curicsity Shop, Great Expectations. The short stories, especially "Christmas Carol", "Cricket on the Hearth", A Child's Dream of a Star".

(*c*) Various editions, biographies, newspaper clippings. "The Dickensian", published quarterly since 1904, by The Dickens Fellowship at the Dickens House, 48 Doughty Street, London, W.C.I. Life (John Foster). Charles Dickens : His Life and Work (Stephen Peacock, 1934). Articles on the Dickens' Centenary.

(*d*) From biographies locate the homes and memorials.

(*e*) Articles in the Saturday Review of Literature and other periodicals.

(*f*) Charles Dickens as a Reader (C. Kent), Pen Photographs of Dickens' Readings in America (Kate Field).

(*g*) The French Revolution (Carlyle), Reds of the Midi (Gras).

Adaptation :

(*a*) Reading done by abler pupils who may also, in cooperation with oral expression department, prepare simple dramatics and puppet shows based on dramatic incidents.

(*b*) For slower groups, shortened editions and individual help to pupils by using illustrations and building up backgrounds. Superior pupils read from following additional list if they have read the others : Little Dorrit, Our Mutual Friend, Dombey and Son, Bleak House, Hard Times or others.

(*c*) Superior students search libraries for material, and report interviews with Dickens' admirers.

(*d*) Slower members do the handwork, lettering, and other objective parts of the work based on the findings of the abler students.

(*e*) Some superior students list types and try to find similar American types :

The Delicate Child : Little Nell vs. Little Eva

The Street Gamin : Jo in Bleak House vs. (?)

The Incompetent Optimist : Micawber vs. (?)

The Struggling Author : David Copperfied vs. (?)

The Brutal Schoolmaster : Squeers vs. (?)

(*f*) Superior students invent games or make objective tests to see how many characters or tags are recognised.

(*g*) Special reports by superior students of "Dickens and Prison Reform", "Dickens as an Educator".

(*h*) Superior students compare Pickwick Papers with other humorous works, such as Don Quixote of Mark Twain's Innocents Abroad. Determine the common elements.

(*i*) Slower students should be helped in the selection of material. Superior students make additional reports on such topics as these : The publishing of The Life of Our Lord and the publicity given to it; Dickens and theatricals (his participation in dramatics and his dramatic recitals); the special values and defects of a Child's Dream of a Star, History of England, A Christmas Carol, a comparison of the portrayal of English society by Dickens and Thackeray; Dickens as a reporter (his actual experiences and the evidences of them in his works); a travelogue on "In Dickens Land", the continuing popularity of Dickens (facts about it and reasons for it); Dickens and America; Dickens and the mystery story.

Appraisal of growth : Ability to compare other authors and works read, especially Victorian, with Dickens' work and personality. Ability to recognise among people known or observed characters whom Dickens would choose to depict. Ability to recognise typical Dickens scenes from books not ready by the pupils.

3. *Becoming acquainted with a Period*

1. *Primary Objective* : To know and to understand the most important literary achievements of the Victorian Age (1832-1890), particularly as an expression of the life of the age.

Enabling Objectives : To know at first hand, through extensive reading, representative contributions to literature by the important writers of the Victorian Age. To know and understand the important aspects of the social background in which this literature was written. To realise how the literature of the age reflects the intellectual unrest and the controversy, which prevailed in the worlds of politics, education, art, science, religion, and ethics. To understand the conflicting points of view presented by different writers. To distinguish between the literature of the age that is timely and the literature that is timeless. To contrast the social attitudes of the Victorian Age with those of our own age. To know what literary types were most successful and effective in the age.

Activities :

(*a*) Individual silent reading of Victorian prose and poetry.

(*b*) Individual silent reading of sufficient secondary sources to make clear the social backgrounds and history of the Victorian Age.

(*c*) Oral reading by the teacher and by members of the class of appropriate selections of Victorian literature.

(*d*) Intensive studies of a few representative selections of Victorian literature, which reflect various aspects of life of the age, as well as selections which, have a universal appeal.

(*e*) Class round-table discussions on particular novels, poems, and essays; on social problems of Victorian society and the literature which reflects these problems.

(*f*) *Group project* : Preparing a class bulletin board on which are kept pictures and cartoons of Victorian authors, pictures of places of special interest in the story of Victorian literature, a literary map of Victorian England, reproductions of the art of the age including such extremes as Cruikshank's cartoons and the paintings of Rossetti and Burne-Jones; articles of criticism and information about the Victorian Age taken from current periodicals.

(*g*) Oral and written reports which summarise the readings of pupils and which show the social significance of the readings.

Material :

Note: The materials for study are divided into two groups : (*i*) Readings which reflect the interest of authors in the various social problems of the Victorian Age; (*ii*) Readings which present the achievements of Victorian authors by types.

(*a*) Some typical problems of social controversy and appropriate literary works in which they are discussed.

In a society that is rapidly becoming industrialised what is happening to the labouring classes and what shall we do to help them?

Novels : Hard Times (Dickens); Alton Locke (Charles Kingsley); North and South (Mrs. Gaskell).

Poems : The Song of the Shirt (Thomas Hood); The Cry of the Children (E. B. Browning); The Voice of Toil (William Morris).

Essays : The Crown of Wild Olive (John Ruskin); "Labor", "Reward", Chapters 11, 12 of Past and Present; (Thomas Carlyle).

What is wrong with our present standards of education and what ought to be the ideal of education in a world growing more complex through the increase of knowledge?

Novels : Nicholas Nickleby (selected chapters), Dombey and Son (selected chapters); (Charles Dickens).

Essays : Literature and Science (Matthew Arnold); A Liberal Education (Thomas Huxley); Selection from the Idea of a University (Cardinal Newman).

What knowledge has scientific investigation given us?

Essays : "On the Advisablness of Improving Natural Knowledge", "A Piece of Chalk" (Thomas Huxley); Selections From the Origin of Species (Charles Darwin).

What is the solution for the many conflicts between our new knowledge and our old faith?

Poems : In Memoriam (Tennyson); "Self Dependence", "Dover Beach" (Mathew Arnold); "Lead Kindly Light" (Cardinal Newman); "Say Not the Struggle Naught Availeth" (Arthur Hugh Clough).

Essays : "Knowledge and faith" in Discourses and Arguments (Cardinal Newman).

What are the prevailing manners and ethical standards of our age?

Novels : Vanity Fair (Thackeray); Jane Eyre (Charlotte Brontë); The Egoist (George Meredith).

(*b*) The most important work of Victorian writers considered by types.

Novels : Vanity Fair (Thackeray); David Copperfield (Dickens); Withering Heights (Emily Brontë); Jane Eyre (Charlotte Brontë); Adam Bede (George Eliot); Barchester Towers (Anthony Trollope); The Ordeal of Richard Feveral (George Meredith); Under the Greenwood Tree (Thomas Hardy).

Poems : Selected Narratives by Tennyson, Browning, William Morris; Monologues by Browning; Lyrics by Tennyson, Robert Browning, E. B. Browning, Matthew Arnold, Dante Gabriel Rossetti, Christina Rossetti, A.H. Clough, W. E. Henley, Edward Fitzgerald.

Essays : Thomas Carlyle, Thomas Babington Macaulay, John Ruskin, Matthew Arnold, Cardinal Newman, Thomas Huxley, Robert Louis Stevenson.

Short Story : Robert Louis Stevenson.

History : French Revolution (Carlyle); History Of England (Macaulay).

Adaptation :

(*a*) For pupils with special interests, the Victorian age provides rich opportunities for reading and reports; *e.g.*, for the art student, the pre-Raphaelite Movement; for the student of biology, the influence of Darwin's Origin of Species; for the music student, the operas of Gilbert and Sullivan.

(*b*) Reading by abler pupils of some of the dramatic monologues of Browning.

(*c*) Staging of a scene from "The Barretts of Wimpole Street."

(*d*) For advanced pupils the reading of books such as Queen Victoria, Eminent Victorians (Strachey); Man of Property (Galsworthy).

(*e*) For slower pupils the reading and the reports will be carefully supervised by the teacher, who will allow the pupils' special interests to guide them in discovering the literature of the period.

(*f*) Superior students may make comparisons of contemporary attitudes to social problems common to both ages with the attitudes of Victorian writers. Similarly they may compare the types of literature; *e.g.*, What differences in the content and the form of the novel of today and the Victorian novel are noticeable?

(*g*) The use where possible of appropriate moving pictures of Victorian, life, *e.g.*, Disraeli, David Copperfield, Great Expectations.

(*h*) Dramatization of scenes from novels depicting Victorian manners. Vanity Fair provides exceptionally fine scenes for this purpose.

6

Reading for Various Purposes

To read is to gather meaning from written or printed symbols. Reading is thus clearly a tool, a skill employed only as part of and for the sake of some larger activity, and therefore it should be taught and practised in school not in isolation but as a part of study or of the enjoyment of literature. Instruction in reading should be regarded as a part of the work in such subject-matter fields as geography, history, science, and literature, whether these are studied separately or integrated through general projects. When this instruction must be separated in time from the class meeting devoted to those subjects, interests already aroused and problems already raised should be carried over - with appropriate reading material. For example, if the geography lesson has aroused curiosity concerning the methods of cotton production the reading lesson may be to get information on this topic, first from the geography text, and then from any other available books, pamphlets, or magazines.

Type of Reading - The distinction between work reading and recreational reading is recognised throughout this report. Although the varieties of reading could be arranged in a scale, with as continuous gradations as the shades of the solar spectrum, most cases can readily be classified as either work or recreational reading. Trying to find out whether Scotch woollens are really better than American is obviously a different sort of activity from enjoying Sara Teasdale's "Barter". Work reading, by and large, seeks information; recreational reading seeks entertainment. Work reading is done for some use, theoretical or practical, to be made of the content; recreational reading is done for present satisfaction. The reason for making the distinction is that the reader's procedure, and therefore the teacher's also, varies with the purpose. The pupils are not to be drilled on the distinction; they are simply to be habituated in behaviour appropriate to the differing situations.

Only work reading is presented in this chapter; recreational reading is handled in the literature chapter, which might well be entitled "Recreational Reading". It does not seem wise to divide the work of the beginning period, which is so informal and occasional and continuous as to make classification impracticable. Since the purposive attitude prevails most of the time in this early period, and since all the later training in mechanics is in this section, beginning reading also has been put here.

Work Reading - The work reading section of the curriculum should consist of experiences in work reading; but at once a difficulty arises. Work reading is distinctly a tool activity; it is always a part of some other activity and cannot be normally experienced in isolation. On the other hand, the teacher of English (or reading) cannot take time to conduct projects or set up problems which naturaly require study reading. If the teachers of history, geography, science, et cetera, cannot stop to give guidance in the reading their work requires, they can sometimes hand over to the teachers of reading both the problems raised and the reading matter bearing upon those problems. Occasionally doing their study reading under the supervision of the teacher of reading, the pupil's soon initiate behaviour patterns, which daily study assignments may be, counted upon to fix and polish.

Because different fields of subject-matter have their special vocabulary and other reading difficulties, each of the units here listed should include some material from each of the fields in which the pupils have textbooks.

Mastering the Skills - It is in work reading that the so-called fundamental skills of reading are to be initiated and practised until they no longer occupy the focus of attention. Recreatory reading ceases to be recreatory when it is burdened with the conscious study of techniques, though it should automatically make use of techniques already acquired and so help to perfect those techniques. Work reading, on the other hand, can very well carry the burden of techniques because it does not depend upon the pleasure of the present activity for its motive, and because as Gates has shown, when work reading is a means to the pupils' own action its interest exceeds that of most recreatory reading.

7

Reading Experiences, Kindergarten - Grades 6

It has been shown conclusively that reading is absolutely essential for school success. It probably bears somewhat this same relationship to all of life. To begin to read at the right time, and in the right way, and to continue in the early years with reading experiences, which lay the foundations for future learnings, become, then, matters of the utmost significance for children.

Getting Ready to Read - Report from centres of research indicate that a child should not begin formal reading before he has reached a mental age of six years. The years before that time may profitably be spent in experiences, which contribute to reading readiness. These beginning experiences may be, probably are, fully as important as the formal reading itself. Their omission, coupled with a too early and formal attack on reading, may account for a large share of the difficulties children encounter in beginnig reading.

The amount of time to be spent upon these reading-readiness experiences will be dependent largely upon the maturity and intelligence of the children. In general, when children are permitted to enter school at five years of age, probably the first year of school is not too much to spend upon these experiences, if they are kept rich and stimulating, and the child himself is permitted to engage whole-heartedly in them. Children who enter at six no doubt need several weeks of the reading-readiness preparation.

See outline of indications that child is ready to read (page 89).

Beginning Reading - Formal reading, which usually is introduced in the first grade, should begin with children's experiences, whether these experiences are furnished by the child's toys, specimen's he brings in science, activities in connection with his school life, projects introduced into the school day, his home his city environment, objects in the room, his dramatic play, or poems and stories told or read to him. Whatever unit is used as an introductory measure, it should at least be one of the same units by which reading is ordinarily done : a word, a phrase, or a sentence. Later, if it seems necessary, words may be analysed into phonetic elements, which compose them. (Possible exceptions to this are certain cases of non-readers, known as "mirror-readers".) However, phonics should always be a means to an end, and not an end in itself. At no stage should first-grade reading resolve itself into word pronouncing. It should continually be thought-getting and thought-giving.

No group of first-grade children will progress at the same rate in learning to read. This necessitates differentiation almost from the beginning. Such differentiation maybe accomplished by grouping, with the groups kept elastic enough for constant shifts back and forth. A better type of differentiation may be made by means of differences of reading materials. Experience charts, pre-primers, primers, and first readers, to say nothing of supplementary materials are needed to supply differing needs. Nor is the first grade the only one in which differentiation is necessary. Since every classroom of children will have a range of three or four years or more in reading ability, any grade room should have books of a wide range of difficulty - that is, books of different grade levels.

Study and Recreational Reading - During this beginning reading period very little differentiation is made between study reading and recreational reading. The dominant purpose throughout is to get acquainted with this new medium of expression, and all other purposes are satisfied in this one. Until the medium (that is, gathering meaning from the printed symbol) is fairly well mastered, the actual literature is supplied by the teacher through story-telling and "reading" poetry.

As soon as the child has "learned to read", or to handle rather adequately this new medium of communication, he begins to differentiate in the purposes for which he reads. Some of the time he is reading only to entertain himself, while at other times he has a study purpose in mind he is definitely looking for answers to questions, for information on a problem, or for directions for doing something. He may be trying to get information from a map, to interpret a statistical table, or to find the definition for a word. In each case the purpose will largely determine the method and materials used. Particularly will this be true if the situations for reading are real. Because of this wide range of purpose in reading, no single book or two can supply all of the reading experiences a child needs. A wide variety of materials, ranging from the textbooks in any of the subjects, pamphlets, maps, dictionaries, and encyclopaedias, to books of fiction, poetry and plays is needed if children are to be introduced to all of the experiences which they can profitably undergo.

Beyond the first two strands, the outline, which follows will be concerned with only the second type of purpose, the study purpose. These purposes are outlined around experiences, which the child has. Ideally each of these experiences should be tied up with a real need which arises in connection with the school life, such as reading to find out what to put in our aquarium or to learn what the pioneers used for lights, or to find out whether our exports of cotton have increased or decreased. Then as the need for more practice on certain involved skills evidences itself, the motive for drill on these skills is furnished. The following outline of experiences is given with such a method in mind.

A. Preliminary Experiences : Developing Reading Readiness

Note : This section of the curriculum might better be regarded as a large and complex unit rather than a strand, because it embraces all the reading activity of the kindergarten and terminates very early in the first grade. Its sub-divisions need not be regarded as sequential. It has certain general objectives in the teacher's mind which cannot become pupil purposes and which are not direct centres of activity. Some of the more important of these are : (*i*) to realise that script and print are mediums of communication (including records), (*ii*) to realise that being able to read makes one more independent, (*iii*) to broaden the background of experience, (*iv*) to enlarge the vocabulary, (*v*) to learn to pronounce words correctly. The units which follow will, if made rich and vital, automatically satisfy these teacher desires.

1. *Primary Objective* : To enjoy stories and poems heard at school or at home.

   Enabling Objectives : *See* "Literature".

2. *Primary Objective* : To place and use labels, *e.g.*, on place to keep different kinds of material and on objects assigned to personal use.

   Enabling Objectives : To understand the purpose of labels. To discriminate between the labels by length, general shape, or some striking letter. To recognise one's own name certainly and quickly.

3. *Primary Objective* : To dictate and use memoranda of things to be done in the classroom.

   Enabling Objectives : To know what the teacher is writing when she puts the memorandum on the blackboard. To recall upon looking at the memorandum what it said. To distinguish two or more memoranda by position and by special characteristics such as a name (with a capital letter), a word already learned, or any peculiarity in appearance.

4. *Primary Objective* : To assist in making records of anything going on in school.

   Enabling Objectives : *See* Composition.

5. *Primary Objective* : To help in composing letters and note to be sent in the name of the class.

   Enabling Objectives : *See* Composition.

6. *Primary Objective* : To exchange information and ideas especially about materials of interest - such as sciences specimens, toys, letters, pets - brought to school.

   Enabling Objectives : *See* Composition.

7. *Primary Objective* : To make and use a library corner.

   Enabling Objectives : To open books properly. To take books in clean hands only. To page from front to back in looking at pictures, etc., to recognise pictures as illustrations of stories and poems.

8. *Primary Objective* : To get information from sources in the room.

   Enabling Objectives : To read the numbers on the calendar so that one can find his own birthday date. To distinguish which card has the word on it which one wants to post designating the weather for the day, such as *cloudy, rain, windy*. To read the numbers posted on articles in the store so that one can be the storekeeper for the day.

9. *Primary Objective* : To enter into guessing games with the other children and to see how well one can do in such games.

   Enabling Objectives : To try to recognise by some characteristic one's favourite poem when posted in the room. To find pictures which illustrate certain poems, or certain words. To remember the words of poems which the teacher has read. To try to think of a good title for a picture by noticing what the picture is about.

Indications that the child is ready to learn to read

1. He has a speaking and understanding vocabulary covering at least the words commonly met in primers and first readers.
2. He is constantly reaching out for additional experiences, and the vocabulary necessary to talk about such experiences.
3. He understands English well enough to communicate with the teacher and others about him.
4. He expresses in clear and connected sentences the ideas gained from his experiences.
5. He has for the most part eliminated any "baby talk" or gross errors of enunciation or pronunciation.
6. He has come to know that ideas are expressed, or communication carried on, by means of symbols (print or script).

7. He is able to give his attention, as one of a group, when not all of the stimulation is directed to him alone.

8. He has built up a desire to read.

B. Introductory Experiences : Learning to Read

Note : This section of the curriculum is not a true strand, but rather a long and complex unit with sub-divisions. Normally, it is entirely contained within the first grade. Its sub-divisions need not be regarded as sequential.

1. *Primary Objective* : To read previously memorised rhymes.

   Enabling Objectives : To follow the lines with the eyes, from left to right, and from top to bottom. To know how much of the rhyme is in each line. To identify words by their positions in known lines. To perceive, when two words are placed one above the other, whether they are alike or different. To form mental pictures (memory images) or some of the words and phrases.

2. *Primary Objective* : To read blackboard or chart compositions dictated by the class.

   Enabling Objectives : To remember what was dictated. To note cues, known words or special visual characteristics, for the identification of each sentence. To identify and visualise key words. To know the meaning of all words used.

3. *Primary Objective* : To read with the aid of picture dictionary very simple directions, for cutting and pasting, for example, or very simple stories.

   Enabling Objectives : To follow lines in book, using a line marker if necessary. To recognise which letters are alike and which are different. To understand the thumb index of the picture dictionary. To recognise the meanings the pictures represent. To put the word meanings together into sentence meanings in reading as in listening.

4. *Primary Objective* : To read with decreasing suggestion by the teacher blackboard compositions in which general content is known and in which some of the words are known.

Enabling Objectives : To recognise old words in new settings. To infer new words from context : the known general content, the teacher's suggestive question, recognised words in the sentence. To ask mentally of each completed sentence, Is this sensible? To realise which words, if any one does not know the meaning of, and to ask for them.

5. *Primary Objective* : To read, with necessary teacher assistance, repetitive primer stories.

   Enabling Objectives : To turn pages one at a time from left to right through the book. To recognise phrase or sentences when repeated. To pick out and identify the new words in each new incident of the story.

6. *Primary Objective* : To enjoy in a library corner or in inter-recitation time very simple picture books.

   Note : This activity continues throughout the year. At first it is examination of the books as motivation for reading but by the end of the year there may be full reading of the stories. The growth, however, is so gradual that its sub-division seems impractical.

   Enabling Objectives : To handle books gently and with clean hands. To recognise pictures of characters in known stories and rhymes. To use reading skill as far as possible.

7. *Primary Objective* : To acquire a means of getting new words for oneself.

   Enabling Objectives : To realize that printed words are made of letters and spoken words of sounds. To note spelling-sound analogies between words. (Authorities disagree as to whether this analysis should be pushed to the recognition of the sounds of individual letters or even of common letter groups.) To pronounce (in a whisper, at most) new words by analogy with old ones, *e.g.*, *some* like the familiar *come*.

8. *Primary Objective* : To read independently a first-reader story all the words of which have been met before (even if some of the words have been presented only in the introduction or motivation of the lesson).

Enabling Objectives : To look for the story. To keep the characters and the succession of incidents straight. To use both phonetic analogy and context in the recognition of forgotten words. To move the eyes in rhythmic sweeps, examining in detail only a few forgotten words. To ask the meanings of words most familiars in speech.

Techniques to be acquired in learning to read

1. To follow the lines from left to right with the eyes, and to return after each to the beginning of the next.
2. To fixate each word or larger portion of the line in order.
3. To recognise many words by their appearance : length, characteristic letters, general shape.
4. To recognise and discriminate between letters upon occasion.
5. To know the sounds represented by most letters and by many letter groups or phonograms.
6. To pronounce new words largely by analogy with familiar ones.
7. To depend upon context to assist direct word recognition or discovery by phonic analysis.
8. To ask mentally concerning each completed sentence, "Is that sensible"?
9. To handle books gently and with clean hands.
10. To turn book pages one at a time from front to back.
11. To recognise known words in new setting.
12. To blend the meanings of the printed words into sentence meanings.

C. Reading in Response to a General Interest

Note : This strand might easily be divided into such sub-types as reading the newspaper, reading travel books or stories, reading on a topic under discussion in class or club, reading to prepare a paper (not a thesis) on a topic. Since, however, the reader's behaviour pattern is relatively constant through all of these, sub-division does not seem necessary.

In most schools this strand probably will not begin below the fourth grade.

1. *Primary Objective* : To secure, in reading a suggested five or six-page chapter or story written in third- or fourth-reader vocabulary and sentence structure, additional bits of information about some topic in which interest has already been aroused.

   Enabling Objectives : (Since this comes in at least the third and probably the fourth grade, the mechanics of reading and even paragraph comprehension's are assumed.) To be alert to many phases of the topic under investigation. To use all one's information and experience in reading about strange landscapes, customs, animals, et cetera. To recognize old facts in new words. To recognise really new material, either details or general features, and to make mental or written notes of it for possible use later.

2. *Primary Objective* : To acquire, in reading a suggested chapter or story of not more than ten pages written in fourth- or fifth-reader vocabulary and sentence structure, new facts in their logical relation to each other or to facts previously known, *e.g.*, the steps in a process, or the reasons for facts already known.

   Enabling Objectives : To think whether each new fact discovered is a result of other facts already known, or possibly an explanation of some of them. When a new series of facts is discovered, to note, which they are, and whether they are held together as causes and effects, as mere followers in time, or by their common relation to some other cause or general fact.

3. *Primary Objective* : To find a suggested book, written with fifth-reader vocabulary and sentence structure, a chapter or story bearing upon a particular interest, and from it to get practically all of the new information in presents on a topic about which the reader knows quite a little.

   Enabling Objectives : To use both tables of contents and index in locating the desired material. To consider the general content indicated by each chapter title rather than to look for specific words. In using the index, to think of several words which might be keys to the sort of information desired. To make notes of new items as found during the reading, and to try to group these for ready recall.

4. *Primary Objective* : To find in encyclopaedias further information on some broad subject in which interest has been aroused.

   Enabling Objectives : To know the general character of each of the available cyclopaedic works available. To think of several headings under which to look. (*See* Strand E.) To make use of sub-heads in very extensive articles such as "England" to locate more promptly the material sought. On scientific, political, and economic topics to note the dates of a available reference books or magazines and to give preference to recent ones.

5. *Primary Objective* : To choose a topic for an individual special report and to gather information about it from textbooks, encyclopaedias and easy, popular books, and even such magazines as the *National Geographic, Popular Mechanics, Technical World.*

   Enabling Objectives : To guess from the titles of books which ones may be worth looking into for the reader's purpose. If there is at hand a classified library, to know where the class of books wanted is. If a book is too difficult for the reader, to recognise this fact soon. To recognize overlappings and disagreements between different books or articles.

Techniques desirable in reading for general interest : A summary

1. To be alert to many phases of the topic under consideration.
2. To use all one's pertinent information in the interpretation of what is read.
3. To recognize previously known material even in new language.
4. To recognise really new material, whether details or general features.

5. To make clear written notes of new information and ideas.
6. To discover relations between new information and that already in hand.
7. To note relations between new facts discovered.
8. To use table of contents and index in locating desired material.
9. To know the character of available reference books especially encyclopaedias.
10. To think of other headings under which to look if the first one tried does not prove productive.
11. To make use of sub-heads to save time in searching for particular items of information.
12. To note publication dates, especially of books and articles about governments, business, industry and science.
13. To estimate from its title the value of a book for a present purpose.
14. To recognise corroborations and contradictions of one writer by another.

D. Reading in Response to a Question

1. ***Primary Objective*** : To look for the answer to a question in a specified paragraph whose main point is the answer.

   Enabling Objectives : To combine sentence meanings into paragraph meanings in explanatory and desriptive as well as in narrative paragraphs. To recognise this meaning as the answer sought.

2. *Primary Objective* : To look for the answer to a question in a paragraph whose main point and supporting details it covers.

   Enabling Objectives : To recognise the dependence of the details upon the main point of the paragraph. To recognize that details as well as main points are called for. To hold the whole paragraph in mind at the conclusion of the reading.

3. *Primary Objective* : To seek the answer to a question in a paragraph in which this is only a minor point.

   Enabling Objectives : To keep attention concentrated on the question. To recognise that the main point and the other minor ones do not belong to the answer.

4. *Primary Objective* : To seek the answer to a question in a group of paragraphs whose central point is the answer to the question.

   Enabling Objectives : To grasp the group of paragraphs as a thought unit. To see that the central idea is the answer sought. To see the relation of the subordinate facts or ideas.

5. *Primary Objective* : To seek the answer to a question in a group of paragraphs whose main point and supporting details it covers.

   Enabling Objectives : To see the relation of the subordinate facts or ideas, each represented by a paragraph, to the central idea. To fix in mind as many as possible of these supporting facts or ideas at a single reading. To glance rapidly from paragraph to paragraph to pick up any one omitted in the mental summary.

6. *Primary Objective* : To find in a specified book the answer to a question either broad or narrow.

   Enabling Objectives : To examine the table of contents if the question is broad. To consult the index, under several heads if necessary, when the question is narrow. To use sub-heads as guides to the location of the desired information or as helps in grasping its organisation.

Techniques desirable in Reading in response to a Question : A Summary

1. To combine sentence meanings into a paragraph meaning.
2. To recognise the main point of a paragraph and the relation of details to it.
3. To perceive the central idea in a group of paragraphs or a chapter and to recognise the relation of the rest of the material to this idea.

4. To reread rapidly in checking up a summary.
5. To use tables of contents, indexes, and sub-heads as guides in locating desired information.
6. To know when one has and when one has not found the answer sought; to know when the answer is partial.

E. Getting Information from Reference Books

1. *Primary Objective* : To look up the pronunciation of a word in the glossary of the book in which it occurs, *e.g*, in a third-reader, or in an elementary geography.

   Enabling Objectives : To know the order of the alphabet. To understand alphabetical arrangement according to first letters. To move swiftly over the letters with which one's word does not begin. To use the pronunciation key provided. To place the accent correctly.

2. *Primary Objective* : To find someone's telephone number.

   Enabling Objectives : To understand that all names beginning with the same letter are arranged according to their second letters. To know that persons of the same last name are listed in the alphabetical order of their first initials. To turn in the correct direction from the point at which one has opened the book.

3. *Primary Objective* : To look up the pronunciation of a word in an elementary dictionary.

   Enabling Objectives : To open the book as near the desired word as possible, *e.g.*, near the back if it begins with W, near the middle if it begins with M. When the proper initial letter has been found to locate the right page by glancing at the guide words in the upper corners.

4. *Primary Objective* : To check one's spelling of a word by finding it in the dictionary.

   Enabling Objectives : To look for it as one has spelled it. If this spelling is not found to guess at other spellings and look them up, *e.g.*, if *accommodate* is not found, to look for the word with a single *c* or with two *m's*.

5. *Primary Objective* : To look up in an elementary dictionary the meaning of a word.

   Enabling Objectives : To choose from the various meanings given the one most appropriate to the context in which the word occurred. To ask help if no clear and appropriate meaning is found.

6. *Primary Objective* : To look up material on a map in the textbook or in an atlas, *e.g.*, the forest areas in the U.S.

   Enabling Objectives : To find the topic in the index. To note how the pages where maps may be found are indicated. To locate the map. To note the legend by which the map is to be interpreted. To interpret the legend in getting the desired information.

7. *Primary Objective* : To look up in tables statistical data needed in regard to some problem.

   Enabling Objectives : To find the table, which will give the most recent or otherwise most appropriate data. To note the headings of the tabular material. To draw conclusions from the data shown.

8. *Primary Objective* : To look in an encyclopaedia for additional information upon some topic, *e.g.*, pottery, or papyrus.

   Enabling Objectives : To find one's topic as in the dictionary. To follow up a cross-reference if necessary, *e.g.*, under papyrus the only information may be "See paper". To use sub-heads, if there are any, to locate the part or parts of the article one wishes to read. To read *carefully* only the paragraphs pertinent to one's present interest.

Techniques Desirable in Getting Information from Reference Books : A Summary

1. To be thoroughly familiar with the alphabetical arrangement (including thumb indexes, guide words, etc., if present) of dictionaries, encyclopaedias, directories, etc.
2. To interpret correctly pronunciation symbols, including accents.

3. To guess at other spellings if the dictionary does not show the spelling which one is trying to verify.

4. To use map indexes successfully.

5. To determine which of several statistical tables contains desired data.

6. To choose among dictionary definitions the one appropriate to the context in which the word in question has occurred.

7. To follow up cross-references.

F. Reading Directions

1. *Primary Objective* : To read and carry out teacher's very simple written or printed commands - such as *Boys, rise,* or *Run to your seats.*

   Enabling Objectives : To realise that the written or printed words may express the commands. To recognise the words for oneself and not merely to imitate others.

2. *Primary Objective* : To read and carry out very simple directions for seat work, using a picture dictionary or its equivalent.

   Enabling Objectives : See Learning to Read, Unit 3, page 90.

3. *Primary Objective* : To read and carry out directions for seat work or other activities consisting of several steps, to be taken one at a time.

   Enabling Objectives : To grasp the purpose of the whole activity. To read and carry out the steps one at a time in proper sequence.

4. *Primary Objective* : To read and carry out directions for more complicated constructions, *e.g.*, in which some general principle such as colour harmony or proportion of parts must be kept in mind while one executes details.

   Enabling Objectives : To grasp the general plan. To pick out and hold in mind the general items while taking specific points one at a time.

5. *Primary Objective* : To read and carry out directions for such chiefly mental activities as studying spelling, performing "long" division, memorising a poem.

   Enabling Objectives : To proceed as systematically as in physical constructions. To make sure of the meaning of any strange words.

6. *Primary Objective* : To read arithmetic problems as directions.

   Enabling Objectives : To visualise (or otherwise image) what is given. To note clearly what is asked for. To recall what one knows about the relations of the items given and the one to be found.

7. *Primary Objective* : To read and help carry out directions, which call for the coördination of the activities of two or more persons, *e.g.*, a game.

   Enabling Objectives : To determine clearly the activities of each participant. To note the relations of each set of activities to the others. To note possible alternatives open to the participants.

8

Reading Experiences, Grades 7 - 12

Typical Reading Situations

It must be remembered that this section of the curriculum does not include the reading of strictly literary material, in which the activity of the reader is dominated by imagination and emotion. Experiences with such material are listed under "Literature". The outlines below deal only with those types of reading in American life in which intellectual apprehension is normally the main element.

The basis on which types of secondary reading can be profitably classified is not the form of the material read. The activity involved in reading so simple a piece of writing as an expository editorial in a daily newspaper differs as widely as do the persons who are reading it. It may vary with the same person at different periods. It is modified radically in the case of the high-school pupil as he expands his intellectual interests. The chief element that differentiates one reading activity from another is the purpose of the reader at the moment. Yet each purpose involves and in fact demands a differing mental activity or reading technique.

Purposes are hard to classify. In the typical reading situations in American life listed below an attempt is made to define each by stating some of the purposes that normally dominate that kind of reading. The resulting divisions are not like city blocks but like the shading of one color into another in a richly coloured sunset. This lack of sharp delimitation does not render less necessary during the period of training the attention to purpose and its concomitant techniques. The goal is the establishment, in the student, of such habits and mind-sets for different reading situations that his intellectual life will proceed economically and efficiently.

Under each situation is sketched an illustrative unit or two of classroom work that tends to establish the necessary procedures and attitudes. The arrangement of these units is intended to indicate the spiral or cyclical nature of reading in high school. The fundamental techniques of recognition, eye-movement, and so on are assumed; those pupils who have not mastered them will have to establish these habits before they can make much progress in the units set forth under the different headings of this high-school report. But within the highschool range there is a constant enrichment of the activities and the addition of new techniques as the intellectual world of the pupil expands. Such essential repetition with growth is suggested by the successive units.

A. Discursive Reading

Informational Reading

Note : This type of reading is largely guided by curiosity. The drive may be illustrated by these purposes.

1. To keep informed concerning current events, as in reading news items, editorial comment, and book and play reviews in the daily newspaper or weekly periodicals.
2. To learn more about events or questions of special interest, as in following the comments and predictions on the sports page or the articles in professional journals.
3. To broaden one's range of information, as in cursory reading of articles in weekly and monthly periodicals or browsing in books.

The procedure to be followed in teaching this type of reading may be illustrated by the commonest of all kinds of reading - the newspaper. It is a life situation in America, which the schools must recognise and prepare for. But in the schools such preparation cannot be achieved in a single term or even a single year. The activities by which the proper work-habits are built up and the essential attitudes induced must be repeated with modifications suitable to the growing capacities of the pupil. These general principles are illustrated in the two units outlined below.

1. ***Primary Objective*** : To determine from the head-line whether one wishes to read a news item of a paragraph or two.

   Enabling Objectives : To learn the nature and purpose of a head-line by studying head-lines to see how they tell the reader the subject of a piece of news and by framing a head-line for the most interesting point in a news item. To gain the power to forecast the contents of a news item from the headlines alone by reading headlines cut from news items and telling the nature of the event, which the item ought to relate.

2. ***Primary Objective*** : To read a news article in the time available.

   Enabling Objectives : To learn how to read "leads" for condensed summaries of news articles of a column or more by comparing and discussing the first paragraphs or "leads" of news articles based on the same event appearing in two or more papers, the purpose of such comparison and discussion being to discover what is emphasised, such as the persons to whom the event happened, where, when, how or why it happened. To find in a news article the parts most interesting to the reader by reading and discussion of the part titles in news articles as a guide to the significant sections of the article and by skimming from paragraph to paragraph to find the most dramatic sections of the article.

Unit 1 is suitable for introducing junior high school pupils to the newspapers. It might easily be covered in a week, but such a brief period would not establish the necessary power even among the brightest pupils. Unit 2 might require two weeks to cover satisfactorily with a normal class in the last year of the junior high school course. However, if the power to read a news article in the time available is to become a habitual reaction of the student, constant recurrence to the suggested types of activity would have to be made throughout the year. These two units illustrate, moreover, the spiral or cyclical nature of reading in high school. Unit 2 is based on the powers gained from the activities in Unit 1, but it is equally a deepening and enrichment of those powers.

It brings into play new techniques and trains in wider comparison and more difficult generalisation.

Reflective Reading

Note : This type of reading is largely guided by the desire not merely to get the facts but to understand or comprehend. It requires a background of facts and general conceptions. The drive may be illustrated by these two purposes :

1. To learn the opinions of others on civic, social, economic and scientific problems, as in reading editorials, discussions in magazines, books on special topics.
2. To discover guiding principles, fundamental interpretations, and the relative importance of various objectives or ideals in the social, economic, scientific or other fields among one's intellectual interests.

A single classroom unit is here given to indicate one of many steps by which pupils might attain purpose 1.

3. ***Primary Objective*** : To arrive at an understanding of the organisation of an editorial.

   Enabling Objectives : To settle upon the central idea after a hasty reading. To determine the main points as distinguished from illustrative detail, examples, and other developmental material. To establish the relationship of the separate divisions to the central idea and to each other (such as causal, adversative, and qualifying). To single out the point of view of the author or his dominant purpose.

Just as Informational Reading merges into Reflective Reading, so this latter often merges into problem reading, in that the reader is constantly estimating the truth, accuracy, and value of statements in what he reads.

B. Problem Reading

Note : This type of reading is largely guided by the expectation of applying the matter to some practical use. The spiral nature of this drive may be illustrated by the following purposes :

1. To follow directions, such as recipes, road guides.

2. To single out the essential items in business letters, telegrams, instructions.

3. To discover specific information connected with efficient ways of doing any definite piece of work that one may be interested in, such as steps in building a model airplane or details relating to the operation of an automobile.

4. To secure general guidance that will help one in making plans in any new situation, such as advice and warning given in special departments of periodicals or in books of special interest (for example, dieting).

5. To increase understanding of one's chosen field of work, such as books on any particular vocation or vocations a student may be considering.

The following classroom unit, suitable to the senior years of the high school, illustrates one step in attaining purpose 2.

1. *Primary Objective* : To read a claim letter so exactly as to be able to answer it.

   Enabling Objectives : To note the circumstances leading to the claim by observing the relation of the claim letter to the purchase in question or to earlier correspondence - points stated at the beginning of perfect claim letters. To arrive at an exact understanding of the writer's claim by checking up the various essential elements in the transaction stated in the body of the letter against order letters to determine the occasion and validity of the claim. To estimate the writer's state of mind and general character by noting phrases in the letter which show whether the writer is angry or clam, fair-minded or prejudiced, and so on. To weigh the advisability of the action suggested or requested in the letter in view of its consequences or the policy of the firm.

C. Reading for Report

Note : This type of reading is largely guided by the desire to organise the material in some definite form, such as : (*i*) To prepare a talk to a class, an address to a club, or a lecture before any audience. (*ii*) To draw up a report for a teacher, a long theme on an assigned topic, or an article for publication.

In such a situation the reader must have at his command many different techniques, as illustrated in the following unit :

1. *Primary Objective* : To gather material for a paper on "The history of a news article - from the occurrence of the event to the last edition".

   Enabling Objectives : To consult the encyclopaedia under such headings as "news agency", "newspaper", "reporting". To consult the card catalogue of school or local library for possible material. To consult the *Reader's Guide* for possible articles in periodicals. To skim through any material that may be available. To determine the main points in articles or chapters that bear on the topic. To select the paragraphs or sections of most significance for this particular paper and to read them with the precision involved in problem reading. To weigh the value of differing accounts of any particular stage in the history of news article.

D. Reference Reading

Note : This type of reading requires several specific techniques, such as the best ways :

(*a*) To secure the different kinds of information to be found in the dictionary, such as *Webster's New International*, Allen's *Synonyms* and *Antonyms*, Krapp's *Comprehensive Guide to Good English*, *The New Century Dictionary*.

(*b*) To locate material in encyclopaedias and other works of reference.

(*c*) To locate material relating to specific points or problems by using card catalogues, bibliographies, *Reader's Guide*, indexes and tables of contents, and similar reference aids.

(*d*) To find the materials so located in the local or school library.

The following illustrative unit may be taken up at any point in junior senior high school for which earlier teaching has prepared the pupil.

Primary Objective : To trace the derivation or history of a word.

Enabling Objectives : To interpret the abbreviations for source languages (as *F, French* and *OE, Old English*). To discover the source words. To note something of the relation between Modern English and Modern French, Spanish, and German words. To identify certain letter combinations as indicative of certain language sources (as *ght* of Teutonic languages, *tion* of Latin, *ph* of Greek). To trace changes in meaning from source word to present form. To identify the chief source languages as either Latin or Teutonic. To comprehend something of the age of languages. To sense something of the relation between word changes and conquests, social systems, scientific discoveries and other elements of history.

9

The Nature and Management of Creative Expression

The word creative has permeated our conceptions of the teaching of English - *creative teaching, creative intelligence, creative living* and *creative composition* - these and many other word combinations suggest new and brave possibilities in the classroom. By all its implications the word *creative* has become in recent years an Open Seasame to a richer and fuller learning experience, and has introduced a new emphasis in our teaching techniques.

Within this happy current of thought are important eddies of educational opinion. *The Play Way* - no one can read the record of creative teaching without encountering this progressive educational shibboleth. *Creative Youth, Singing Youth, The Children Sing in the Far West* - such titles as these remind us that the creative process is deeply rooted in our instinctive nature and that creative expression is the birthright of every child. The glamour of this conception has caught hold of our teaching imagination, and enlivened the word with an aura of generous enthusiasm.

As first, fearful lest laboratory analysis would unweave the rainbow, teachers of creative expression were contemptuous of the scientific method applied in the field of art. But even the most dubious had only to scan the pages of June Downey's *Creative Imagination* to realise that a psychologist need not do violence to the sensitivity of the port. A new set of titles now looms on the horizon : *An Approach to Composition through Psychology* by Phyllis Robbins. We can no longer escape the fact that writing is a "psychological enterprise" and as such lies well within the field of scientific inquiry and systematic, though informal, cultivation.

A Definition of Creative Expression

Creative expression is the translation of experience into words - It occurs when a person recognises the dignity of his own experience and when he imposes upon his experience the discipline of expression in an effort to share it with others. Creative expression is differentiated from other forms of composition by the absence of an external or utilitarian motive, by the fact that it is done primarily for its own sake, and proceeds from experience which is recognised as possessing *intrinsic* rather than "practical" value. Business letters, news items, reports of investigations, debates - all these forms of composition have some external reason for being, have a motive of practical use, of objective value. In creative expression, on the other hand, the reason for transferring the experience lies not in some material benefit to be attained by the writer or the speaker, but in his pleasure and interest in the experience itself.

We need to recognize here that both "actual" and imaginative experience afford valid material for creative expression. A child playing in the snow experiences immediate sensations; a child imagining himself on a trip to the Arctic experiences derived and newly combined sensations through his imagination. Both types of experience are real. For reasons that will be made increasingly clear, however, the emphasis should be placed upon actual first-hand experience.

The temptation to live vicariously is a strong impulse, often overpowering in its appeal to youth. It is easier for the imagination to accept the ready-made reactions of others, described in books, than it is for the senses and the imagination to respond to original stimuli. Too often pupils deceive themselves and their teachers by merely echoing or imitating pieces - especially poetry - which they have heard praised, without having any genuine content in their own minds. We may exclude from the field of creative expression any writing or speaking in which no detail of the individual's first-hand experience is present. Expression becomes increasingly creative as the emphasis is placed upon the interpretation of the writer's own experience.

Nothing could be farther from the truth than the rather frequent assumption that certain literary forms are in themselves creative, that the arrangement of words in fourteen iambic pentameter lines with a certain rhyme scheme makes them a poem and thereby an example of creative expression. On the contrary, thousands of so-called poems are written, and not a few are published, in which there is no evidence of any genuine esthetic experience whatsoever, no indication that the writer had seen anything so sharply or felt anything so deeply that he was sincerely impelled to try to share his experience. Too many verse-makers are patching together the traditional poetic ideas, the conventional words and phrases and forms, in wholly derivative and imitative fashion, and asking us to accept the result as poetry, especially if it shows some mechanical facility. The fact that a piece of writing happens to have traditional literary form does not mean that it is creative.

Ends to Be Served in the Teaching of Creative Composition

The most dangerous fallacy in the teaching of creative expression lies in the assumption that it is of importance only to the "gifted" child, and hence is only a frill, a bit of embroidery for the "regular course". Let us say at once that the making or training of professional writers or speakers is not the business of creative composition in the schools. The real object is *the development of the pupils' capacity to value experience for its own sake* and not for some utilitarian end or practical consideration. His pleasure in the experience is increased and deepened through the increased grasp of the experience developed by the effort to transfer it.

This intrinsic reward of the creative process must be carefully differentiated, especially under usual classroom conditions, from the external motive of social advantage, which may accrue in composition. When a child tells a story or recounts an experience *primarily* to gain admiration of the teacher or his fellows, to impress or astonish, rather than because of his delight in the experience itself, and a genuine desire to share that delight, his act is losing creative significance, and acquiring the external value of social aggrandisement. Other external and utilitarian consideration, such as prizes, grades, or credits to be earned, are wholly alien to the genuine creative impulse. They can be justified only as a means of breaking down inhibiting and conditioning forces which might otherwise prevent the appearance of creative composition at all. When these material and utilitarian motives become paramount, the work ceases to be creative.

There is an important difference between the man who measures everything he feels and does by material standards, and the man who values the activities and impressions of each day in and for themselves. The first man asks, "Will it get me ahead?" The second, "Is it worth while for its own sake?" On the one hand is the ideal of outward achievement - of doing and getting. On the other hand is the ideal of experience, of being, of feeling richly and truly, of thinking clearly.

The enlargement of pupils' vocabularies and command of sentence patterns which results from sincere attempts at self-expression is to be regarded merely as a by-product, valuable and a further justification if we must defend the allotment of time to creative expression, but not an end toward which the activity is to be guided.

Specific Objectives in Stimulating Creative Expression

1. *To help pupils recognize the value of their own experience* - Every student is a bundle of interests, enthusiasms, moving daily through a world of infinitely varied stimuli to all his senses. These interests, enthusiasms, and sensory experiences are his materials, the things he should write and talk about - always different from those of everybody else. Under no circumstances should the excuse, "There is nothing in my experience interesting enough to write about" be accepted as valid. Even the most commonplace experience abounds in possibilities, as the Jane Austins, the Ruth Suckows, the Susan Hales, and the Emily Dickinsons of literature testify. And probably no one really lacks imagination. An "unimaginative" boy may be experiencing secretly the imaginative shock to knuckles and shoulder from the impact of a blow in a boxing ring, but fail to react poetically to clouds and trees and flowers.

2. *To amplify the range of pupils' experience* - The degree to which people react keenly and adequately to stimuli depends in part upon their inherent sensory equipment. But it depends, also, on

their interest in their own reactions. Such an interest can be aroused by a variety of teaching devices.

3. To improve the quality of pupils' experience by encouraging more discriminating observation.

4. *To aid pupils to fit words to the details of experience* - The extension of observation and discrimination and the improvement of vocabulary are reciprocal. The new sensory experience demands a new word; the search for new words makes possible new sensory experience.

5. *To help pupils discover suitable forms for the transfer of experience to others* - In order to express experience words must be arranged, combined, related to each other in patterns so that the experience as a whole can be participated in by the reader. The experience itself must determine the choice, not only among the generic patterns - story, play, poem, and essay - but also of specific patterns such as free verse or the sonnet monologue or dialogue, logical or associational organization.

Caution : Form should never be an end in itself. "Experience creates substance, and substance creates form", said Emerson. For purposes of school work simple and natural forms are preferable to elaborate and artificial forms. Sincerity is more important than literary ostentation.

Poetry : Some Special Dangers

The writing of poetry is perhaps the most prominent and widely discussed of the activities included in the general field of creative writing. It is also an activity especially subject to difficulties and dangers encountered in all attempts to deal with creative writing in the school. For this reason the writing of poetry may deserve some specific consideration in these introductory comments.

He is a hardy person who will assert that he can teach children to write poetry. Equally wrong, however, is the view that nothing can be done about it that the writing of poetry by children must be left to luck. It cannot reasonably be denied that the teacher can produce situations in which creative expression, including poetry, will be easy, natural, and enjoyable. That this can be done most readily in schools where teachers have small classes and special facilities is obvious. But that it can be done even in schools which are deplorably overcrowded and understaffed has been demonstrated repeatedly.

One of the difficult things demanded of teachers in this work is the realisation that the truest poetic experience of children is not limited to the traditional poetic material of the literature of the past. The teacher who looks only for poems about fairies, flowers, and sunsets will miss what are for many children the best possibilities for poetic expression. Machines, sports, the sights and events of city streets, are legitimate parts of poetic experience. Whatever moves a child most deeply, means most to him, and is his best material for poetic expression.

However, in the particular field of poetry, the greatest single problem and danger lies in the easy and general confusion between traditional poetic forms and poetry itself. It is too easy for us to regard anything, which rhymes as poetry, and anything, which scans passably as a distinguished achievement. In so doing we miss the main point. Poetic experience is the thing to be sought, the exercise of the child's capacity to see the real world about him - things, people, events - freshly and intensely, to enter into the mind-built world of reading and imagining richly and vitally. The facility to put words together into jingles will mean little to him. A developed capacity for poetic experience - for seeing, feeling, imagining - will enrich every day of his life.

Hence the purpose of the teacher will be to bring about favourable conditions for the recognition of poetic values in experience and for the sharing of this recognition. Special procedures will be useful for breaking down inhibitions, for emphasizing poetic kinds and qualities of experience, and for familiarizing children with modes of expression. Specific assignments and special occasions will seldom call forth anything of real poetic value. The teacher will be careful, therefore, not to refer in such cases to "writing poetry" but to speak rather of "putting words together with rhyme and meter". Indeed, we shall probably make more progress if we talk scarcely at all about writing poetry as such. If attention is kept directed toward the experience to be recognized and shared, and poetic expression can be shown to be one of the natural and normal and enjoyable reactions to experience, we can hope with some assurance that our pupils will draw valuable rewards from the work.

The Relation of Creative Expression to Composition and Literature

Since its goal is to develop pupils' capacity for creative experience, creative expression should be interpreted primarily as a *point of view* rather than as a separate course in the curriculum. Not all students will be equally sensitive to the worth of their own experience, nor equally artistic (if at all) in interpreting it. But the discovery that experience in and for itself is both reason and reward for living is the birthright of every child. Creative composition as a teaching problem therefore, is the *setting up* of this point of view, in both composition and literature classes, and *emphasising it* in special classes, wherever school administration permits. The experiences listed in this section of the curriculum differ from those under communication chiefly in breadth of opportunity, which they offer for development of this point of view.

Suggested Teaching Methods

What means shall we use to induce students to realise the value of their own experience, and to interpret it artistically? Seriously hampering a practical answer to this question is a sentimental faith in the "natural" functions of the child - our much-abused heritage from Rousseau - and a reluctance to interfere with "free" self-expression. "Let Nature speak to you!" We have said in effect in the past, and if the student protested "But I hear nothing!" There was only a mournful wail at the false teaching which had unfettered his spirit. This point of view negates the whole teaching problem and reduces it to a mere "setting of the stage for the creative process".

The problem of self-expression is as much a problem of self as of expression. There must be a self to express, and the problem of creative teaching is a problem of developing that self by a direct stimulation of the senses, of the imagination, and of judgement. To turn students back on their own undeveloped powers, assuming that they already are what they are trying to become, is to beg the whole teaching question. Freedom of any kind is appreciated only by the person of abundant resources, by the person who has already learned to start himself observing, imagining or reflecting.

One of the simple facts of psychology is that the trained eye or ears notices what it is prepared to notice. A woodsman, for example, sees signs of deer or moose not because his vision is superior to that of the novice but because his attention is better trained by experience. A curious phenomenon, which anyone may observe, is that which follows the first hearing of a new and interesting word. "How strange!" We say to ourselves. "Until today I never heard that word. Now I hear it on every hand". The explanation of this apparent mystery is not difficult to find. The same word was doubtless "heard" or "seen" many times before, as far as physical reception was concerned; but it was only after the mind knew what to listen for that the ears distinguished the sounds. It is part of the function of the teacher to supply the senses of his pupils with such definite clues. There is some danger, of course, that the teacher in such stimulation will give too much of himself. But there is the greater danger that he will give too little - too little to lure the senses of his students to follow. Almost everyone can trace much of his sensory interest back to the person of poem or situation, which first aroused it.

A popular notion among students is that their own experience is unworthy or imaginative interpretation. Herein lies the challenge to the teacher of creative expression. However difficult, this problem of helping pupils to see the art possibilities of their own experiences, like that of sharpening the senses, yields to specific procedures by which students may be led to perceive meaning and significance in their own experience. There is no more reason to suppose that a student's emotional susceptibility to life about him cannot be heightened than that his senses cannot be awakened. But just as the senses need clues to follow. so, often, in order to spin its web, does the imagination need those first frail filaments stretched across space from one easily recognised perception to another. Without those first gossamer threads (supplied by the teacher?), the student very often is powerless to start his design.

The problem of freedom and independence, therefore, can perhaps best be disposed of by regarding the teaching device merely as a point of departure, not as an inflexible assignment. Someone has said that no matter what you teach, students will learn something else. This quip is to a criticism of teaching method, it is a cryptic comment about the learning process. Specific suggestions, have the advantage over general suggestions of focusing attention, and of precipitating thought. It is on this basis that the following units of learning are offered.

It should be obvious that the specific suggestions for classroom procedure must be used with discretion. The mind, even at its best, is coy, whimsical, uncertain, and capricious. It does not produce ideas on demand. It must be cajoled into action, not bullied. Before such suggestions as the following can be used effectively, therefore, a word or two of caution is imperative :

1. *Teachers themselves must see in each unit a wealth of possibility* before they suggest such an assignment, if it is to yield the kind of results anticipated. They may well omit those units which fail to elicit enthusiastic responses in themselves. Furthermore, they must not take such assignments mechanically; *i.e.*, without preparation, elaboration, illustration, and adaptation, as though each unit were an exact formula.

2. *The atmosphere of the classroom will in large measure determine the success of the units suggested.* Ideas are generated in a classroom, which is electric with stimuli and interaction. It sometimes takes a long and patient preliminary process to charge pupils' minds. Only when pupils feel a genuine interest in thinking or reacting or imagining, however, will they respond to *any* suggestion.

   Methods of establishing the right atmosphere for creative activity are various. Perhaps no book has been so helpful in this connection as Hughes Mearns' *Creative Youth*. From this account of a vivid classroom experience, we learn that the pupils' confidence in his teacher, with all its attendant incentives; his confidence in himself, with all the ramifications implied; and his confidence in the value of expression are of equal importance with teaching techniques.

3. *The materials used in the classroom to stimulate response should be vividly and compellingly pertinent to pupils, own experience.* The following list of materials suggests the wide range of direct stimulation, which is possible to the ordinary classroom.

Objects of sensuous interest brought to class : a piece of cloth, pottery, etc., of rich colour and distinctive texture.

"Field trips" to the school greenhouse, to the creek, museum, etc., actual observations out the window, at school, at home, etc., pre-arranged views of industrial life.

Pictures emphasising colour, action, etc., photographs, rotogravure section of newspaper; photographs from family album; statuary

Victrola records; voices cover the radio

Artistic reproductions, which interpret our machine - age

Newspaper clippings recording dramatic incidents

Volumes of sensuous verse and prose

Collection and examples of student writing of sensuous verse and prose

Anthologies in which such classifications as "People", "City", etc. are designated.

4. *The pupils should be familiar with simple patterns, which they can adopt and adapt for their own purposes.* The child in whom surges a realisation of the joy of skating is more likely to attempt to tell his joy if in the background of his consciousness are some patterns of lyric expression into one of which, modified to suit his purpose, he can pour his experience. And he is much more likely to achieve such satisfying expression as will

lead him to try again with a new experience. Probably the best means to bring about possession of such patterns without obsession by them is to read much good literature and to give the patterns there employed a moderate amount of attention. For some children attempts to imitate these patterns will prepare the way for self-expression; for others such imitation will overemphasise the patterns.

5. *Pupils should be trained to catch an inspiration when it comes and to work it out then so far as time and present insight permit, and to revise carefully.* The sentimental attitude toward creative expression is that the "first fine careless rapture" will be lost in "the discipline of expression". If the writer keeps his eye on his experience, no reasonable effort to perfect his expression of it will fatally cool his ardor. True artists rarely publish first drafts. Even correctness in such mechanics as spelling and punctuation should be a matter of pride, because it contributes to the effectiveness of the expression.

6. *Publication and public praise are advisable only when they are necessary to destroy an inhibiting group attitude.* Such stimulation may easily produce shallowness or absolute insincerity by diverting attention from experience to what teacher or editor wants.

References

1. Henry Caldwell Cook (Frederick Stokes, 1917).
2. Hughes Mearns (Doubleady, Doran, 1925).
3. Mabel Mountsier (Harper Brothers, 1927).
4. Mary Austin (Houghton Mifflin, 1928).
5. (Harcourt, Brace, 1929).
6. *Harvard Studies in Education*, V. 12 (1929).
7. Overstreet in *Influencing Human Behavior*.
8. For a fuller discussion see *Creative Writing in American Schools*, John

T. Frederick, in *The English Journal* (January 1933). See also *To Have or To Be*, by Hendrick Willem Van Loon, one of the John Day Pamphlets.

9. For a fuller discussion see "Is the Whole the Sum of its Parts?" by Luella B. Cook, *English Journal* (September 1933).

10. Helen Keller's *Midstream, Footfalls* by Wilbur Daniel Steele, *Jungle Peace* by William Beebe.

11. *Younger Poets*, by Nellie Sergent (D. Appleton and Co., 1931). A very excellent volume of this sort.

12. See, for example, *Modern Verse*, by Anita Forbes (Henry Holt and Co., 1921).

10

Creative Expression Experiences, Kindergarten - Grades 6

Note : To divide this group of experiences into strands seems undesirable. Consequently each class will normally do two consecutive units each year.

1. *Primary Objective* : To explore the world of sensory impressions and to tell about what is interesting in it.

   Enabling Objectives : To observe accurately number, form size and action. To plan, with materials at hand, in imitation of something known - a house or an engine out of blocks. To choose something related to the work or play at hand to tell about, and to concentrate on the experience. To sue an adequate vocabulary of name and descriptive words. To enjoy the activity.

   Typical Activities : To handle objects in the classroom (bunnies, little chickens, kittens, flowers, blocks, etc.) and to tell what one has discovered by looking and touching. To play with objects - making new arrangements (as with blocks), sorting (materials, colours, sizes), and imitating (playing house, store, fire engine) - and to tell about what one is doing. To tell short accounts of experiences with objects, play and home activities.

2. *Primary Objective* : To express feeling and illustrate action by pantomime.

Enabling Objectives : To listen attentively. To tell what the music or the poem "says". To choose appropriate and suggestive actions for interpreting the thought or feeling of the poem, etc., in pantomime.

Typical Activities : To listen attentively to the reading of poems and to music; to tell what actions the poems or the music suggest, or what feeling that can be shown by action. To say little poems, with attention to interpretation. To act out in pantomime rhymes, games, music, poems, stories. To relate personal experience with dramatic effect, acting out such parts as lend themselves to acting.

3. *Primary Objective* : To respond to the appeal of simple, natural rhythms.

   Typical Activities : To march, skip, or dance to music or poetry. To beat time with hands, pencil, drum. To say or sing poems with simple rhythm forms. To listen to the reading of poems with obvious rhythms.

4. *Primary Objective* : To participate in a period of telling bits of personal experience.

   Enabling Objectives : To choose details for their connection with one's emotion. To sue action words that make the experience clear to the audience.

   Typical Activities : To report happenings at home, on the playground, on trips, etc., to tell an incident illustrating how surprised, pleased, proud, etc., one was upon occasion.

5. *Primary Objective* : To report in writing (one paragraph) a short and definite unit of experience in which emotion, either one's own or another's is the centre of interest.

   Enabling Objectives : Same as for 4. To report honestly.

   Typical Activities : To report an observation (description): How My Dog Acts When I Have Hurt His Feelings, How My Dog Acts When He Wants To Go With Me, How My Dog Acts When He Has a Bone That Another Dog Wants, Etc. To report happenings at home, on the playground, on trips, etc. *See also* other items under Typical Activities for 4, above.

6. ***Primary Objective*** : To express another person's experience through dramatisation or first-person narrative.

   Enabling Objectives : The ability to put one's self imaginatively into a situation or a part. To observe people and how they act and speak under various circumstances. To make a choice from much material, keeping requirements of the assignment in mind. To use accurate words of sight, touch, sound, feeling, and action so that the experience may be vividly told.

   Typical Activities : To identify one's self with a character and take part in a simple dramatisation (a single incident). To read poems aloud and to enjoy the action as if it has happened to the reader. To select from many experiences of which one has read one specific incident to tell or write about as vividly as possible as if it has happened to the narrator.

7. ***Primary Objective*** : To express some quality of experience by means of comparison.

   Enabling Objectives : The ability to recall sense impressions vividly enough so that comparisons may be made with present impressions. To note essential characteristics. To find a common element or characteristic in two or more unlike objects or experiences.

   Typical Activities : To make simple comparisons, based on direct observations. (The silk of this milk-weed is as soft as my little sister's hair.) To note imaginative comparisons encountered in reading. To use an occasional imaginative comparison in oral or written reports, in an attempt to transmit an experience vividly.

8. ***Primary Objective*** : To organise experience in story form (written).

   Enabling Objectives : To select portions of experience (*a*) interesting and (*b*) appropriate or relevant to the topic under discussion. To limit the account, keeping out the non-essentials. To follow an order. To keep to the assumptions or conditions implied in the beginning of the story.

Typical Activities : To report, in writing, a definite unit of personal experience. To report, in writing, a definite unit of imaginative experience. To finish a story told by the teacher or read in part.

9. *Primary Objective* : To organise experience in dramatic form.

Enabling Objectives : To plan in accordance with the requirements of the dramatic form, the available actors, and the physical equipment. To make characters life-like. To have a sense of proportion.

Typical Activities : To plan the dramatisation of a story (original or otherwise) requiring several scenes; to decide upon the number of scenes necessary, the characters, the stage properties, the assignment of parts. To prepare the play for presentation.

10. *Primary Objective* : To recognise rhythm and to express feeling in rhythmical patterns.

Enabling Objectives : To distinguish between an accented and an unaccented beat. To feel rhythmic patterns. To adhere to rhythmic patterns once adopted.

Typical Activities : To listen to the reading of highly rhythmical poems and mark the rhythm by gestures. To note the fact that the sense of the poems is often realised by the rhythm. To observe rhythmic patterns in street noises, machines, nature. To select fitting speeches for the use of strong rhythm, as, prayers, ceremonial speeches, etc. To find rhythms in harmony with a purpose.

11. *Primary Objective* : To project one's self in time or in space to a different period or a different place.

Enabling Objectives : To reconstruct a situation or a character from scattered clues. To hold to facts in making such a reconstruction.

Typical Activities : To plan the dramatisation of a scene from history, the material to be collected from various sources. To write a story of life in a different country or period. To write a letter in the person of a child of a different country or period. To write a dialogue between imaginary people.

12. *Primary Objective* : To express a strong emotional preference or feeling.

Enabling Objectives : To be sincere in expressing sentiment. To have an ear for rhythms and rhymes. To be willing to try something new.

Typical Activities : To express in writing a sincere feeling for home, parents, country, school, friendship. To read short songs and short poems of feeling. To practice making imaginative comparisons, to add to the beauty or the effectiveness of the expression of feeling. To make a song or a short poem expressing sincere feeling for some loved (or despised) object.

13. *Primary Objective* : To plan something new and to describe one's invention.

Enabling Objectives : To observe with the intention of finding discrepancies between needs and conditions. To exercise original fancy in supplying these needs. To keep one's object in mind. To be clear and concise.

Typical Activities : To invent something needed, *e.g.*, detachable handles for hot pans and kettles. To plan something different, *e.g.*, a new sort of animal or a new country. To plan something better, *e.g.*, an improvement in the school, a rearrangement of a room, an ideal room. To plan something new to do, *e.g.*, a new game.

14. *Primary Objective* : To organise experience for the specific purpose of creating mood.

Enabling Objectives : To recall and sort experience. To select concrete details in accordance with the dominant mood. To use words that give strong sense impressions.

Typical Activities : To write or tell a single-phase story of personal experience, choosing details with a definite intention of creating mood. To make a book of memories in an attempt to recapture the thrill of the experience, the disappointment, the surprise, etc. (*Summers in My Childhood, My First Memories,* etc.)

15. *Primary Objective* : To make an original contribution for a special occasion or purpose.

Enabling Objectives : To enter into the spirit of the occasion. To express sentiment sincerely. To feel sufficiently at home with the various forms of expression so that the appropriate form may be chosen for a given expression.

Typical Activities : To compose an original play or pageant for a special occasion. To write an original anecdote for the school paper. To write a class poem, or a poem celebrating a special event. To write appropriate verses for Christmas cards, Valentines, etc.

Desirable Techniques in Creative Writing : A Summary

1. To be willing and eager to experiment with expression.
2. To be aware in all the senses.
3. To be accurate in observation.
4. To be sincere in expression of individual thought or feeling.
5. To be willing to take infinite pains, especially in finding the concrete detail or the exact word.
6. To identify one's self-imaginatively with a character or a situation.
7. To plan, always keeping the fixed requirements in mind.
8. To see relationships. To make new combinations and relationships.

11

Creative Expression Experiences, Grades 7 - 12

The creative process has three phrases : *observation, imagination,* and *reflection.* Observation is regarded as the gathering of sense impressions; imagination and reflection, as personal reactions to the experience of the senses.

Both imagination and reflection are dependent upon observation. Every bit of material they use is picked up by the senses. Robert Frost has said "A poet must lean hard on facts, so hard sometimes it hurts". When we lean hard on facts (observation) we react in a special way (imagination or reflection).

Imagination is like a moving picture that never stops : a recollection or image does not start up singly in our memories; it is always introduced by a preceding picture and it never fails to draw a third. The force that moves this succession of photographs in our minds is quite mechanical, and independent of reflection. With sleepy ease the imagination associates one object with another into a long chain of impressions. When we are half-asleep, or ill with a fever, when the will falters, our imagination thus holds full sway.

Reflection, on the other hand, says "Halt ! I resume command!" Reflection introduces a rational connection between images : order, logic, meaning, significance and so forth.

These three behaviour patterns - observation, imagination, and reflection - are obviously blended in the creation of a work of art. In the analysis that follows they are separated merely on the grounds of teaching expediency. No attempt has been made, furthermore, to keep the categories air-tight; there are obvious overlappings of one pattern on to another. Whatever consistency has been achieved has been in the interest of teaching facility, rather than of psychological exactness.

The units presented do not pretend to be an exhaustive list. They aim merely to suggest the kind of sub-division possible for each behaviour pattern.

No distinction is made in the objectives which follow between written and oral expression. Some units will obviously lend themselves better to written composition than to oral; some can be deliberately assigned as oral, in order to lift conversation to a creative level; and some can be assigned as a combination of oral and written work - a story to be read aloud to the class, for example.

A. Creation Stimulated by Observation

1. *Primary Objective* : To develop an interest in one's own sense-reactions to nature and the objective world, and to communicate them to others in sense-arousing diction.

   Enabling Objectives : To observe more fully and accurately colour, sound, rhythm, texture, odour, taste, etc., in nature and to express reactions in concrete and specific diction. To discriminate more accurately between impressions received through the different senses, and express such impressions with well-chosen words of the senses. To choose from a mass of sense-data details, which create a special sensory effect - for example, intense gloom, or intense heat - and to use these details to build up the impression for the reader.

2. *Primary Objective* : To become more observant of people and to share such observation with others.

   Enabling Objectives : To become more aware of individual differences in appearances and movements among people : gait, gesture, facial expression, eyes, mouth manners, hands, etc. To choose specific words, similes, and metaphors which describe these vividly. To become aware of contrasts in conversation : tone, pitch, vocabulary, emphasis, etc. To select typical examples of these contrasts.

3. *Primary Objective* : To become more aware of significant detail peculiar to occupation, and to emphasise such detail in communicating the impression to others.

Enabling Objectives : To observe the routine of different occupations and to note one's own reaction to it. To observe significant paraphernalia for occupations. To observe in detail the effects of life-long occupation on people.

4. *Primary Objective* : To become more aware of the beauty and power of machines and to express such reactions in words.

Enabling Objectives : To observe a machine at work (a steam shovel, a newspaper press, etc.), noting size, power, precision, rhythm, colour, and line. To observe one's own reactions to driving an automobile, adjusting a radio set, etc. To devise verse or prose forms to communicate the subjective as well as objective aspects of these experiences.

5. *Primary Objective* : To become more sensitive to details of form, colour, rhythm, symmetry, balance, proportion, etc., in artistic portrayal and to communicate the pleasant experience as vividly, suggestively, and briefly as possible.

Enabling Objectives : To observe the artistic spacing of pictures and photographs (balance, symmetry, proportion, etc.). To observe the consistency or contrast or harmony of colour in paintings. To find (as with camera finder) artistic "composition" of objects in landscape, room, etc. To observe the lines and shapes of buildings. To find concrete non-technical words to express the qualities of the art works. To make suggestive combinations of words.

6. *Primary Objective* : To become more discerning of details of sound, rhythm, melody, tone, etc., in musical arts, and to share one's perceptions with others.

Enabling Objectives : To find examples of correspondence between rhythm and idea expressed in poetry and music. To find in poetry words with particular sound qualities (onomatopœia, alliteration, etc.). To identify the qualities of voice of radio singers, opera stars, etc. To observe one's own emotional reactions to favourite songs, hymns, verse. To find sensory words for the sounds, and kinaesthetic or tactile images for the subjective effects of the sounds.

B. Creation stimulated by Imagination

1. *Primary Objective* : To discover and communicate an imaginative interest in words.

   Enabling Objectives : To discover the *mood values,* which certain words have for you because of their association, and to use them appropriately. To discover the *sound values of words* and employ them in appropriate description. To discover the rich imaginative thought content of words - words like *transgression, precipitate, supercilious,* etc., whose literal meanings are picturesque - and employ them appropriately.

2. *Primary Objective* : To see resemblances in unlikely places and communicate impression to others in imaginative comparisons.

   Enabling Objectives : To find resemblances to something else in any situation that impresses you. To express this resemblance as a comparison. To list common similes of experience : *still as a mouse,* etc. To find imaginative resemblances expressed in familiar slang : *bookworm, wallflower,* etc. To play with metaphor and simile.

3. *Primary Objective* : To discover the associative power of detail to evoke pictures, and to communicate impressions objectively.

   Enabling Objectives : To discover in your own experience *moments of heightened susceptibility,* when small details seem to possess for you significant meaning, and let your imagination complete a story. To tell the story in the poets' way, as a series of pictures (though not necessarily in verse). To read *Creating the Short Story* edited by Henry Goodman (or books serving similar purpose) and notes the explanations by authors of how a story gets started. (See in particular those of Kumroff, Williams, Babcock, Hurst.)

4. ***Primary Objective*** : To discover the suggestive power of places to incite imaginary action, and to relate what might have happened as a story - a short story or a ballad.

   Enabling Objectives : To discover actual places in one's observation that arouse one's imagination (a lonely stretch of road, a deserted cabin, a brightly painted kitchen, a cobblestoned alley, etc.) and suggest appropriate action. To tell one's story in ballad measure. To tell one's story as a short story in any of the following ways : as a story of incident, a story of atmosphere, a story of fantastic impression, etc.

5. ***Primary Objective*** : To extend forward or backward in time, imaginatively, actual happenings, and to relate the total sequence as continuous action.

   Enabling Objectives : To find in one's own experience or observation significant happenings or situations and to interpret their meaning. To imagine the explanation or outcome of such observations and relate the total sequence as a story of incident.

6. ***Primary Objective*** : To invent circumstances to illustrate proverbs, and to share such imagined development with others in the form of a story.

   Enabling Objectives : To find incidents to illustrate familiar proverbs, as for instance "It's an ill wind that blows no one any good", etc. To arrange such incidents in the form of a short story with the proverbs as title.

C. Creation Stimulated by Reflection

1. ***Primary Objective*** : To translate into words peculiar reactions to person, place or thing.

Enabling Objectives : To analyse your own prejudices (against *snakes*, for example, or in behalf of the *prairie*) and to describe whimsically your attitude. To describe, in the manner of Rupert Brooke, familiar items that you like or dislike. To "listen in" on yourself during reverie, and see what attitudes, moods, preferences, etc., you can discover which indicate contrast with the moods, attitudes, etc., of others. To read a volume of personal or informal essays and note the opportunity for capricious expression of opinion. To look for analogies between machine operation and human behaviour, and to describe your reactions in metaphor and simile. To interpret the actions of people, look for motives, hidden causes, explanations, etc., and express your interpretation in well-chosen words, including metaphor and simile.

2. *Primary Objective* : To interpret the actions of people, and to share such impressions with others.

   Enabling Objectives : To find the "key" to some character that you know well (his dominant ambition, for example, or his most persistent trait) and to show how such a characteristic expresses itself in action. To trace the consequences of some act you have observed to its logical, dramatic conclusion. To relate such a sequence of events according to a dramatic, rather than a chronological, order of events. To discuss in the form of a logical analysis some character whom you know well. To invent a story to account for certain persons you have observed and analysed.

3. *Primary Objective* : To discover a social problem and to set it forth imaginatively.

   Enabling Objectives : To collect data from observation on some topic (football enthusiasm, for example, or "crushes" in high school) and interpret imaginatively the significance of such a body of facts. To express your opinion on such a subject and use your facts as illustrative material. To look for *trends* in any significant body of facts that come under your observation (signs of the times, for example) and to express your opinions as though your mind were a search-light revolving slowly on its axis. To illuminate some brief incident of history by descriptive detail so that a "dry" fact becomes a living and breathing episode.

4. *Primary Objective* : To infer the causes of a present phenomenon and to present them imaginatively.

Enabling Objectives : With the aid of information from books and from your own observation, to think through some disputable question to a satisfying conclusion (for example, the place of women in the world, the relationships between parents and children, the need of "protective colouring" in human contacts, etc.). To try to justify your opinion by the logic of your analysis, the fairness in considering the other side, and the pertinence of your illustrative material.

5. *Primary Objective* : To discover and reveal the laws of life and communicate ideas to others.

Enabling Objectives : To amplify or illuminate quotations from Shakespeare (or another) as though they were "texts" or themes of a discourse. To enlarge upon the significance of some utterance heard over the radio, read in the newspaper.

6. *Primary Objective* : To sharpen critical faculties' in relation to music, literature, painting, etc., and to share opinions with others.

Enabling Objectives : To discover specific reasons *why* you "appreciate" a certain movie, book, picture. To explain, within some field of special knowledge, what constitutes good quality. To discern what is wrong with a "poor" short story, or musical comedy, or magazine cover, etc., and explain your objections clearly to others.

References

1. The reflection was originally made by Phyllis Robbins in her book, *An Approach to Composition Through Psychology*; Harvard Studies in Education, No. 12.

2. *See A Gossip of Romance*. Robert Louis Stevenson; or "Flint and Fire", by Dorothy Canfield in *Americans All*, Heydrick (Harcourt, Brace).
3. See *Cargoes* by John Masefiled for illustration.
4. "The Great Lover", in *Collected Poems* (Dodd, Mead).
5. See Joseph Conrad's preface to *Victory* for detailed explanation.

12

Purposes and Problems in Teaching Communication

The exchange of ideas and information is the very lifeblood of society. The art of communication must therefore occupy a prominent place in any modern curriculum. And within the curriculum the assignment of communication to the English department is expedient, because the use of language is a constant and important feature of normal communication.

The Social Nature of Language - Experiences in the use of language are never limited solely to language; they are always social contacts, involving social adjustments the control of body and voice, knowledge of and skill in the use of subject-matter and language forms. Successful conversation, for example, is much more than a matter of composing, more than merely communication of one's ideas; it obviously includes choosing which ideas to communicate and which, for the time at least, to suppress. It may involve finding a topic in which the *vis-à-vis* is interested. It involves tone of language; tone of voice, manner, all suited to the occasion and personalities involved. And in addition it involves the ability to anticipate the effect produced. In most instances all of this teaching falls to the English teacher, who must be trained to distinguish between language for writing and language for speaking, must know how to teach bodily control and voice improvement, and must be able to guide students in using these tools.

The art of communication can be mastered only through experience in actual, normal communication and mere practice in speaking and writing is valueless unless it arises directly from real communication and issues promptly in further communication. When pupils, for example, are preparing an assembly programme, they see the need of good voices, clear-cut enunciation, accurate pronunciation, and correct usage, and are ready for some related habit-forming drill. On the contrary, practising voice and enunciation exercises and correcting pronunciation and usage errors accomplishes approximately nothing if pupils lack desire and determination to improve. When a boy decides to learn to play golf, he plays the game, goes in person or through a book to a professional for suggestions, practices driving, putting, and approaching, and continues to play the game. Practice swings and the advice of a professional will never make a skilful golfer out of a boy who lacks either interest in the game of frequent opportunity to play real golf. Make - believe letters and other ordinary "themes" neither draw out the pupil's full power nor prepare him to meet the emotional and moral element in the real situations of life. Classroom experience that is itself real and is as close as possible to the reality of extra-school and post-school life, without deception or pretense, must be the actual basis of any realistic curriculum.

Representative Language Experiences - The actual experiences in communication which go into the curriculum should be representative of the present experiences of most pupils outside the English class - in other school classes, in clubs, on the playground, at homes at the store. Many of these may depend for their reality upon the social situation in the English class itself, but they should parallel quite closely the experiences that do and will occur elsewhere.

In the construction of this pattern curriculum investigations of the language experience of high school pupils by Baker and by Starbird, Williams and Hatfield have been used, and the Clapp study of *The Place of English in American Life* has been allowed to influence the emphasis upon various experiences normal to children. The items of the elementary school outline have been determined only by informal observation. Besides those experiences which pupils usually have, others which it is thought would be natural to them under favourable circumstances, such as writing news items or announcements for publication, have been included.

Creative Expression - The term *communication* includes creative expression, but it seems expedient to separate experiences of that sort from purely utilitarian and social communication. Although there is no definite boundary between creative expression and utilitarian communication, the general distinction is between the writing and speaking which is done to relieve one's own mind and feelings, to share some outward or inner experience that is too good to keep, and the writing or speaking which is done for a purpose beyond itself. The distinction does not imply that utilitarian writing and speech must lack charm or that either communication or expressionistic writing is superior to the other.

Social and Language Skills - Among the techniques or enabling objectives are not only the traditional items of rhetoric, grammar, and mechanics, but also such vitally important skills or qualities as open-mindedness, self-control, consideration for the thought and feelings of others, direction of all means and efforts toward achieving a desired effect upon those to whom the language is addressed. The traditional items will often need redirection. Thus, in the arrangement of material the traditional "logical order" must frequently give way to a psychological order made necessary be a consideration of the human element involved in the situation. All these techniques, social as well as linguistic, have been listed as "enabling" objectives in order to keep them in their place as means rather than ends.

Grammar - Grammar is not, of course, presented as a separate discipline - except as an eleventh- or twelfth-grade elective for the philosophically minded. Since grammatical concepts are valuable chiefly as tools for the improvement of expression, only such items of grammar are introduced as serve immediately and importantly in the building of more effective sentences. The desired new types of construction are included among the enabling objectives of the oral and written communication units and accompanied by references to the grammar summary.

A Typical Classroom Procedure - A curriculum of actual experiences in communication implies typical (not invariable) classroom procedures somewhat like these : (The order of the activities should vary with circumstances and pupils).

1. Making the pupils conscious of a present, worthy occasion for communication. Sometimes this occasion must be created by the teacher; frequently it needs only to be brought to attention.
2. Letting pupils attempt to meet the situation by speaking or writing.
3. Giving advice and assistance as the pupils prepare (if the occasion permits preparation) and as they write (if the occasion calls for writing). This includes helping them to perceive the techniques, which they can use to advantage.
4. Helping pupils to realise that the excellence of their work must be measured in terms of the effect of their efforts upon their audience, and pointing out the causes of their (usually partial) success or failure.
5. Introducing at any favourable time specific practice in a skill which the pupils realise the worth of but which they have not mastered.
6. Noting growth, chiefly by comparing success on this and previous similar occasions.

Conventional Correctness - The problem of securingcorrectness - observance of our language customs - is discussed at length in the chapter on Corrective Teaching. Here it is sufficient to say that constant nagging about the infraction of the many sound rules of usage, not to mention the countless taboos purists have set up, is unlikely to produce correctness. Usage's to be made habitual or errors to be eliminated are not listed in the communication outlines; they are to be found in the Corrective Teaching section.

Teachers who feel that the development of sentence sense is not merely a remedial procedure are urged to note this caution : Children should learn to speak and write in sentences. In the development of this skill, however, teachers should recognise the fact that in conversation, and to some extent in other forms of oral communication, a single word or phrase may make sense in its setting and context. On such occasions the so-called "sentence fragment" is not only acceptable but often preferable to a complete sentence. In writing, however, except of dialogue in stories, the sentence, which is complete in structure, is usually desirable. Furthermore, in both speaking and writing the careless run-on sentence is to be regarded as objectionable, though it is probable that in speech the sentence may be longer and looser in structure.

The Division of Time between Speech and Writing - Pupils in elementary grades and students in high schools and colleges should have more experience in spoken than in written communication. Throughout life, occasions for speaking are more frequent than those for writing, more varied in type, often more important, and in many ways more difficult to meet. As one progresses in school achievement, his opportunities widen, so that the necessity for the advanced student to have mastery of oral as well as written language for more complex and important occasions constantly increases. Although in the following outline the speaking and writing units are printed separately, these activities may be closely related, and often they may be included in the same unit of work. We should neither completely divorce speaking from writing nor treat either of them as an end to be served by the other. Both should be vitally related to the needs of life. The time devoted to oral and written composition will vary in different schools, but should always be determined by the needs of life and the abilities of the class and the individual.

Voice and Body in Speech - It is extremely important that the teacher be educated in oral language and the less technical aspects of speech. She must know how to discover the speech difficulties of her pupils and to help them overcome the commoner ones. (The technical aspects of speech will doubtless have to be committed to specialists in speech.) She should be skillful not only in methods of dealing with voice and bodily control, but also in handling attitudes, emotions, and the intangible responses which make up the situations in which language must be used.

The use of voice and body in expression must be taught as definitely and intelligently as the language skills, and may become matter for special exercises or drills when teacher and pupils both see the need to them. These skills are listed among the enabling objectives of the Speech units or, if they should have been acquired before school life began, among the Speech items for Corrective Teaching.

13

Speech Experiences, Kindergarten - Grades 6

Note : The grammatical terms used in the statement of enabling objectives may (and should) be used by the teacher after the pupils have had experience in the manipulation of the constructions to which the terms apply, but the pupils should not be required to define or to use the terms.

A. Conversation

1. *Social Objective* : To talk with a familiar small group about home experiences.

   Enabling Objectives : To take an informal attitude toward the group. To wait until the preceding speaker has finished. To speak audibly. To speak in sentences, marking them with appropriate pauses and inflections. (If Instrumental Grammar Units 1 and 2 have not already been introduced, they may well be related to this composition experience.)

2. *Social Objective* : To talk with a familiar small group about shared experiences.

   Enabling Objectives : To show interest in others' contributions to a conversation. To speak with reasonable distinctness. (Any difficulty due to missing teeth should be ignored.) In incidental narratives or explanations to put only one complete thought into a sentence. (Instrumental Grammar Unit 3 may be needed in connection with this composition experience.)

3. *Social Objective* : To be a good host to visitors from another room or from outside the school.

Enabling Objectives : To plan for the entertainment of expected guests. To receive guests graciously. To dismiss guests graciously, perhaps asking them to come again. To speak in pleasant tones.

4. *Social Objective* : To be a satisfactory guest.

Enabling Objectives : To accept the welcome of the host graciously. To show interest in the host's hobbies and plans for amusement by questions and favourable comment - if only, "That is nice". To express appreciation to the host at parting. To look squarely at the person to whom one is talking. If children's structure is too monotonous, it may be well to introduce such initial expressions of times as *yesterday, just then, at eight o'clock* (I.G.U. 4).

5. *Social Objective* : To converse interestingly and pleasantly with mere acquaintances, *e.g.*, classmates not intimately known.

Enabling Objectives : To begin with some topic all know about. To talk naturally about things in which one is interested. To ask questions if necessary to draw out a shy acquaintance. To sit or stand at ease without slouching. To avoid choppiness by sometimes combining two sentences with same subject into a single simple sentence with a compound predicate (I.G.U. 5).

6. *Social Objective* : To converse during "refreshments" served at a table, to not more than eight persons at once.

Enabling Objectives : To speak at least part of the time to the whole table. To think of remarks or incidents interesting to all, *e.g.*, news of someone they know, a new game, an interesting photoplay or radio programme, someone else's (not one's own) pet or collection, appreciation of decorations or refreshments. To use discretion in teasing and boisterous joking. To avoid *gee! gosh! you see, you know, say! listen!* To secure sentence variety and paragraph coherence by learning to use initial adverbial clauses, especially those introduced by *when* and *if* (I.G.U. 6).

7. *Social Objective* : To meet strange children gracefully and graciously.

   Enabling Objectives : To acknowledge introductions properly. To follow up any topic which seems to interest the strangers. To talk about pleasant things and people liked, rather than about unpleasant things and people disliked. To increase effectiveness and accuracy of expression by learning to use adverbial clauses in the predicate position (I.G.U. 7). To increase the vividness and colour of statement by means of adverbs (modifiers of verbs) in the predicate position (I.G.U. 8).

8. *(Optional) Social Objective* : To converse with a group of boys *and* girls not intimately known, about school, sport, or local-event topics.

   Enabling Objectives : To look at all members of the group when one is speaking, even addressing by name anyone who seems to be "left out". To speak favourably, or not at all, or races, or religions, and of harmless individual in the community. To use fresher words of approval than *nice* and *fine e.g., interesting, thrilling, beautiful, exciting, surprising, bright, clever, showing endurance, strong, daring.* To improve ease and clarity of statement by employing simple relative clauses (I.G.U. 10).

9. *(Optional) Social Objective* : To introduce child friends to adult friends.

   Enabling Objectives : To present the children to the adults. To give full names, if needed. To pronounce names distinctly. To give any information that will help the newly introduced to find a topic of conversation. To act as if introducing people were an everyday matter.

10. *(Optional) Social Objective* : To be a satisfactory host or guest.

    Enabling Objectives : To introduce guests who do not know each other. To joke without "slamming" or personal "wise-craking", *e.g.*, to repeat clever remarks, anecdotes, limericks.

11. *(Optional) Social Objective* : To converse naturally with a single mere acquaintance, *e.g.*, a classmate of opposite sex, or a teacher one has not seen recently.

Enabling Objectives : To centre one's attention primarily on the other person's thoughts and thus reduce self-consciousness. To "break the ice" if necessary with a remark about activities in your class or school. To realise that occasional silences are natural.

Techniques Desirable in Conversation : A Summary

Social Techniques :

1. To adopt an easy and natural attitude.
2. To reduce self-consciousness by :
   a. Centering one's attention primarily on the other person's thought.
   b. Realizing that occasional silences are natural.
3. To make and acknowledge introduction properly and gracefully, giving full names when needed, and such information as will help a stranger to find a topic of conversation.
4. To attempt to put others, especially if they are strangers, at their ease, by :
   a. Beginning the conversation with a topic familiar or interesting to all.
   b. Following up topics which seem of interest to others.
   c. Showing interest in the contributions of others to the conversation by listening courteously, by questions, and by favourable comment.
5. To talk about pleasant things and people liked.
6. To speak favourably or not at all about races and religions and about harmless individuals in the community.
7. To introduce humour without becoming boisterous and without hurting the feelings of others.
8. To wait until the preceding speaker has finished.
9. To plan for the entertainment of expected guests.

10. To receive and dismiss guests graciously.

11. To greet and take leave of the host gracefully.

Language Techniques :

1. To Speak in sentences, marking them with appropriate pauses and inflections.
2. To put only one complete thought into a sentence in incidental narrative or explanation.
3. To employ, for smoothness, variety, clarity, and effectiveness the following devices :
   (*a*) Initial adverbs and adverbial clauses.
   (*b*) Compound predicates.
   (*c*) Adverbs and adverbial clauses in the predicate position.
   (*d*) Simple relative clauses.
4. To avoid *gee! gosh! you see, you know, say ! listen!*
5. To use various words of approval.

Speech Techniques :

1. To look squarely at the person one is addressing.
2. To sit or stand at ease without slouching.
3. To speak audibly and distinctly and in a pleasant voice.

B. Telephoning

1. *Social Objective* : To receive a telephone call for another member of the family.

   Enabling Objectives : To state one's telephone number or street address clearly. To reply courteously to the inquiry for the parent, brother, or sister. To speak directly into the transmitter.

2. *Social Objective* : To receive and invitation by telephone.

   Enabling Objectives : To show pleasure at the invitation, even if one must decline it. To avoid interruption. To allow the one who called to close the conversation. To speak in a well modulated voice.

3. *Social Objective* : To extend an invitation to a friend.

   Enabling Objectives : To introduce one's self and ask for the person wanted. To use correct procedure in placing a call. To give all the necessary information : place, time, and nature of the occasion.

4. *Social Objective* : To telephone a message for someone else.

   Enabling Objectives : To use correct procedure in placing a call. To formulate messages and inquiries before taking down the receiver. To explain graciously who one is and for whom he is telephoning.

5. *Social Objective* : To give a tradesman an order.

   Enabling Objectives : To be as polite as if receiving the order. To speak very distinctly and slowly enough for him for write.

6. *Social Objective* : To telephone thanks for a favour.

   Enabling Objectives : To make it clear that the favour really helped. To substitute some fresher synonyms for *good* and kind, *e.g., generous, thoughtful, gracious, obliging, friendly.*

7. *Social Objective* : To seek the use of another's telephone in giving or receiving a message.

   Enabling Objectives : To ask permission to use the telephone. To avoid bringing inconvenience to the person who own the phone by calling at inopportune times, or using the telephone a long time, or using it very frequently. To express appreciation for the privilege which has been extended.

Techniques Desirable in Telephoning : A Summary

Social Techniques :

1. To use correct procedure in placing a call.
2. To formulate messages, inquiries orders, and detailed information before making the call.
3. To explain clearly and courteously who one is and what the purpose of the call is.

4. To give necessary information definitely.
5. To be as courteous and gracious as if one were speaking with the person face to face.
6. To allow the one who called to close the conversation.
7. To ask permission to use another's telephone, to use it with discretion, and to thank for the privilege extended.

Language Techniques :

To increase one's vocabulary of words of appreciation and approval.

Speech Techniques :

To speak distinctly and in a well-modulated voice, and when necessary, slowly enough to allow the person at the other end to write down the information.

C. Discussing and Planning

1. *Social Objective* : To plan under teacher leadership some simple classroom or school-yard activity of the group.

   Enabling Objectives : To keep the purpose of the activity in mind. To give courteous and thoughtful consideration to suggestions offered by others. To feel responsible for assisting by offering suggestions. To speak so that all may hear. To speak in sentences, marking them with appropriate pauses and inflections. (If Instrumental grammar Units 1 and 2 have not already been introduced they may well be related to this composition experience.)

2. *Social Objective* : To join in the development of such social and scientific topics as : How Letters Are Sent; Where Butter Comes From; Why We Celebrate November 11.

   Enabling Objectives : To stick to the topic. To recognise one's own thought when expressed by another in different language, and to avoid repetition. To be very careful to tell the exact truth. To speak in sentences. To provide variety in sentences by learning to shift adverbs and adverbial phrases (I.G.U. 4).

3. *Social Objective* : To participate in the organisation of a formal project, such as an assembly programme, after information and suggestions have been gathered.

   Enabling Objectives : To distinguish main features of the undertaking from details. To eliminate irrelevant detail. To seek effectiveness of the project rather than opportunity for one's self. To yield without sulking to majority opinion. To speak in pleasing, natural tones. To secure speed and ease by combining sentences with the same subjects into sentences with compound predicates (I.G.U. 5).

4. *Social Objective* : To plan an activity, which requires division of labour and coordination of activities.

   Enabling Objectives : To propose definite divisions of work, using the blackboard to help the class to follow the plan. To consider first the effects of each plan, and second the cost of the most effective ones in time, labour, and perhaps money or materials. To plan for coordination. *E.g.*, preliminary reports, date for completion of work, a general chairman. To maintain easy posture, without slouching. To secure sentences variety and paragraph coherence by learning to use initial adverbial clauses, especially those introduced by *when* and *if* (I.G.U. 6).

5. *Social Objective* : To discuss, after outside study, two definite plans, which have survived from a number of earlier suggestions.

   Enabling Objectives : To ask for explanation of any part of a proposal, which is not clear. To think for one's self. To distinguish between important and unimportant arguments on a debated point. To look the class or committee in the eye while speaking. To increase effectiveness and accuracy of expression by learning to use adverbial clauses in the predicate position (I.G.U. 7).

6. *Social Objective* : To plan an activity under the direction of a pupil chairman.

Enabling Objectives : To obey the chairman as the representative of the group, even if one thinks the chairman is wrong. To refrain from speaking when anyone else is speaking. To take not more than one's share of the time. To decide general question, such as the organisation of the activity first, and details, such as the names of participants, later.

7. *Social Objective* : To discuss the results of an undertaking just completed by the class.

Enabling Objectives : To praise as much as sincerity permits. To criticise tactfully, without sarcasm or cattiness. To criticise only important shortcomings. To raise questions freely. To increase vividness and colour by increased and more accurate use of modifying adjectives (I.G.U. 9).

8. *Social Objective* : To discuss such a topic as might arise in the history or geography class, *e.g.*, the development of transportation, the difficulties, Columbus had to overcome, or how our state serves the rest of the U.S.

Enabling Objectives : To have clearly in mind the point to be discussed. To use visual aids to make one's contribution clear and interesting. To contribute facts from independent reading, stating one's sources of information. To omit from one's remarks whatever has already been said in substance by someone else. To improve ease and clarity of statement by employing simple relative clauses (I.G.U. 10).

Techniques Desirable in Discussing and Planning : A Summary

Social Techniques :

1. To keep clearly in mind the purpose of discussion.
2. To show one's sense of responsibility by offering suggestions and by listening attentively to the proposals of others.
3. To seek the success of the group rather than opportunity for one's self.
4. To praise as much as sincerity permits.
5. To criticise tactfully, when criticism is necessary.

6. To think for one's self.
7. To distinguish between important issues and unimportant details.
8. To raise questions and ask for explanations freely.
9. To omit from one's remarks what has been said in substance by others.
10. To keep cool when one's opinions are attacked and to yield gracefully to majority opinion.
11. To state opinions honestly and directly, but impersonally.
12. To state proposals clearly and definitely.
13. To state facts accurately, giving the sources of the information when necessary.
14. To obey the chairman.
15. To wait for recognition by the chair before speaking.
16. To refrain from speaking while others are speaking.
17. To speak no more than one's share of the time.
18. To support arguments with fact or illustration.
19. To use visual aids to make one's contribution clear and interesting.

Language Techniques :

1. To speak in sentences, marking them with appropriate pauses and inflections.
2. To employ, for speed, ease, vividness, and variety, the following devices :
    (*a*) Adverbs and adverbial phrases in various positions.
    (*b*) Initial adverbial clauses.
    (*c*) Adverbial clauses in the predicate position.
    (*d*) Modifying adjective in increased and more accurate use.

(*e*) Compound predicates.

(*f*) Simple relative clauses.

Speech Techniques :

1. To speak to that all may hear and in a pleasant voice.
2. To look directly at those to whom one is speaking.
3. To maintain in easy posture.

D. Telling Stories

1. *Social Objective* : To retell all or part of a story that the class wishes to hear again.

   Enabling Objectives : To recall events in proper sequence. To retain picture words and phrases. To forget one's self in the story. To speak loudly and distinctly enough for all to hear. (If Instrumental Grammar Unit 1 has not already been introduced, it may well be related to this composition experience.)

2. *Social Objective* : To tell to a familiar group, as part of a conversation, a short interesting bit of personal experience.

   Enabling Objectives : While talking, to concentrate one's mind on the experience, in order to avoid (*a*) wandering from the topic and (*b*) becoming self-conscious. To reduce the tendency to speak fragmentary sentences by acquiring the concept of the sentence as a group of words which makes sense (I.G.U. 1). To show by unstudied gestures the movements of people or objects in the story. To tell the story *to* the group, not merely before them.

3. *Social Objective* : To participate in a season (period) or telling bits or personal experience.

   Enabling Objectives : To recall experiences in some way similar to those that others have encountered. To stick to the truth, avoiding exaggeration. To use well-modulated tones. To stand erect but not stiff. To provide variety in sentences by learning to shift adverbs and adverbial phrases (I.G.U. 4).

4. *Social Objective* : To tell a one-paragraph, single-phase story of a personal experience.

   Enabling Objectives : To select an interesting yet simple experience. To choose details in accord with a definite view of the experience as funny, surprising, thrilling, embarrassing, etc. to introduce direct quotations in order to gain vividness. To use such time words as *when, before, until, after, since, while.*

5. *Social Objective* : To retell a brief story read independently or heard outside the classroom.

   Enabling Objectives : To start the action in the first sentence. To cause the voice to express different feelings. To introduce the adversative *but, and yet,* and for the brilliant children, also *however, although, nevertheless, though.* To secure sentence variety and paragraph coherence by learning to use initial adverbial clauses, especially those introduced by *when* and *if* (I.G.U. 6).

6. *Social Objective* : To narrate a personal experience of some particular sort suggested by teacher or classmates.

   Enabling Objectives : To keep the pitch of the voice low most of the time. To end strongly either with the climax of the action or with some comments so natural as not to seem a tag. To increase effectiveness and accuracy of expression by learning to use adverbial clauses in the predicate position (I.G.U. 7).

7. *Social Objective* : To retell a story read independently which is of the length and difficulty found in the grade reader.

   Enabling Objectives : To mark the beginning of each new incident by a pause and some verbal sign post such as, *One year later or During all this time.* To substitute sentences with compound predicates for series of coordinate clauses with the same or equivalent subjects (I.G.U. 5). To increase vividness and colour by increased and more accurate use of modifying adjectives (I.G.U. 9).

8. *Social Objective* : To retell an anecdote with an obvious "point".

Enabling Objectives : To make all explanations early in the story, so that the "point" will instantly be clear. For the most part, to show personal reaction to the experience through the language of narration rather than by direct comment. To improve ease and clarity of statement by employing simple relative clauses (I.G.U. 10).

9. *(Optional) Social Objective* : To describe an incident with the accuracy required in court testimony.

Enabling Objectives : To use diagrams if they will help the listeners to understand. To use comparisons with familiar objects of actions to secure clearness.

10. *(Optional) Social Objective* : To retell a conversation, as, for example, on oral agreement, a quarrel, an interview, vividly and accurately.

Enabling Objectives : To substiture more specific synonyms for overworked verbs, especially for *said*. To omit non-essential repetitions. To use both direct and indirect quotations.

11. *Social Objective* : To retell an incident from a book as a sample or appetiser for other pupils.

Enabling Objectives : To identify the characters at the beginning or as they appear. To being some sentences with dependent clauses.

Techniques desirable in Telling Stories : A Summary

Social Techniques :

1. To overcome self-consciousness by concentrating on the story one is telling.
2. To relate a story or a personal experience in keeping with the spirit of the occasion.
3. To recall events in proper sequence.
4. To start action in the first sentence.
5. To identify characters at the beginning or as they appear.
6. To make all explanations early in the story so that the point, will be instantly clear.

7. To choose the details with an eye to the effect one wishes to produce.
8. To omit non-essential repetition.
9. To use diagrams if they will help the listeners to understand.
10. To make comparisons with familiar objects for clarity.
11. To end the story with the climax of the action or with a natural comment.
12. To show personal reactions in the narrative rather than by direct comment.

Language Techniques :

1. To mark the beginning of each incident by a pause of by some verbal time post.
2. To speak in sentences.
3. To employ, for clarity, accuracy, ease, effectiveness, and variety, the following devices:
   a. Adverbs and adverbial phrases in various positions.
   b. Initial adverbial clauses.
   c. Adverbial clauses in the predicate position.
   d. Time words.
   e. Adversatives.
   f. Direct and indirect quotations.
   g. Compound predicates.
   h. Modifying adjectives in increased and more accurate use.
   i. Specific verbs.
   j. Simple relative clauses.
   k. Initial dependent clauses.

Speech Techniques :

1. To speak to the audience, not merely before it.
2. To speak audibly and distinctly in a pleasant voice.
3. To cause the voice of express feeling.
4. To use spontaneous gestures.
5. To stand erect but not stiff.

E. Dramatisation

1. ***Social Objective*** : To engage in dramatic play.

   Enabling Objectives : To make use of such properties and bits of custom as are available. To converse in character and in situation. To speak with ordinary loudness and distinctness. To think of new phases of the same dramatised activity.

2. ***Social Objective*** : To act out, under teacher leadership, a nursery rhyme or primer story.

   Enabling Objectives : To increase the use of gesture, pantomime and dialogue. To lose consciousness of self in the imagined action.

3. ***Social Objective*** : To act out, under teacher leadership, a first-reader or second-reader story.

   Enabling Objectives : To plan the play : scenes, characters, properties. To retain colourful phrases in the dialogue. To use tones and inflection appropriate to characters and situations.

4. ***Social Objective*** : To act out, without adult guidance, a very short story or a rhyme.

   Enabling Objectives : To conduct the planning in a systematic fashion : scenes, characters, details of action, properties; speaking one at a time. To work out dialogue and stage business in free rehearsals, rather than through memorisation of written lines of directions. To use posture and gesture appropriate to characters and situations.

5. *Social Objective* : To make up and act out a simple story, as for example, an additional incident in a story read, an act for some historical programme, a demonstration of social life in another country.

   Enabling Objectives : To recognise that drama is a story told through the speeches and actions of characters. To avoid conversation which does not advance the plot or deepen the characterisation.

6. *Social Objective* : To stage for classmates a short story or play, or an incident from a longer story, which they have not read.

   Enabling Objectives : To make the dialogue full enough to seem natural but not slow. To determine the pronunciation and meaning of unfamiliar words.

7. *Social Objective* : To make up and perform brief plays with plot, as for instance, illustrating proverbs or qualities of character.

   Enabling Objectives : To work out detail with increasing regard for truth. To place the climax near the end. To deliver speeches distinctly and yet with conversational effect.

8. *Social Objective* : To present a playlet as part of a programme for outsiders : at any assembly, before another room, or at a parents' party.

   Enabling Objectives : To deliver memorised lines as if they were spontaneous. To increase the power of the voice as far as necessary, without raising the pitch.

Techniques Desirable in Dramatization : A Summary

Social Techniques :

1. To overcome self-consciousness by losing one's self in the imagined action.
2. To plan the play or dramatisation in a systematic fashion.
3. To avid conversation which does not advance the plot or deepen the characterisation.

4. To use properties and costumes which are available.

Language Techniques :

1. To tell the story through the speeches and actions of the characters.
2. To make the dialogue natural but not slow.
3. To work out details with increasing regard for the truth.
4. To place the climax near the end.
5. To determine the pronunciation and meaning of unfamiliar words.

Speech Techniques :

1. To work out dialogue and stage business in free rehearsals rather than by memorising written lines or directions.
2. To use tones and inflections, posture and gestures appropriate to the characters and situations.
3. To deliver speeches audibly and distinctly, yet with a conversational effect.

F. Reporting

1. *Social Objective* : To report individual observations made during some class excursion or similar activity.

   Enabling Objectives : To call attention to something no one else has mentioned. To state one's point in a sentence not merely to name an object or activity. To speak loudly and distinctly enough that all may hear easily. (If Instrumental Grammar Unit 1 has not already been introduced, it may well be related to this composition experience.)

2. *Social Objective* : To report to the class such independent observations, as of making flour, cooking at home a rabbit's (or other animal's) behaviour.

   Enabling Objectives : To think through the activity before starting to speak. To follow the time order closely, for the sake of clearness. To further guard against fragmentary sentences by extending the concept of the sentence (I.G.U. 2). To reduce the tendency to speak and especially to write run-on-sentences whether with or without *and*, by sharpening the concept of the sentence as the expression of a single thought (I.G.U. 3). To use gesture when it will contribute to clearness. To stand easily erect.

3. *Social Objective* : To secure through observation or inquiry information, which the class desires, and to report this orally.

   Enabling Objectives : When inquiry is necessary, to state the problem or question clearly and definitely. In reporting to tell first the source of one's information and then, very simply and directly, what one found out. To use pleasant and varied tones. To provide variety in sentences by learning to shift adverbs and adverbial phrases (I.G.U. 4).

4. *Social Objective* : To report items of information upon a topic before the class gained from reading material not accessible to all.

   Enabling Objectives : To tell only that which is new to the class. To make the report in one's own words rather than in those of the material read. To secure speed and ease in narrative by combining sentences with the same subjects into sentences with compound predicates (I.G.U. 5).

5. *Social Objective* : To be one of a committee to assume responsibility for a certain phase of observation during class excursion or experiment, and to report.

   Enabling Objectives : In reporting to stick to one's own field. If opinion is included, to distinguish between it and observed fact. To talk directly to the class. To secure sentence variety and paragraph coherence by learning to use initial adverbial clauses, especially those introduced by *when* and *if* (I.G.U. 6).

6. *Social Objective* : To find and report the answer to a definite question raised in class, *e.g.*, the pronunciation and meaning of a word, the size of the Hoover of Muscle

Shoals Dam, what white man first explored this part of the country.

Enabling Objectives : To present accurately the information as found. To include details or illustrations which will make clearer the fact or its significance. If statistics are involved to give round numbers only. To increase vividness and colour by increased and more accurate use of modifying adjectives (I.G.U. 9).

7. (*Optional*) *Social Objective* : To present the report of a committee appointed to make a plan for some class activity.

Enabling Objectives : To put the reasons for a recommendation all before or all after the statement itself. To present the whole programme in connected form either at the beginning or at the end of the report. If notes are necessary, to use them only as reminders. To improve ease and clarity or statement by employing simple relative clauses (I.G.U. 10).

8. (*Optional*) *Social Objective* : To describe a book to one's classmates or a club.

Enabling Objectives : To begin directly by describing a character (or characters), or the place of the action, or by telling what kind of things the people do. To give a brief statement of the theme. To compare or contrast the book with others familiar to many of one's hearers. To quote or read thrilling, artistic, or humorous passages. To show one's approval in the description of the book rather than in a direct statement at the end.

9. (*Optional*) *Social Objective* : To report the substance of talk (or an address) either summarising or choosing the most important part of it.

Enabling Objectives : To maintain the lecturer's organisation and emphasis. If there are a number of points, to mark them by *first*, *second*, etc., or some other expressions, which will help the audience, keep the organisation clearly in mind.

Techniques Desirable in Reporting : A Summary

Social Techniques :

1. To think through an activity before starting to speak.
2. To give a brief, clear, and definite statement of the theme, problem, or question.
3. To tell only what is new to the class.
4. To put all explanatory material, such as the reasons for a recommendation or the sources of information, in one place, either before or after the statement itself.
5. To use illustration, comparison, and contrast when they will contribute to clarity and understanding.
6. To present information accurately.
7. To distinguish between opinion and observed fact.
8. To maintain the original organisation and emphasis in reporting a lecture.
9. To begin book reports directly.
10. To quote passages of merit.
11. To use notes only as reminders.
12. To give statistics in round numbers only.

Language Techniques :

1. To mark the various points in a report by expression which will help the audience to keep the organisation in mind.
2. To show approval by the language of narration or description rather than by direct comment.
3. To speak in sentences.
4. To employ, for economy, variety, clarity, and effectiveness, the following devices :
   (*a*) Adverbs and adverbial phrases in various positions.
   (*b*) Initial adverbial clauses.

(c) Modifying adjectives in increased and more accurate use.

(d) Compound predicates.

(e) Simple relative clauses.

5. To make reports on material read or heard in one's own words rather than in those of the original.

Speech Techniques :

1. To talk directly to one's audience.
2. To speak audibly and distinctly in a pleasant, well-modulated voice.
3. To use gestures when they contribute to clearness.
4. To stand easily erect.

G. Speaking to Large Groups

1. *Social Objective* : To recite a memorised poem.

   Enabling Objectives : To learn the poem thoroughly, as a whole. To recite the poem with both rhythm and expression. If the voice seems weak, to recite to some individual seated well back in the room.

2. *Social Objective* : To participate in a planned and rehearsed dramatisation.

   Enabling Objectives : To think primarily of the play, rather than of one's self of the audience. To speak loudly enough and distinctly enough to be herd in the large room.

3. *Social Objective* : To make a short original speech, rehearsed but not memorised, as for example, explaining some part of the programme, or presenting one part of a long informational statement.

   Enabling Objectives : To keep the succession of ideas in mind, not trying to remember phrases. To carry in the hand a card of notes to be consulted if necessary. To speak in complete. clearly separated sentences. To speak directly to the audience.

4. ***Social Objective*** : To make an isolated announcement.

   Enabling Objectives : To pause a moment after reaching position, before beginning the announcement. To speak more slowly than in conversation. To restate at the close the details which must be remembered, such as time and place. To stand well forward on the platform. To pitch the voice normally.

5. ***Social Objective*** : To participate in a play.

   Enabling Objectives : To speak the lines conversationally. To make even the last of every sentence audible. To maintain posture and facial expression and to use gestures expressive of the thought and feeling.

6. ***Social Objective*** : To make a speech in a support of some school project.

   Enabling Objectives : To think of one's self as part of the group, and to say "we" instead of "I" as much as possible. To explain some one result of the project vividly, using effective details. To close strongly with an expression of opinion or an appeal for action.

7. ***Social Objective*** : To speak, "read", or act in a programme for parents or others from outside the school.

   Enabling Objectives : To adopt a team spirit toward the whole programme, refraining from criticism of other participants. To be more than usually deliberate and distinct in speech. To present an animated countenance, as pleasant as the subject-matter permits.

Techniques Desirable in Speaking to Large Groups : A Summary

Social Techniques :

1. To identify one's self with the group when supporting or taking part in a school activity.
2. To identify one's self with the character one is portraying in a play.
3. To carry a card with notes to be consulted when necessary.

4. To keep the succession of ideas in mind, not trying to remember phrases.
5. To close strongly with an expression of opinion or an appeal for action.
6. To restate at the end of an announcement details which must be remembered, as time and place.
7. To memorise poems thoroughly.

Language Techniques :

1. To speak in complete, clearly separated sentences.
2. To explain vividly.

Speech Techniques :

1. In addressing a large group formally, to pause a moment after reaching position.
2. To stand well forward on the platform.
3. To speak audibly and distinctly, and as deliberately as the occasion requires.
4. To present an animated countenance.
5. To speak directly to the audience.
6. To recite poems with rhythm and expression.
7. To speak the lines of a play conversationally.
8. To use posture, gestures, and facial expression appropriate to the character one is portraying.

14

Speech Experiences, Grades 7 - 12

A. Social Conversation

1. *Social Objective* : To converse easily and interestingly with a small group of slightly known classmates.

   Enabling Objectives : To have something worthwhile to talk about. To introduce a new topic gracefully, where an old one grows tiresome. To avoid unnecessary, stereotyped expressions such as *see, listen, and all like that, and everything like that, don't you know, I don't know, you know, say*. To increase vividness and colour by increased and more accurate use of modifying adjectives. To use adjective prepositional phrases for effective description or identification (I.G.U. 11). To speak in well-modulated tones and distinctly. To maintain easy yet polite posture.

2. *Social Objective* : To converse in a group of young people chiefly strange to each other, *e.g.*, schoolmates from other rooms.

   Enabling Objectives : To introduce one's self properly. To use a variety of appropriate forms of presentation in introducing others. To use conventionalities as the weather, the occasion, or an important current event as an introduction to fresher topics. To address and draw out anyone who seems shy or crowded out of the conversation. To improve ease and clarity of statement by employing simple relative clauses (I.G.U. 10).

3. *Social Objective* : To converse in a group of young people and parents or older friends.

Enabling Objectives : To keep to subjects known and interesting to both ages. To show deference to the elders, standing until they are seated, yielding them the right of way in conversation and avoiding direct contradiction of their opinions. To employ more dignified equivalents for such expressions as *swell, O.K., fine and dandy, rocky, not so hot, crazy* (about something), *pooch, eats, gay* (person), *mut, peach* (anything excellent) and *peachy*. To secure directness and force in discussing actions by using infinitives and other verbal nouns (gerunds) as sentence subjects (I.G.U. 13).

4. *Social Objective* : To put a friend and a new acquaintance at ease.

   Enabling Objectives : To include the third person in the conversation already in progress or to mention a common interest, such as a "mutual" friend. To introduce a joke or humorous anecdote to relieve stiffness. To keep hands still (and out of pockets) excepts when they are used in gestures. To secure conciseness by using infinitives as adjective and adverbial modifiers (I.G.U. 14).

5. *Social Objective* : To leave a group gracefully, especially before the others are ready to break up.

   Enabling Objectives : To express or imply clearly regret at having to go. To withdraw uncbtrusively, interrupting the conversation as little as possible. To go promptly after saying one must. To say *Goodnight* or *Goodbye* rather than *So long* or *I'll be seein' yuh.*

6. *Social Objective* : To apologise graciously and with dignity for an accident or an unintentional discourtesy.

   Enabling Objectives : To assume the responsibility squarely and to express regret. To explain only if your unfortunate behaviour would otherwise seem intentional. To avoid self-disparagement. To speak quietly and only to the person offended or injured.

7. *Social Objective* : To be host or guest at dinner (not more than eight at the table).

Enabling Objectives : To observe the proprieties in siting down to the table. To engage for a while in general conversation, host or hostess leading. To hold briefer conversations with each neighbour. To find fresher words than *awful, nice, lots, terrible, fine.*

8. *Social Objective* : To take part acceptably in a jocular conversation.

Enabling Objectives : To have a sufficient stock of jokes, anecdotes and limericks. To slip in an occasional pun or amusing comparison of something mentioned by another. To yield to the comic spirit and enjoy the fun making by others. To gain conciseness by substituting participial phrases for adjective and even adverbial clauses (I.G.U. 16).

9. *Social Objective* : To converse acceptably in a group composed of familiars and one or two strangers.

Enabling Objectives : To avoid topics known only to familiars. To be well enough informed to talk about general topics, rather than local or personal ones. To increase clarity and brevity in the discussion of ideas by the use of subject clauses (I.G.U. 19).

10. *Social Objective* : To congratulate a schoolmate upon achievement or good fortune.

Enabling Objectives : To see and to say why he deserved success or good fortune. To express good wishes without exaggeration of manner of language. To increase exactness and ease by using verbal nouns (gerunds) as objects of verbs and prepositions (I.G.U. 13). To use the present perfect (perfect) tense always and only to indicate indefinite past time or action just completed (I.G.U. 18).

Techniques Desirable in Social Conversation : A Summary

Social Techniques :

1. To be sufficiently well informed to discuss common topics of interest to all.

2. To have a sufficient stock of humorous material.
3. To yield to the spirit of the occasion.
4. To introduce one's self properly.
5. To use a variety or appropriate forms of presentation in introducing others.
6. To put others, especially strangers, at their ease by :
   (*a*) Addressing the whole group at least part of the time.
   (*b*) Using conventionalities as to the weather or the occasion as an introduction to other topics.
   (*c*) Introducing a fresh topic gracefully when the old one grows tiresome.
   (*d*) Avoiding topics unfamiliar or uninteresting to all or part of the group.
   (*e*) Introducing humour to relieve stiffness.
   (*f*) Addressing or drawing out anyone who seems shy.
   (*g*) Following the lead of the host in conversation at table.
7. To show deference to elders.
8. To assume squarely the responsibility for accidents or un-international discourtesies, and to express regret without self-disparagement.
9. To explain accidents only if they would otherwise seem intentional, and then only to the person injured or offended.
10. To express good wishes without exaggeration, and to see and to say why they are deserved.
11. In withdrawing from a party still in progress, to express regret, and to go unobtrusively and promptly.
12. To observe the proprieties in sitting down to table.

Language Techniques :

1. To avoid unnecessary and stereo typed expressions, especially the more common slang terms.
2. To employ, for economy, conciseness, emphasis, colour, and variety, the following devices :
   (*a*) Modifying adjectives in increased and more accurate use.
   (*b*) Adjective prepositional phrases for description and identification.
   (*c*) Verbal nouns and infinitives as sentence subjects.
   (*d*) Infinitives as adjective and adverbial modifiers.
   (*e*) Verbal nouns as objects of verbs and prepositions.
   (*f*) Participial phrases in place of adjective and adverbial clauses.
   (*g*) Simple relative clauses.
   (*h*) Subject clauses.
   (*i*) Appositive noun clauses.
   (*j*) The present perfect tenses always and only to indicate indefinite past time or actions just completed.

Speech Techniques :

1. To speak in well modulated tones, distinctly.
2. To maintain easy but polite posture.
3. To keep the hands still except when they are used in gestures.

B. Telephone Conversation

1. *Social Objective* : To plan with a friend for some activity, such as picnicking, getting up a surprise party, or giving a club programmeme.

   Enabling Objectives : To stick to the business in hand, in order to finish promptly. To state clearly one's own understanding of each decision, or to approve definitely such a statement by one's friend. To take notes of decisions and to rehearse the whole plan at the close of the conversation. To improve ease and clarity of statement by employing simple relative clauses (I.G.U. 10).

2. *Social Objective* : When calling a friend, to converse briefly with another member of his family who answers.

   Enabling Objectives : Upon learning who has answered to tell one's own name and ask the usual, "How are you today"? To inquire about or comment upon some matter of interest to the person who has answered. To ask for one's friend reasonably soon but not abruptly. To increase vividness and colour by increased and more accurate use of modifying adjectives (I.G.U. 9). To use adjective prepositional phrases for effective description or identification (I.G.U. 11).

3. *Social Objective* : To inquire about a friend who is sick.

   Enabling Objectives : To be brief. To express pleasure at or hope for improvement.

4. *Social Objective* : To do shopping which requires decision on the basis of information secured in the conversation.

   Enabling Objectives : To have clearly in mind the information wanted and the basis upon which one will decide. To repeat for verification prices, sizes, or other easily misunderstood details. To persist in questioning, if necessary, until facts are clear. To secure variety by substituting participial phrases for adjective and even adverbial clauses (I.G.U. 16).

5. *Social Objective* : To make a business complaint or ask for an adjustment

   Enabling Objectives : To ask at once for the proper authority. To tell the story in orderly fashion without comment or show of temper. To show confidence that the business house will correct this *mistake*. To use the past (imperfect) tense always and only to indicate definite past ime (I.G.U. 17). To use the present perfect (perfect) tense always and only to indicate indefinite past time or action just completed (I.G.U. 18).

6. *Social Objective* : To make arrangements for a party, a school programmeme, a club or other meeting.

   Enabling Objectives : To know just what one wants each person to do. To present suggestions or ask for favours rather than to give orders or to assume obligation upon others to do these things. To consider generously suggestions made in return. To secure directness and force in discussing actions by using verbal nouns and infinitives as sentence subjects (I.G.U. 13) and as objects of verbs and prepositions (I.G.U. 15).

7. *Social Objective* : To get railroad, express, or other similar information by telephone.

   Enabling Objectives : To insure understanding of proper nouns by spelling, for example, *Buffton* : *B* for Boston, *u* for Under, *f* for Frank, *t* for Thomas, *o* for Oscar, *n* for Nora. To tell first what *kind* of information one wants. To organise inquiry in relatively short sentences, without repetitions. To increase clarity and brevity in the discussion of ideas by the use of subject clauses (I.G.U. 19).

8. *Social Objective* : To arrange with a representative of another group for a game debate, or rally.

   Enabling Objectives : To phrase courteously any necessary refusals. To speak as the representative of one's group, saying *we* rather then *I*.

9. *Social Objective* : To telephone a long or difficult message for someone else.

   Enabling Objectives : To organise the material very thoroughly beforehand. To make sure that each point is clear before proceeding to the next. To dictate in phrases any message to be written down *verbatim*.

10. *Social Objective* : To make a long distance call for any purpose.

Enabling Objectives : To name clearly (*a*) the town and (*b*) the name of the person or the number of the "station" (or both) that you wish. To indicate quite clearly whether you wish to place a station-to-station or a person-to-person call. To be as direct and brief as courtesy permits.

Techniques Desirable in Telephone Conversation: A Summary

Social Techniques :

1. To have clearly in mind the purpose of the call.
2. To tell one's name, and, if a relative of the person one wishes to speak to answers, to converse briefly but courteously with him before asking for one's friend.
3. To be brief in inquiries about a sick person, and to express pleasure at or hope for improvement.
4. To stick to the business in hand, outlining and discussing it in orderly fashion, and repeating detailed information to make sure that it is clearly understood.
5. To persist in questioning, if necessary, until the facts are clear.
6. To present suggestions and ask for favours rather than to give orders.
7. To consider generously the suggestions of others, and definitely approve or disapprove them.
8. To phrase necessary refusals courteously.
9. To say "we" rather than "I" when making a call as the representative of a group.
10. In business calls, to ask at once for the proper authority or to state at once and definitely the purpose of the call.
11. To be especially courteous in making complaints, assuming that the business house will show equal courtesy.
12. To use proper procedure in placing long distance calls.
13. To be as brief as courtesy permits in making or answering long distance calls.

Language Techniques :

1. To employ, for ease, clarity, conciseness, emphasis, and effectiveness, the following devices :
   (*a*) Simple relative clauses.
   (*b*) Clauses introduced by relative pronouns in the oblique cases.
   (*c*) Adjective prepositional phrases for description and identification.
   (*d*) Participial phrases in place of adjective and adverbial clauses.
   (*e*) Gerunds and infinitives as sentence subjects.
   (*f*) Gerunds as objects or verbs and prepositions.
   (*g*) Subject and appositive clauses.
   (*h*) Parallel form for coordinate ideas and subordinate clauses for subordinate ideas.
   (*i*) The past (imperfect) tense always and only to indicate definite past time.
   (*j*) The present perfect tense always and only to indicate indefinite past time or action just completed.

Speech Techniques :

1. To speak directly into the transmitter
2. To use moderate force and pleasant tones.
3. To speak quite distinctly.
4. To dictate slowly messages to be written down.

C. Interviews and Conferences

1. *Social Objective* : To secure information, *e.g.*, for a class report or for publication.

   Enabling Objectives : To introduce one's self simply, without shrinking or aggressiveness. To state or suggest a reason that the person interviewed should give time or information. To thank the person interviewed. To ask, from a checklist, for items of information not covered in the general reply. To increase vividness and colour by increased and more accurate use of modifying adjectives (I.G.U. 9). To use adjective prepositional phrases for effective description or identification (I.G.U. 11).

2. *Social Objective* : To secure permission, authority, or advice.

   Enabling Objectives : To state one's desire clearly. To state clearly the reasons which will appeal to the authority, putting them first if a refusal is feared. To give courteous thanks for the consideration of the request, even if the request itself is refused. To discover and, if possible, to overcome any objection of the authority which may lead to refusal. To improve ease and clarity of statement by employing simple relative clauses (I.G.U. 10).

3. *Social Objective* : To buy a stock article.

   Enabling Objectives : To be as definite as possible in one's first request of the salesperson, to save time. To state frankly wherein any article offered differs from one's desires. To avoid argument, especially comparison with a competing article elsewhere. To secure conciseness by using infinitives as adjective and adverbial modifiers (I.G.U. 14). To reduce formality by substituting participial phrases for adjective and even adverbial clauses (I.G.U. 16).

4. *Social Objective* : To apply for a part-time position.

   Enabling Objectives : To look the interviewer in the eye. To state one's qualifications effectively, the strongest last. To answer all questions frankly. To use the past (imperfect) tense always and only to indicate definite past time (I.G.U. 17). To use the present perfect (perfect) tense always and only to indicate indefinite past time or action just completed (I.G.U. 18).

5. *Social Objective* : To help to frame a committee report.

   Enabling Objectives : To seek the general good rather than to try to get one's own way. To avoid personal remarks and other digressions. To discover as soon as possible the issues which will determine the report. To secure directness and force in discussing actions by using gerunds and infinitives as sentence subjects. To increase exactness and ease by using gerunds (infinitives in *ing*) as objects of verbs and prepositions.

6. *Social Objective* : To solicit support for a candidate or proposal.

   Enabling Objectives : To persuade, rather than to beg or to dictate. To praise one's own candidate, rather than to disparage another. To appeal to the special interests and motives of the person whose support is sought. To use appositives as shorter and less emphatic substitutes for relative clauses (I.G.U. 20). To increase clarity and brevity in the discussion of ideas by the use of subject clauses (I.G.U. 19).

7. *Social Objective* : To arrange (with a representative of another group) a game, contest, or rally.

   Enabling Objectives : To assume a spirit of fairness in the other conferee. To work out together a written statement of the final plan.

8. *Social Objective* : To solicit advertising or other patronage.

   Enabling Objectives : To make some disarming opening, as praising a merchant's attractive store. To describe what one offers showing its attractiveness or possibilities, rather than to argue. To persist, sweetly, in the face of indifference or rudeness. To use the active voice habitually for vigour and the passive occasionally to minimise the action of the agent (I.G.U. 24).

9. *Social Objective* : To apply for a position.

   Enabling Objectives : To show respect without subservience. To show enthusiasm for the prospective employment. To express coordinate ideas in parallel form and subordinate ideas in subordinate clauses (I.G.U. 25).

Techniques Desirable in Interviews and Conferences : A Summary

Social Techniques :

1. To introduce one's self without shrinking or aggressiveness.

2. To show respect without subservience.
3. To state clearly one's desire or request, giving reasons why it should be granted, and appealing, when appropriate and possible, to the self-interest of the hearer.
4. To discover and, if possible, to overcome beforehand conditions which would make for a refusal of one's request.
5. To persuade rather than to argue, beg, or dictate.
6. To point out the merits of what one has to offer rather than to disparage other ideas or persons.
7. To discover and recognise main issues.
8. To avoid digression.
9. To answer all question frankly.
10. To arrange beforehand a checklist of questions to be asked in an interview.
11. To work out with conferees written statements of detailed plans.
12. To remain courteous in the face of indifference or rudeness.
13. When acting, as a member or representative of a group, to seek the general good rather than one's own way.
14. To assume a spirit of fairness in others.
15. To be as definite as possible in making requests of a salesperson.
16. To thank courteously for the time and consideration given one, even when the results are disappointing.

Language Techniques :

1. To employ, for smoothness, clarity, conciseness, emphasis, and vividness, the following devices :
   (*a*) Simple relative clauses.
   (*b*) Clauses introduced by relative pronouns in the oblique cases.

(*c*) Adjective prepositional phrases for description and identification.

(*d*) Modifying adjectives in increased and more accurate use.

(*e*) Participial phrases in place of relative clauses.

(*f*) Gerunds and infinitives as sentence subjects.

(*g*) Gerunds as objects of verbs and prepositions.

(*h*) Subject clauses.

(*i*) Appositives in place of relative clauses.

(*j*) Infinitives as adjective and adverbial modifiers.

(*k*) Parallel form for coordinate ideas and subordinate clauses for subordinate ideas.

(*l*) Active verbs habitually for vigour and passive verbs occasionally to minimise the action or the agent.

(*m*) The past (imperfect) tense always and only to indicate definite past time.

(*n*) The present perfect tense always and only to indicate indefinite past time or actions just completed.

Speech Techniques :

1. To look directly at the person one is addressing.
2. To be particularly careful about voice quality and enunciation.
3. To maintain a dignified bearing.

D. Discussion

1. *Social Objective* : To discuss under teacher leadership a story, poem, play or essay that all the group have read.

Enabling Objectives : To speak upon the phase of the selection under consideration at the moment, saving other comments for their proper time. To indicate, in a variety of tactful ways, whether one is supporting or attacking views already expressed. To begin some sentences with adverbs or adverbial phrases. To increase vividness and colour by increased and more accurate use of modifying adjectives (I.G.U. 9). To use adjective prepositional phrases for effective description or identification (I.G.U. 11).

2. *Social Objective* : To discuss some subject-matter topic, such as the cause of the American Revolution, or the effects of cyclones and anti-cyclones.

   Enabling Objectives : To cite authority in a variety of graceful manners, as for instance, "Merritt's Dictionary gives...". "In Bacon's Encyclopaedia I found that...". To distinguish between fact and opinion (interpretation of fact) in authorities, and to quote hearsay or one's general information as tentative facts. To link one's contribution to any previous remarks upon the same point. To improve ease and clarity of statement by employing simple relative clauses (I.G.U. 10).

3. *Social Objective* : To discuss, under teacher chairmanship, specific recent events.

   Enabling Objectives : To recognise and allow for the bias of each newspaper or magazine. To assume that all present, however biased they appear to be, are trying to see the truth. To attack the acts and opinions of public men, but not their motives. To use rhetorical questions. To secure conciseness by using infinitives as adjectives and adverbial modifiers (I.G.U. 14). To use appositives as shorter and less emphatic substitutes for relative clauses (I.G.U. 20).

4. *Social Objective* : To join in the discussion preceding the adoption of a course of action by the class group.

   Enabling Objectives : To use initial or final (frequently hortatory) exclamations, such as, "Let's keep out of debt!" "Only a first class play for us !" To make a single point and to support it by such citation of facts or such description of the consequences of a course of action as will give that point moving power. To increase exactness and ease by using verbal nouns (gerunds) as objectives of verbs and prepositions (I.G.U. 15).

5. ***Social Objective*** : To discuss some broad factual topic, such as changes in styles of clothes, present conditions in some foreign country.

   Enabling Objectives : To begin some sentences with adverbial clauses. To use metaphors, similes, blackboard diagrams, and gestures to assist understanding. To quote accurately, especially avoiding generalisation of specific statements. To use the past (imperfect) tense always and only to indicate definite past time (I.G.U. 17). To use the present (perfect) tense always and only to indicate indefinite past time or action just completed (I.G.U. 18).

6. ***Social Objective*** : To discuss a book or an author and the issues, esthetic and ethical that arise.

   Enabling Objectives : To make a point with reasonable thoroughness without speaking more than sixty seconds. To brighten the talk with literary quotation and allusion. To agree to as much as one honestly can of the opinion or argument of those from whom he differs. To seek by questions to locate the basic reason for a difference of opinion. To increase clarity and brevity in the discussion of ideas by the use of subject and appositive clauses (I.G.U. 19, 21).

7. ***Social Objective*** : To discuss a current problem of government, social customs, or ethics, after preparatory reading or investigation.

   Enabling Objectives : To avoid the imputation of stupidity or moral obliquity to any party, religion, or social group. To use with precision such terms as *fascist, communist, fundamentalist*, etc., to illustrate with good-humoured stories as means of preventing emotional tension. To use appositives as shorter and less emphatic substitutes for relative clauses (I.G.U. 20). To express coordinate ideas in parallel form and subordinate ideas in subordinate clauses or in phrases (I.G.U. 25).

Technique Desirables in Discussion : A Summary

Social Techniques :

1. Stick to the phase of the material under discussion the moment, leaving other comments for their proper time.
2. To make a single point and support it by such citation of facts as will give it moving power.
3. To indicate in a variety of tactful ways whether one is supporting or attacking views already expressed.
4. To link one's contribution to previous remarks on the same subject.
5. To distinguish between fact and opinion, and to recognise and allow for bias.
6. To quote accurately.
7. To use blackboard diagrams where they will help understanding.
8. To assume that all present are seeking the truth.
9. To avoid the imputation of stupidity or moral obliquity to any party, religion, or social group.
10. To agree to as much as one honestly can of the opinions of arguments of those from whom one differs.
11. To illustrate with good-humoured stories as a means of preventing emotional tension.
12. To attack the acts and opinions of public men, not their motives.

Language Techniques :

1. To cite authority in a variety of graceful ways.
2. To brighten one's talked with literary allusion and quotation.
3. To use with precision words denoting a set of ideas or principles.
4. To use initial and final exclamations.
5. To employ, for clarity, ease, conciseness, accuracy, and vividness, the following devices :

(*a*) Modifying adjectives in increased and more accurate use.

(*b*) Clauses introduced by relative pronouns in the oblique cases.

(*c*) Adjective prepositional phrases for description and identification.

(*d*) Simple relative clauses.

(*e*) Infinitives as subjects and as adverbial modifiers.

(*f*) Gerunds as objects of verbs and prepositions.

(*g*) Subject clauses.

(*h*) Appositives in place of relative clauses.

(*i*) Appositive noun clauses.

(*j*) Initial adverbs and adverbial phrases.

(*k*) Initial adverbial clauses.

(*l*) The past tense always and only to indicate definite past time.

(*m*) Present perfect tense always and only to indicate indefinite past time or action just completed.

(*n*) Rhetorical questions.

(*o*) Metaphors and similes.

Speech Techniques :

1. To speak in pleasant, tones, distinctly.
2. To look at the audience.
3. To use gestures where they will help understanding.

E. Questions and Answers

1. *Social Objective* : To inquire how to find a certain place or object.

Enabling Objectives : To ask the information politely, as a favour. To identify clearly the place of object you wish to find, describing it if necessary. To repeat the instructions, if complicated, to insure accuracy. To use adjective prepositional phrases for effective description or identification (I.G.U. 11).

2. *Social Objective* : To give directions for finding a certain place or object.

Enabling Objectives : To show a genuinely friendly spirit. To give the directions slowly, one point at a time. To pronounce any necessary names distinctly. To improve ease and clarity of statement by employing simple relative clauses (I.G.U. 10).

3. *Social Objective* : To ask for explanation of a difficulty encountered in reading as, for instance, in a school lesson.

Enabling Objectives : To point out the place of difficulty as specifically as possible. To tell whether the difficulty is lack of meaning or apparent contradiction. To secure directness and force in discussing actions by using verbal nouns (gerunds) and infinitives as sentence subjects and as objects of verbs and prepositions (I.G.U. 13, 15).

4. *(Optional) Social Objective* : To answer requests for explanations of the difficulties in reading.

Enabling Objectives : To question the applicant for help if he has not made clear his difficulty. To explain slowly, step by step, encouraging questions as one goes along. To use, if necessary, more familiar examples of or parallels to the explanation read. To increase clarity and brevity in the discussion of ideas by the use of subject clauses (I.G.U. 19).

5. *Social Objective* : To answer specific test questions in a school subject.

Enabling Objectives : To decide upon the main point of the answer before beginning to speak. To use words exactly, avoiding any terms one does not understand. To reduce formality by substituting participial phrases for adjective and even adverbial clauses (I.G.U. 16). To use the past (imperfect) tense always and only to indicate definite past time (I.G.U. 17).

6. *Social Objective* : To present some specific problem arising outside of books, *e.g.*, the explanation of some physical phenomenon.

   Enabling Objectives : To explain clearly what one has noticed. To state definitely the question these facts raise. To improve clarity in the discussion of ideas by the use of appositive noun clauses (I.G.U. 21).

7. *(Optional) Social Objective* : To offer a solution of a problem presented.

   Enabling Objectives : To begin with the facts known to the questioner. To assume no further knowledge, especially of terminology. To use diagram and to use similes where they are helpful. To express coordinate ideas in parallel form and subordinate ideas in subordinate clauses (I.G.U. 25).

8. *Social Objective* : To ask test questions, especially upon an explanation one has just given.

   Enabling Objectives : To choose the central point and the main supports for questioning. To confine each question to *what, when, how* or *why*. To make sentences rather simple, with never more than one modifying clause.

Techniques Desirable in Questions and Answers : A Summary

Social Techniques :

1. To ask questions politely and as definitely and specifically as possible.
2. To repeat, if necessary to insure accuracy, instructions or detailed information given or received.
3. To answer, questions with genuine friendliness and in an orderly and definite fashion.
4. To begin difficult explanations with the facts known to the questioner or audience, and to proceed with explanation step by step, using familiar examples or parallels to make one's self clear, and defining terms when necessary.

5. To decide on the main point of the answer before beginning to speak.

Language Techniques :

1. To use words precisely.
2. To employ, for ease, clarity, conciseness, emphasis, and effectiveness, the following devices :
   (*a*) Clauses introduced by relative pronouns in the oblique cases.
   (*b*) Adjective prepositional phrases for description and identification.
   (*c*) Simple relative clauses.
   (*d*) Gerunds and infinitives as sentence subjects.
   (*e*) Gerunds as objects of verbs and prepositions.
   (*f*) Participial phrases in place of adjective and adverbial clauses.
   (*g*) Appositive noun clauses.
   (*h*) Subject clauses.
   (*i*) Parallel form for coordinate ideas and subordinate clauses for subordinate ideas.
   (*j*) The past tense always and only to indicate definite past time.
   (*k*) Similes.

F. Organizations

1. *Social Objective* : To propose action by the class, club, or other body.

Enabling Objectives : To address the chairman for permission to speak. To use the conventional locution : "I move that..." or "I move you that...." To state the proposal in a single sentence which is not confusingly long or complex. To address the chair and make a nomination during an election. To increase vividness and colour by increased and more accurate use of modifying adjectives (I.G.U. 9). To use adjective prepositional phrases of effective description or identification (I.G.U. 11).

1a. (For superior pupils) Social Objective : To preside over a club or similar meeting.

Enabling Objectives : To call the meeting to order, and to maintain order. To recognise members to speak or to present motions. To put motions clearly and to announce the result promptly.

2. *Social Objective* : To debate a motion before the house.

Enabling Objectives : To give a reason, which is likely to influence one's fellows to vote either for or against the motion. To explain one's point fully enough to make it effective, using specific illustration. To improve ease and clarity of statement by employing simple relative clauses (I.G.U. 10).

3. *Social Objective* : To secure a change in someone else's proposal.

Enabling Objectives : To "move to amend" by inserting, striking out, or both. To state the exact place in the sentence and the exact words of the insertion or omission. To secure directness and force in discussing actions by using verbal nouns (gerunds) and infinitives as sentence subjects and as objects of verbs and prepositions (I.G.U. 13, 15).

3a. (Optional) Social Objective : To preside during the consideration of amendments to motions.

Enabling Objectives : To repeat each amendment, and to state clearly how the motion will read if the amendment is adopted. To call for a vote first upon any amendment to the amendment, then upon the (perhaps amended) amendment and finally upon the (perhaps amended) original motion.

4. *Social Objective* : To present a committee report.

Enabling Objectives : To read the formal report of the committee and hand it to the secretary. To "move the adoption of the report" one has just presented. To claim one's right to speak first in discussion of this motion to adopt the report. To use the past (imperfect) tense always and only to indicate definite past time (I.G.U. 17). To use the present perfect (perfect) tense always and only to indicate indefinite past time or action just completed (I.G.U. 18).

5. *Social Objective* : To hold a formal debate, with decision either by appointed judges, or by audience vote on the "merits of question" before and after the debate.

   Enabling Objectives : To reduce the case to a few fundamental issues, usually not more than three, rather than to present a dozen scattered points. To arrange with one's team-mates a plan for presenting the whole case, dividing the phases of the argument among the speakers. To cite facts, with authority for them, but not to cite opinion. To avoid sarcasm, particularly personal sarcasm upon one's opponents. To increase clarity and brevity in the discussion of ideas by the use of subject and appositive noun clauses (I.G.U. 19, 21).

6. *Social Objective* : To force a decision when it is unduly delayed.

   Enabling Objectives : To "move the previous question" if simple calls of "Question! Question!" do not produce a vote. If one wishes the motion defeated, to move to adjourn, or to move to lay the motion on the table. To move "that nominations be closed".

6a. *(Optional) Social Objective* : To preside justly when parliamentary manoeuvring is going on.

   Enabling Objectives : To know and apply the table of precedence of motions. To explain to anyone rising for information the effect of the proposed parliamentary action. When the result of a vote seems doubtful, to ask for a rising vote. To announce the result of any close vote deliberately enough to permit a protest : "The ayes seem to have it. ...The ayes do have it.... The motion is carried".

7. *Social Objective* : To postpone decision.

   Enabling Objectives : To move to lay the motion on the table until a certain time. If the organisation will meet again, to move to adjourn or to move to adjourn to a certain time.

8. *Social Objective* : To maintain one's parliamentary rights, especially against an unfair chairman.

Enabling Objectives : To rise to a point of order. To "call for a division" when the result of a vote seems doubtful. To "appeal from the decision of the chair" when the chairman rules incorrectly on a point of order or on a *viva voce* vote.

9. *Social Objective* : To debate a motion before the house.

Enabling Objectives : To give one's whole attention to one of the few big issues upon which the decision should rest. To outline, if only mentally, the course of one's argument. To describe as persuasively as possible the results of the action one advocates. To phrase sentences condemning some one else's proposal "to fall upon their softest sides". To use the active voice for vigour and the passive to soften statements (I.G.U. 24).

10. *Social Objective* : To secure, in spite of opponents, a vote upon just the proposal one wishes.

Enabling Objectives : To move the division of a motion, which couples something desirable with something undesirable. To "move to substitute for the motion before the house the following : ... "

Techniques Desirable in Organizations : A Summary

Social Techniques :

1. To concentrate on important points and main issues, disregarding unimportant details.
2. To give reasons and explanations, which are likely to influence the hearers in the direction of one's wishes, using specific illustration.
3. To outline, if only mentally, the course of one's argument.
4. To cite facts, with the authority for them, but not to cite opinions.

5. To avoid sarcasm, particularly personal sarcasm.
6. To phrase tactfully sentences condemning the proposals of others.
7. To arrange with one's team-mates in a debate a plan for presentation.
8. To become familiar with and apply parliamentary law and procedure as follows :
   (*a*) To use the conventional parliamentary locutions.
   (*b*) To address the chairman for permission to speak.
   (*c*) To use the proper procedure in presenting and discussing a committee report.
   (*d*) To "move to amend".
   (*e*) To "move the previous motion".
   (*f*) To move to adjourn, or to move to lay the motion on the table.
   (*g*) To move that nominations be closed.
   (*h*) To rise to a point of order.
   (*i*) To "call for a division".
   (*j*) To "appeal from the decision of the chair".
   (*k*) To move the division of a motion.
   (*l*) To "move to substitute for the motion before the house the following".
9. For strong students, as presiding officer :
   (*a*) To call a meeting to order and to maintain order.
   (*b*) To recognise members to speak or to present motions.
   (*c*) To know and to apply the table of precedence of motions.
   (*d*) To put motions, including their amendments, clearly, and to announce the results promptly.
   (*e*) To explain to anyone rising for information the effect of the proposed parliamentary action.

(*f*) To ask for a rising vote if the result of a vote seems doubtful.

(*g*) To announce the result of a close vote deliberately enough to permit protest.

Language Techniques :

1. To state a proposal in a single and relatively simple sentence.

2. To be clear and precise in moving insertions and omissions.

3. To employ, for clarity, ease, economy, emphasis, and vividness, the following devices :

   (*a*) Clauses introduced by relative pronouns in the oblique cases.

   (*b*) Adjective prepositional phrases for description and identification.

   (*c*) Simple relative clauses.

   (*d*) Gerunds and infinitives as sentence subjects.

   (*e*) Gerunds as objects of verbs and prepositions.

   (*f*) Modifying adjectives in increased and more accurate use.

   (*g*) Appositive noun clauses.

   (*h*) Subject clauses.

   (*i*) Parallel form for coordinate ideas and subordinate clauses for subordinate ideas.

   (*j*) The past tense always and only to indicate definite past time.

   (*k*) The present perfect tense always and only to indicate indefinite past time of action just completed.

G. Special Occasion Speeches

1. ***Social Objective*** : To make an announcement, as of an entertainment or a lecture.

Enabling Objectives : To know the facts. To make an interesting beginning. To study the audience so as to make the event announced attractive to them. To repeat for emphasis. To suit the language to the occasion. To increase vividness and colour by increased and more accurate use of modifying adjectives (I.G.U. 9). To use adjective prepositional phrases for effective description or identification (I.G.U. 11).

2. *Social Objective* : To make a speech for some school activity.

   Enabling Objectives : To shape the speech for the purpose of encouraging loyalty to your school and the activity, without stirring antagonism for any other school. To appeal to the feelings of the students. To give good reasons for the promotion of the activity. To improve ease and clarity of statement by employing simple relative clauses (I.G.U. 10). To reduce formality by substituting participial phrases for adjective and even adverbial clauses (I.G.U. 16).

3. *Social Objective* : To make a nomination speech for the candidate whom you favour for the presidency of your class.

   Enabling Objectives : To analyse the requirements of the office, and in a definite, concrete way, measure your candidate by these requirements. To avoid saying anything derogatory about another candidate. To keep within a time limit. To secure conciseness by using infinitives as adjective and adverbial modifiers (I.G.U. 14).

4. *Social Objective* : To make an installation address, as when being installed as president of your class.

   Enabling Objectives : To express appreciation of the honour in other than a stereo typed way. To foresee the work of the year and give a bird's-eye view of it to the class. To express graciously your appreciation of the work of your predecessor. To encourage loyalty by stimulating pride in the past of the organisation and interest in the work to come. To increase exactness and ease by using verbal nouns (gerunds) as objects of verbs and prepositions (I.G.U. 15).

5. *Social Objective* : To make a talk of five minutes or less in length, for some occasion such as the celebration in school assembly of the birthday of your principal.

   Enabling Objectives : To direct all your efforts toward the promotion of friendly feeling. To learn the facts about your subject. To distinguish between appreciation and flattery. To include touches of feeling. To use the present (perfect) tense always and only to indicate indefinite psat time or action just completed (I.G.U. 18). To use appositives as shorter and less emphatic substitutes for relative clauses (I.G.U. 20).

6. *Social Objective* : To make speeches of presentation and acceptance on such occasions as the receiving of a trophy won by your school in some contest.

   Enabling Objectives : To keep in mind that the purpose of the ceremony is to encourage loyalty to the school and the activity, which won the award. To give due appreciation or honour to those to whom the school is indebted. To keep your language on a high level. To improve clarity in the discussion of ideas by the use of appositive noun clauses (I.G.U. 21).

7. *Social Objective* : To introduce a speaker, as, for instance, a person of distinction who will address your school assembly.

   Enabling Objectives : To keep within about two minutes. To say only what will make the audience eager to hear what the speaker has to say. To speak his name distinctly, and repeat it incidentally in the body of the speech. To obviate awkwardness on the stage by arranging beforehand where each person will sit or stand. To plan a gracious close. To use the active voice habitually for vigor (I.G.U. 24).

8. *Social Objective* : To make an after-dinner speech, or serve as toast-master; as on the occasion of a banquet given in honour of last year's graduates.

Enabling Objectives : To learn the procedure so as to be ready. To avoid comment on a speech just made. To speak in a natural, conversational manner. To bend all efforts to promoting friendly feeling. To know the value of a light touch and a pleasant smile, and to have on hand some appropriate nonsense. To keep within the limits of your time previously set. To express coordinate ideas in parallel form and subordinate ideas in subordinate clauses (I.G.U. 25).

Techniques Desirable in Special Occasion Speeches : A Summary

Social Techniques :

1. To keep in mind the main purpose of the speech.
2. To stay within the time limit.
3. To know the facts and to state them clearly.
4. To direct all efforts toward promoting a feeling of friendliness and ease.
5. To being interestingly and to close gracefully.
6. To give definite and concrete reasons for one's advocacy of a cause.
7. To stimulate desirable emotions, as loyalty, justifiable pride, enthusiasm for or interest in a cause or activity, without disparaging or stirring antagonism, toward other persons or causes.
8. To introduce light touches and amusing anecdotes when appropriate.
9. To express appreciation when it is due, and to do so without flattering and in other than a stereotyped way.

Language Techniques :

1. To use repetition for emphasis.
2. To use language suitable to the occasion - informal and lively or formal and more dignified.
3. To employ, for ease, economy, conciseness, clarity, and vividness, the following devices :

(*a*) Clauses introduced by relative pronouns in the oblique cases.

(*b*) Adjective prepositional phrases for descritpion and identification.

(*c*) Simple relative clauses.

(*d*) Gerunds and infinitives as sentence subjects.

(*e*) Gerunds as objects or verbs and prepositions.

(*f*) Infinitives as adjective and adverbial modifiers.

(*g*) Modifying adjectives in increased and more accurate use.

(*h*) Participial phrases in place of adjective and adverbial clauses.

(*i*) Appositives in place of relative clauses.

(*j*). Appositive noun clauses.

(*k*) Parallel form for coordinate ideas and subordinate clauses for subordinate ideas.

(*l*) Active verbs habitually for vigour and passive verbs occasionally to minimize the action or the agent.

(*m*) The present perfect tenses always and only to indicate indefinite past time or action just completed.

Speech Techniques :

1. To speak in a natural, conversational tone.
2. To pronounce names with particular distinctness.

15

Writing Experiences, Elementary Level, Kindergarten - Grades 6

A. Social Letters

1. *Social Objective* : To compose as a group an informal invitation or the reply to such an invitation.

   Enabling Objectives : To show a genuine friendliness toward the guest or host. To include all necessary facts or details - *viz.*, the hosts, the place, the date, the hour, and the kind of party. To write in sentences, using beginning capitals and closing periods.

2. *Social Objective* : To compose as a group a note of thanks, of request, etc.

   Enabling Objectives : To express the purpose of the note clearly and graciously. To begin some sentences with adverbial modifiers, usually such expressions of time as *yesterday, just then, at eight o'clock.* To include and arrange conventionally the following details of the superscription (address on the envelope) : the person's name, the street or rural route address or the post office box, the city or town, and the state. To capitalise the names of persons and the pronoun *I.* To use the conventional, or customary, arrangement of the parts of a note - *viz.*, the heading, including the place and date of writing; the appropriate salutation; the body of the note, with the first line properly indented; the appropriate complimentary close; and the signature.

3. *Social Objective* : To copy such an invitation as is composed under *1* to take to a parent or to be sent to others.

   Enabling Objectives : To note relative positions of parts of a note, as in 2. As a matter of courtesy to write as neatly and legibly as possible. To copy spellings accurately. To leave appropriate margins. To proof-read the note, looking for omitted or repeated words, capitals, and periods.

4. *Social Objective* : To write an informal invitation or a reply to such an invitation.

   Enabling Objectives : To employ in original individual work the techniques already used in *1*, *2* and *3*. (If I.G.U. *1* and 2 have not already been introduced, they may well be related to this composition experience). To capitalise the names of days, months, and holidays.

5. *Social Objective* : To write a note of thanks or of request.

   Enabling Objectives : To express gratitude and appreciation of the favour in simple, sincere phrases. To gain speed by occasionally combining sentences having the same subject into a single simple sentence with a compound predicate. (If I.G.U. 5 has not already been introduced, it may well be related to this composition experience.) To examine each sentence for clearness. To ask for the spelling of doubtful words.

6. *Social Objective* : To write a simple letter to a relative or friend.

   Enabling Objectives : To write about topics of interest to the recipient of the letter. To avoid writing exclusively about one's self. To use occasional adverbs or adverbial clauses in the predicate position, especially those showing the manner in which the action is done (I.G.U. 6 and 7). To capitalise the names of places. To capitalise words which are part of names, whether of persons or places, for example, Doctor Jones, State Street.

7. *Social Objective* : To write a "newsy" letter to a relative, friend, or "shut-in".

Enabling Objectives : To enliven the letter by giving interesting descriptive details. To employ such descriptive adjectives as will add vividness to the narrative (I.G.U. 9). To make use of direct discourse where it contributes to economy in statement. To mark each direct (undivided) quotation with quotation marks, a comma, and an initial capital. To discuss each main topic in a separate paragraph. To indent the first line of each paragraph. To use apostrophes to mark the omission of letters in contractions. To follow convention in the choice of stationery and ink and in the folding of the letter.

8. *Social Objective* : To write a note of greeting or congratulation, as for a birthday or some good fortune.

Enabling Objectives : To express the sentiment with spontaneity, warmth, and sincerity. To use occasional exclamations, one word or whole sentence, for the sake of force and variety. To write all nouns in the possessive singular with's.

9. *Social Objective* : To write a social letter to a group of acquaintances, such as a class or a club.

Enabling Objectives : To adopt a friendly attitude oward the group. To select topics of interest to the various members of the group. To think of the feelings of one's readers when expressing an opinion. To use relative clauses where they make the relations of ideas clearer (I.G.U. 10). To set off with commas the words *yes* and *no*, and nouns in direct address. To capitalise titles of books.

Techniques Desirable in Writing Social Letters : A Summary

Social Techniques :

1. To adopt a friendly attitude, expressed in sincere and simple terms.
2. To express opinions tactfully.
3. To mention all necessary facts or details.
4. To express thoughts with clarity.
5. To use descriptive detail for vividness.

6. To write about topics of interest to the recipient, rather than exclusively about one's self.

Language Techniques :

1. To write in complete sentences.
2. To employ occasionally, for clarity, variety, and economy, the following devices :
   (*a*) Adverbial modifiers at the beginning of sentences.
   (*b*) Compound predicates.
   (*c*) Adverbs and adverbial clauses in the predicate position.
   (*d*) Exclamations.
   (*e*) Direct discourse.
   (*f*) Relative clauses.
3. To paragraph properly.
4. To punctuate direct quotations properly.
5. To use commas to set off *yes* and *no*, and nouns in direct address.
6. To use apostrophes to indicate contractions, and for nouns in the possessive singular.
7. To capitalise words beginning sentences, proper nouns, titles that are part of name's the pronoun, *I*, and the titles of books.
8. To spell correctly.
9. To write neatly and legibly.
10. To follow convention in the choice of ink and stationery, in the arrangement of the parts of the letter, including the superscription, in leaving margins, and in folding the letter.

B. Business Letters

1. ***Social Objective*** : To compose as a group a request for information.

Enabling Objectives : To state the request courteously and clearly. To write in sentences. To use an appropriate heading, consisting of place and date of writing, and a proper salutation, courteous close, and signature. To write in sentences, marking sentence beginnings with capitals and sentence endings with periods. (If I.G.U. 1 and 2 have not already been introduced, they may well be related to this composition experience.)

2. *Social Objective* : To compose as a group an order or request for merchandise.

   Enabling Objectives : To state clearly and definitely the kind and amount of material desired. To tell how much money is enclosed, and in what form. To use business-letter form, including the inner address. To keep a copy of the letter. (If I.G.U. 4 has not already been introduced, it may well be related to this composition experience.) To capitalise the names of persons and the pronoun I. To capitalise the names of places.

3. *Social Objective* : To write a request for information.

   Enabling Objectives : To use in individual work techniques already practised in 1 and 2. To leave proper margins. To sign the full name legibly. To inclose a stamp, without comment. To begin some sentences with adverbial modifiers, usually such expressions of time as *yesterday, just then, at eight o'clock.* To use some adverbs or adverbial clauses, especially initial *when* and *if* clauses (I.G.U. 6). To capitalise the names of days, months, and holidays.

4. *Social Objective* : To write an order or request for a single item of merchandise.

   Enabling Objectives : To describe the article desired, accurately and definitely, giving the appropriate indentifying details, such as the number or amount required, the exact name of title, the catalogue number, the price, the colour or the size. To use adverbial clauses of occasional adverbs in predicate position, especially those are showing the manner in which the action is done (I.G.U. 7). To follow convention in folding the letter and addressing the envelope.

5. *Social Objective* : To write an order or request for merchandise of more than one type.

   Enabling Objectives : To state the purpose of the letter at the beginning. To paragraph separately each item in an order for goods. To capitalise abbreviations of words which would be capitalised. To indent the first line of each paragraph. To put a return address in the upper left corner of the envelope.

6. *Social Objective* : To change or cancel by mail an order for merchandise or a subscription.

   Enabling Objectives : To read the letter carefully to make sure that it says exactly what it should say. To consider the advantages of the following types of service and to select the proper one : regular mail, air mail, special delivery, and registered mail.

7. *Social Objective* : To write a letter requesting an interview.

   Enabling Objectives : To state in the first sentence the reason for seeking the interview. To make the letter so courteous and attractive that it will win a favourable reply.

8. *Social Objective* : To make by mail a complaint or remonstrance.

   Enabling Objectives : To state clearly and concisely the nature of the complaint. To select the essential details of the complaint. To state the facts truthfully and courteously.

Techniques Desirable in Writing Business Letters : A Summary

Social Techniques :

1. To be courteous in all business, letters, and as brief as is consistent with perfect clarity.
2. To state the purpose of the letter at the beginning.
3. To state all essential facts.
4. To state facts truthfully.

5. To refer definitely to enclosures.
6. To enclose a stamp without comment when requesting information.
7. To keep a copy of every business letter.

Language Techniques :

1. To write in complete sentences.
2. To employ occasionally, for clarity and economy, the following devices :
   (*a*) Adverbial modifiers at the beginning of sentences.
   (*b*) Adverbs and adverbial clauses, initially and in the predicate position.
3. To paragraph properly.
4. To give each items in an order for goods a separate paragraph.
5. To capitalise words beginning sentences, proper nouns, abbreviations of words that would be capitalised, and the pronoun *I*.
6. To follow convention in the arrangement of the parts of the letter, including the superscription, and in leaving margins.

C. Blank Forms

1. *Social Objective* : To furnish personal data required on record-cards for school files.

   Enabling Objectives : To supply complete and accurate information concerning all names, addresses, dates, and other items required. To capitalise the names of persons, streets, towns, and state or countries.

2. *Social Objective* : To write the personal data required in printed examinations and tests.

   Enabling Objectives : To write the surname first when so directed. To follow all directions explicitly. In writing a date, to use a comma between the day of the month and the year.

3. *Social Objective* : To fill the blanks in a printed application, such as for a library card.

   Enabling Objectives : To give the requested information in concise form. To write legibly with ink in the proper blank. To capitalise words which are part of names, whether of persons or places, *e.g.*, Doctor A. J. Jones, State Street.

4. *Social Objective* : To pay a bill with a postal or express money order.

   Enabling Objectives : To fill with the proper data all blanks of the application for the money order. To enclose the bill. To address the envelope properly. To place a return address on the envelope. To capitalise abbreviations of words which would be capitalised.

5. *Social Objective* : To give a receipt for money paid - *e.g.*, for class or club dues.

   Enabling Objectives : To fill out properly the blanks of a printed receipt. To fill out properly the stub of the receipt.

6. *Social Objective* : To fill out questionnaires, school record cards, etc.

   Enabling Objectives : To answer all questions accurately and concisely. To proof-read each answer carefully, making sure that it answers the question asked.

Techniques Desirable in Filling Blanks : A Summary

Social Techniques :

1. To supply completely, accurately, and concisely all information required by blank forms, following directions explicitly.
2. To enclose the bill when making payment by mail.
3. To give or require receipts for all money received or paid out.

Language Techniques :

1. To write legibly with ink.

2. To capitalise all proper nouns, words that are part of names, and abbreviations of words that would be capitalised.

3. To punctuate dates properly.

D. Labels, Titles, and Signs

1. *Social Objective* : To assist in labeling lockers, tablets, books, drawings, etc. with the owners' names.

   Enabling Objectives : To identify individual property by affixing appropriate labels. To initiate the habit of reading and heeding labels. To use capitals for the initial letters of each name.

2. *Social Objective* : To devise as a group labels for boxes, shelves, cabinets, drawers and other receptacles for equipment.

   Enabling Objectives : To select, if possible, a single significant word for use on the label. To begin this word with a capital letter.

3. *Social Objective* : To devise and write the placards and labels needed for the class post office, grocery, garden, etc.

   Enabling Objectives : To determine what labels and placards are necessary. To print or write all inscriptions neatly and legibly. To spell all words correctly. To capitalise the first word of each inscription.

4. *Social Objective* : To design as a group a cover page for booklets made by the class.

   Enabling Objectives : To select a short title. To include such essential details as the title, the full name of the owner, and the date. To arrange these details effectively on the page.

5. *Social Objective* : To label each specimen in a collection of seeds, stones, etc.

   Enabling Objectives : To use labels as records or memoranda. To put each item on a separate line or to separate the items by periods, and to begin each with a capital.

6. *Social Objective* : To design a title page for a class or

individual book, such as a Junior Red Cross Book, a journal, a scrap-book, a book of original stories or poems.

Enabling Objectives : To select a concise title appropriate to the nature and purpose of the book. To make the page attractive through the use of the appropriate size and type of lettering and the artistic arrangement and spacing of the necessary details.

7. *Social Objective* : To label appropriately articles or specimens for an exhibit.

Enabling Objectives : To use labels and placards to give information to others. To present the significant facts clearly and accurately.

8. *(Optional) Social Objective* : To design and make posters and signs needed to protect children, pets and property : *Keep to the Right, Park Bicycles Here,* health and safety posters, etc.

Enabling Objectives : To use posters and signs to influence the thinking and actions of others. To make posters and signs courteous and attractive.

9. *Social Objective* : To make a simple vertical file of pictures, music, bibliography, clippings, etc.

Enabling Objectives : To devise brief, simple, significant headings for various classifications of material. To inscribe legibly on each manila folder the proper heading. To code each article, *i.e.*, to write on it the inscription or label of the folder in which it will be filed. To arrange the folders alphabetically.

Techniques Desirable in Writing Labels,
Titles and Signs : A Summary

Social Techniques :

1. To use labels for identification, records, memoranda, and information.

2. To devise brief but significant inscriptions.

3. To use posters and signs purposefully.
4. To make cover pages, posters, and signs attractive through arrangement and lettering.

Language Techniques :

1. To capitalise proper nouns, single identifying words, and the first word of each item in a list of items.
2. To print or write inscriptions neatly and legibly.
3. To spell all words correctly.
4. To separate properly the items in a list.
5. To code all articles for a file.
6. To arrange folders and other materials alphabetically.

E. Announcements, Notices, and Advertisements

1. *Social Objective* : To compose a simple announcement of interest to the class, to be written or printed on the blackboard by the teacher - *e.g., Peter Smith has a new brother.*

   Enabling Objectives : To furnish accurate information answering such questions as, *Who? What? Where? Why?* (If I.G.U. 1 has not already been introduced, it may well be related to this composition experience.)

2. *Social Objective* : To make, as a group, with the teacher as scribe, a memorandum of room duties or other tasks to be performed by individuals or committees.

   Enabling Objectives : To use an appropriate heading, such as *Room Duties,* followed by the date. To compose concise sub-headings, naming particular duties. To list under or opposite such headings the names of pupils responsible for the duties.

3. *Social Objective* : To write and post a simple announcement of interest to the group.

   Enabling Objectives : To tell only the major fact. To write in sentences using beginning capitals and closing periods. (If I.G.U. 2 and 3 have not already been introduced, they may well be related to this composition experience.) To capitalise the names of persons and places. To leave appropriate margins. To place it on the bulletin board so that it will look best.

4. *Social Objective* : To compose as a group a notice for the school bulletin board or for the boards in other rooms concerning an article lost or found.

   Enabling Objectives : To use elliptical sentences to express the details - *e.g.*, "*Lost* : A copy of *Just So Stories* by Kipling". To capitalise the names of days, months and holidays. In writing a date, to use a comma between the day of the months, and the year. To capitalise words which are part of names, whether of persons or places : *Doctor Jones, State Street.*

5. *Social Objective* : To compose as a group a simple announcement to persons outside the class, such a notice to parents of a class picnic, etc.

   Enabling Objectives : To decide what items of information the reader will need or want. To give these items definitely and accurately. To gain compression by occasionally combining sentences having the same subject into a simple sentence with a compound predicate (I.G.U. 5). To use some adverbs or adverbial clauses in the predicate position, especially those which show the manner in which the action is done (I.G.U. 7). To copy the announcement neatly and legibly.

6. *Social Objective* : To prepare for mimeographing or posting a simple programme for a concert, dramatisation, puppet show, or other entertainment.

   Enabling Objectives : To include along with other essential information a list of the events, with the name of the performer opposite each. To give the cast of a play in the order of appearance. To write all nouns in the possessive singular with 's.

7. *Social Objective* : To advertise a puppet show, a Girl Scout cooky sale, a candy sale, etc., by means of simple

posters.

Enabling Objectives : To express the essential facts in concise phrases. To place these phrases in separate paragraphs. To emphasise by illustration or lettering the most appealing reason for attendance. To employ such descriptive adjectives as will really add to the force of the appeal (I.G.U. 9). To use an attractive and appropriate illustration.

8. *Social Objective* : To write an announcement of a puppet play, an exhibit, etc., to be read at an assembly.

Enabling Objectives : To include a brief recital of the chief merits of the events, in order to arouse the interest of the audience. To be truthful in all statements. To use relative clauses when their use makes clearer the relations of ideas (I.G.U. 10). To use occasional exclamations, one word or whole sentence, for the sake of force and variety. To separate by commas the members of a series of words in the same construction.

Techniques Desirable in Writing Announcements, Notices, and Advertisements : A Summary

Social Techniques :

1. To furnish definite and accurate information answering all relevant questions.
2. To give only the essential facts in concise terms.
3. To be truthful in all statements.
4. To list in the order of occurrence the events of a programme, with the name of the performer opposite each item.
5. To gain attractiveness and emphasis in posters by lettering, illustration, and the use of margins.

Language Techniques :

1. To write in complete sentences.
2. To employ occasionally, for clarity, effectiveness and economy, the following devices :

   (*a*) Elliptical sentences.
   (*b*) Compound predicates.
   (*c*) Adverbs and adverbial clauses in the predicate position.
   (*d*) Exclamations.
   (*e*) Relative clauses.
3. To paragraph separately all major points.
4. To use commas :
   (*a*) In dates.
   (*b*) To separate the members of a series of words in the same construction.
5. To write all nouns in the possessive singular with 's.
6. To capitalise proper nouns, abbreviations of words that would be capitalised, and the pronoun *I*.
7. To write neatly and legibly.

F. Memoranda; Rules, Recipes and Directions; Records, Notes and Diaries

1. *Social Objective* : To make as a group a shopping lists for a class picnic or a list of objects to be looked for during an excursion.

   Enabling Objectives : To make a complete list. To organise the items so as to save time and steps, *e.g.*, to list together articles located in the same shop or department.

2. *Social Objective* : To make as a group, with the teacher as scribe, a rule or reminder necessary for the care and use of materials.

   Enabling Objectives : To make the reminder courteous. To state it in a clear, concise sentence.

3. *Social Objective* : To keep a class record of interesting events, such as a bird or flower record, the diary of a robin, etc.

   Enabling Objectives : To select the most important events for the record. To begin each day's record with the date of the month. To write in sentences, using beginning capitals and closing periods. (I.G.Us. 1, 2, 3). To begin some sentences with adverbial modifiers, usually such expressions of time or place as *yesterday, just then, in the park, at eight o'clock.* (If I.G.U. 4 has not already been introduced, it may well be related to this composition experience.) To capitalise the names of persons and the pronoun *I*. To capitalise the names of days, months, and holidays.

4. *Social Objective* : To keep individual journals or diaries.

   Enabling Objectives : To discover in one's daily life incidents worth recording. To state one's opinions and reactions frankly. To choose exactly the right word to express one's meaning. To gain speed by occasionally combining sentences having the same subject into a single simple sentence with a compound predicate (I.G.U. 5). To capitalise the names of places. To leave appropriate margins. In writing a date, to use a comma between the day of the month and the year.

5. *Social Objective* : To keep an individual record of books read.

   Enabling Objectives : To give the name of the author and then the title of the book. To underline the title with a single continuous, straight line. To record next the date of finishing the book. To tell in a single sentence what kind of book it is. In a second sentence to point out the most interesting feature of the book - such as the best scene, or the most interesting character - or to tell why the book is dull. To use occasional adverbs or adverbial expressions in the predicate position, especially those showing the manner in which the action is done (I.G.Us., 7 and 8). To write all nouns in the possessive singular with's. To capitalise titles of books.

6. *Social Objective* : To make a memorandum of costumes or properties needed for a play, or books lent or borrowed, etc.

   Enabling Objectives : To list the articles alphabetically. To list each in a separate paragraph, allowing space below, or to the right, for the following data : the name, the address, and the telephone number of the person from whom the article is secured, and the date of the loan and of the return of it.

7. *Social Objective* : To make brief notes for a talk or a written report.

   Enabling Objectives : To list each point to be made on a separate slip of paper. To decide upon the chief point to be made in the report. To arrange the slips in such order as will best contribute to the chief point. To copy all points in outline form upon cards or a sheet of paper.

8. *Social Objective* : To write out directions to aid a friend in making some object or in using apparatus, etc.

   Enabling Objectives : To arrange the steps in the order of action. To list all materials together, at the beginning or the end. To make the directions as definite as possible. To explain all technical terms used. To use relative clauses when their use makes the relations of ideas clearer (I.G.U. 10). To separate by commas the members of a series of words in the same construction.

9. *(Optional) Social Objective* : To take brief notes for an oral report on an article read.

   Enabling Objectives : To outline the chief points of the article. (See Strand G, Unit 3.) To select the sub-topics or points treated under each chief point in the article. To express each of these sub-topics in a concise phrase or sentence. To mark the points under each main topic. A, B, C, etc.

10. *(Optional) Social Objective* : To take notes on a programme, a play, a concert, etc., from which to write an article for the school paper.

    Enabling Objectives : To secure a programme or to record accurately titles of numbers and names. To jot down in phrases or single words, in order to keep up with the programme, important features of qualities of each performance.

11. *(Optional) Social Objective* : To take notes on a club meeting, from which to write the secretary's minutes.

Enabling Objectives : To include accurately the following details : the place, date, and hour of the meeting; the name of the person presiding; and all important parts of the meeting, such as appointments of committees, reports of committees, election of officers, and motions that have passed. To quote verbatim each motion passed or to take full and accurate notes on it.

Techniques Desirable in Writing Memoranda: Rules, Recipes, and Directions; Records, Notes and Diaries : A Summary

Social Techniques :

1. To select the most important events or data.
2. To express opinions and reactions frankly and courteously.
3. To record accurately names, dates, and titles, and place of action.
4. To make lists complete and accurate.
5. To organise directions, recipes, etc., so that they can be efficiently carried out.
6. To make directions definite, defining technical terms if necessary.
7. To characterise books in a single sentence.

Language Techniques :

1. To write in clear, concise sentences.
2. To employ occasionally, for economy and clarity, the following devices :
   (*a*) Adverbial modifiers at the beginning of sentences.
   (*b*) Compound predicates.
   (*c*) Adverbs and adverbial expressions in the predicate position.
   (*d*) Relative clauses.
3. To use commas :
   (*a*) In dates.

(*b*) To separate the members of a series of words in the same construction.

4. To capitalise proper nouns, and the pronoun *I*.
5. To capitalise and underline titles of books.
6. To write nouns in the possessive singular with 's.
7. To list each item in a separate paragraph.
8. To arrange lists in alphabetical, chronological, or other convenient order.
9. To use slips of paper in collecting material for reports or talks.
10. To arrange these slips in such order as will best contribute to the main point.
11. To use outlines for effective organisation.

G. Reports, Reviews, Summaries and Outlines

1. ***Social Objective*** : To compose as a group. With the teacher writing on the board, a summary of a class conversation which may serve as a reading lesson, *e.g.*, The Colours We Like, The Birds We Saw in the Part.

Enabling Objectives : To use, under the teacher's guidance, the chronological or some other good order. To write in sentences, using beginning capitals and closing periods. (If I.G.Us. 1, 2 and 3 have not already been introduced, they may well be related to this composition experience.)

2. ***Social Objective*** : To write for a class journal or individual record an account of a visit, and excursion, a project, etc.

Enabling Objectives : To select the most important incidents or details of the excursion. To begin some sentences with adverbial modifiers, usually such expressions of time as *yesterday, just then, at eight o'clock*. (If I.G.U. 4 has note already been introduced, it may well be related to this composition experience.) To capitalise the names of persons and the pronoun *I*. In writing a date, to use a comma between the day of the month and year.

3. *Social Objective* : To make as a group a simple topical outline of a short article read.

   Enabling Objectives : To select after a preliminary reading the chief points of the article. To express each of these points in a concise, original phrase'. To number these statements, in the order of their occurrence, with Roman numerals.

4. *Social Objective* : To compose as a group a summary of what has been learned about some topic, *e.g.*, Eskimos.

   Enabling Objectives : To make and use a simple topical outline, in order to get the important points and a good order. To tell it all in the third person. To combine sentences having the same subject into a single simple sentence with a compound predicate (I.G.U. 5). To capitalise the names of places. To leave appropriate margins.

5. *Social Objective* : To write, in preparation for a reading, science, social studies, or other class, a single sentence summarising each paragraph or section of a factual article.

Enabling Objectives : To express the chief point of each paragraph in a clear, concise sentence. To summarise the author's statements accurately. To use some adverbial clauses, especially initial *when* and *if* clauses (I.G.U. 6). To use occasional adverbs or adverbial expressions in the predicate position, especially those showing the manner in which the action is done (I.G.Us. 7 and 8). To capitalise the names of days, month and holidays. To capitalise abbreviations of words which would be capitalised.

6. *Social Objective* : To write individually for a notebook a summary of what has been learned about some topic studied by the group.

   Enabling Objectives : To apply alone the techniques used by the group in Unit 4. To use descriptive or demonstrative adjectives for the sake of clearness or definiteness (I.G.U.

9). To capitalise words which are part of names, whether of persons of places, *e.g.*, Doctor Jones, State Street. To separate by commas the members of a series of words in the same construction.

7. ***Social Objective*** : To make, in preparation for a discussion or a written report, a topical outline of an article read.

   Enabling Objectives : To select the sub-topics or points treated under each chief point in the article. To express each of these sub-topics in a concise phrase or sentence. To number the points under each main topic, A, B and C etc.

8. ***Social Objective*** : To answer satisfactorily examination questions in elementary science, social studies, reading, etc.

   Enabling Objectives : To jot down all the facts essential to each answer. To arrange these in the most effective order. To state these facts in clear, concise sentences in a single paragraph. To use relative clauses where they aid in condensation or contribute to clearness (I.G.U. 10).

9. ***(Optional) Social Objective*** : To write for the school paper a brief review of a book or article.

   Enabling Objectives : To give information about the book, including such points as the following : the title, the name of the author, the setting, and a very brief synopsis of the book. To place in quotation marks all expressions quoted. To give a frank, courteous opinion of the book, including the reasons for the opinion.

10. ***(Optional) Social Objective*** : To write for the school paper an account of a programme, a play, a concert, etc.

    Enabling Objectives : To be especially careful of names and of titles of numbers on the programme. To report important or human-interest details. To praise or else to avoid comment.

11. ***(Optional) Social Objective*** : To write the minutes of a club meeting.

    Enabling Objectives : To include all important details recorded in the notes taken during the meeting. (*See* Strand F, Unit 11). To quote verbatim or to summarise accurately each motion passed. To summarise concisely and accurately each committee report. To use a heading including the following details : the name of the city and state and the date of the meeting. To sign the minutes, following the signature with a comma and the title *Secretary.*

Techniques Desirable in Writing Reports, Reviews, Summaries and Outlines : A Summary

Social Techniques :

1. To select the chief points, or the most important incidents or events.
2. To summarise accurately the statements of others.
3. To be frank and courteous in expressing opinions, giving the reasons for these opinions.
4. To praise, or else to avoid comment, in reporting on school programmes or similar events.
5. To record accurately names, titles, dates, and places.
6. To sign minutes properly.

Language Techniques :

1. To write in complete sentences.
2. To employ occasionally, for economy and clarity, the following devices :
   (*a*) Adverbial modifiers at the beginning of sentences.
   (*b*) Compound predicates.
   (*c*) Adverbial clauses.
   (*d*) Adverbs or adverbial clauses in the predicate position.
   (*e*) Relative clauses.
3. To use commas :
   (*a*) In dates.
   (*b*) To separate the members of a series of words in the same construction.

4. To capitalise proper nouns, and the pronoun *I*, and abbreviations of words that would be capitalised.
5. To enclose in quotation marks all direct quotations.
6. To make and use a simple topical outline, employing Roman numerals to indicate the chief topics, and letters to indicate sub-topics.
7. To write topic sentences.
8. To write in the third person.
9. To leave appropriate margins.

H. Bibliographies, Indexes, Tables of Contents, and Title Pages

1. *Social Objective* : To make as a group a table of contents for a class booklet.

   Enabling Objectives : To include such details as the title *Contents or Table of Contents,* the title of each selection included in the booklet, and the page number on which each selection begins. To write the title of the booklet in larger letters. To leave a wider space at the top than at the bottom of the page.

2. *Social Objective* : To make a table of contents for a class or individual book.

   Enabling Objectives : To make a perfect alignment of the titles along the left margin and of the page numbers along the right. To make the page attractive and easily read through the use of the appropriate size and type of lettering and the spacing of items. To number this page at the bottom.

3. *Social Objective* : To make as a group an alphabetic list of the books in the class library. books borrowed from the school or public library, etc.

   Enabling Objectives : To write on a slip of paper, approximately 3"×5", the following information : the name of the author, with the surname first, followed by a comma and the given name, and the exact title of the book, underlined with a single, continuous, straight line. To arrange the slips alphabetically by authors' surnames. To compile these items into a single list, the teacher serving as scribe.

4. *Social Objective* : To make as a group an index for a volume of children's poems or stories or for a portfolio of pictures, clippings, etc.

   Enabling Objectives : To write accurately on a slip of paper the title of a single selection and the page on which it occurs. To make a slip for each author encountered and to add the page number for each additional selection by him. To arrange these slips alphabetically, using the first word of each title and the author's surnames. To copy the inscriptions on these slips upon sheets of paper, arranging the material in columns.

5. *Social Objective* : To make a simple bibliography of books consulted on a single topic or problem.

   Enabling Objectives : To write on slips of paper the following information for each book : the name of the author, the exact title of the book, and the date of the copyright. To write the author's name, surname first, in the upper left-hand corner of the slip. To arrange the slips alphabetically be author's surname's and to number the slips in order. To copy the entire inscription from each card upon a sheet of paper, writing each as a separate paragraph, *e.g.*, 1. Kelty, Mary G. The *American Colonies. 1932.*

6. *Social Objective* : To make an author and title index for a class or individual book, such as a Junior Red Cross Book, or a book or original poems or stories, of clippings, etc.

   Enabling Objectives : To apply individually the techniques used by the group in Unit 4.

Techniques Desirable in Writing Bibliographies, Indexes, Tables of Contents, and Title Pages : A Summary

Social Techniques :

1. To use the conventional card or slip system.

2. To give completely and accurately all necessary information, as author's name, page numbers, and date of copyright.
3. To make title pages and lists attractive through suitable lettering, appropriate margins, and perfect alignment.

Language Techniques :

1. To use alphabetical order whenever suitable.
2. To write first the author's surname, followed by a comma.
3. To underline all titles of books or magazines.

16

Writing Experiences, Grades 7 - 12

A. Social Letters

1. *Social Objective* : To write appreciative and tactful notes of thanks.

   Enabling Objectives : To evidence cordial and sincere gratitude for the gift or favour or hospitality and appreciation for the consideration of the tastes and interests of the recipient. To write prompt acknowledgement as an evidence of appreciation. To use adjective prepositional phrases to add colour unobtrusively (I.G.U. 11). To use appropriate paper with matching envelope, and ink, never pencil. To say "Dear John", or "My Dear May", but never "Dear Friend". To end the letter "Sincerely Yours", or "Cordially Yours", avoiding "Respectfully yours".

2. *Social Objective* : To write informal and courteous notes of invitation and acceptance or regret.

   Enabling Objectives : To write interesting, persuasive invitations. To make definite and concise statements concerning place, time of arrival, and extent of visit. To specify the type of entertainment and the size of party, which will suggest appropriate dress. To give directions and suggest convenient transportation. To arrange items in orderly sequence and to express them with direct simplicity. To omit confusing items and superfluous words. To accept or to decline graciously and sincerely so that appreciation for the invitation is evidenced. To capitalise important words in titles. To use infinitives as subjects for variety and vigour (I.G.U. 13). To capitalise proper adjectives.

3. *Social Objective* : To write friendly and informal letters of news and gossip to friends of the writer's age or to older relatives.

   Enabling Objectives : To give a natural, conversational tone to the letter, quoting occasionally from those persons referred to in the letter. To use simple and direct language and to avoid both stilted and vulgar forms. To answer the queries of the correspondent. To comment on his present life, or changes occurring since his visit, or news items of special interest to him. To limit the subjects introduced. To increase smoothness and conciseness by the use of relative pronouns in the possessive (genitive) and objective (accusative) cases. To use pronouns which agree in person and number with their antecedents.

4. *Social Objective* : To write an interesting and informing travel letter to one's family, to friends, or to strangers in other cities or other countries.

   Enabling Objectives : To select from the day's or the week's varied experiences those details which the family and friends would find interesting, and to omit less important happenings. To share the new scenes and the new acquaintances with the old friends. To find and describe the centre of interest and to give the mood produced in the writer. To interpret and relate the new to the shared old. Or, to see with the traveller's eye the familiar scenes of one's own village. selecting points of interest and describing them to the contemporary in another city or a far country (students' international correspondence). To use specific nouns and vivid verbs. To use gerunds for compactness and smoothness (I.G.U. 15). To use subject noun clauses in statements *about* ideas (I.G.U. 19). To practise consistently the use of the comma to punctuate parenthetical expressions (including non-restrictive modifiers), expressions out of order, appositives, direct quotations, and the members of compound sentences.

5. ***Social Objective*** : To write sincere and simple letters of sympathy, or to entertain a shut-in.

   Enabling Objectives : To show sympathy and sensitive understanding through sincere and simple language. To adapt the message to the recipient, saying what will encourage him. To avoid commiseration and anything doleful. If possible, to offer specific help without intruding. To use participial phrases for light descriptive touches (I.G.U. 16). To use the perfect tense for indefinite past time (I.G.U. 18). To make the letter pleasing to look at and especially easy to read.

6. ***Social Objective*** : To write friendly and informal letters of news and gossip to friends of the writer's age, or to relatives. To visit by mail.

   Enabling Objectives : To limit the subjects written about to those of essential interest to the reader, and to treat these adequately. To omit trivial, dull details. To plan a simple organisation of material, and to begin and end interestingly. To remember that the letter should approximate good talk in matter and manner. To mark doubt or supposition by using the sub-junctive forms of verbs (I.G.U. 22). To use the apostrophe to form plural possessives. To use divided quotations. To use the colon before numerations. To use the hyphen in compound words, and in dividing a word into syllables.

7. ***Social Objective*** : To write friendly and tactful "bread and butter" notes.

   Enabling Objectives : To acknowledge the hospitability with cordial gratitude. To recall some of the happy experiences shared by host and guest. To include the family of the host in the appreciation of the pleasant time. To sketch informally the chief experiences of the journey home. To choose conjunctions which will show accurately, the relations between the sentence elements they connect (I.G.U. 25). To make use of the compound sentence without conjunction, punctuating with the semi-colon.

8. *Social Objective* : To write correct formal letters of invitation, acceptance, and regret.

Enabling Objectives : To use third person, full name, and complete statement of the place, hour, day, and month in the invitation. To accept and to decline invitation following the form used in the invitation. To answer promptly.

9. *Social Objective* : To write to friends or relatives a letter of news, gossip and opinion which is an expression of the writer's friendliness and personality.

Enabling Objectives : To discuss in vivid and concrete detail news, which is pleasurably shared by the correspondent. To add to the enumeration of facts the writers comment, observation, and interpretation. To give clear expression to opinions, feelings and attitudes. To use active verbs for vigour and passive verbs for minimising the doer of the action (I.G.U. 24). To use appositive noun clauses, *e.g.*, "the fact that..." "the hope that..." for clarity in speaking of ideas (I.G.U. 21).

Techniques Desirable in Writing Social Letters : A Summary

Social Techniques :

1. To adopt a friendly and cordial attitude, expressed in simple terms.
2. To put one's self into the recipient's place and write what would interest, please, or encourage him, or what he needs to know.
3. To adopt a style in keeping with one's relations with the correspondent and with the occasion; intimate, conversational, friendly, or formal.
4. To express clearly, opinions, feelings, and attitudes.

5. To state definitely, where necessary, place. hour, date and names.
6. To be prompt, especially in acknowledging hospitality or gifts, and in accepting or declining invitations.
7. To plan a simple organisation, selecting the important items and omitting trivial details.
8. To begin and end letters properly.
9. To use appropriate ink and stationery.
10. To make the letter attractive and legible.

Language Techniques :

1. To use the conventional form in writing or answering formal invitations.
2. To employ occasionally, for smoothness, vigour, variety, and compactness, the following structural devices :
   - (*a*) Subject noun clauses.
   - (*b*) Verbal nouns (gerunds).
   - (*c*) Adjective prepositional phrases.
   - (*d*) Subject infinitives.
   - (*e*) Participial phrases.
   - (*f*) Relative pronouns in the oblique cases.
   - (*g*) Appositive noun clauses.
3. To employ, for vividness and colourfulness, the following rhetorical devices :
   - (*a*) Specific nouns and vivid verbs.
   - (*b*) Conjunctions that show relationships accurately.
   - (*c*) Compound sentences without conjunctions, punctuating with semi-colons.
   - (*d*) The perfect tense to indicate indefinite past time.
   - (*e*) Sub-junctive forms of the verb to indicate doubt or suspicion.

(*f*) Active verbs for vigour, and passive verbs for minimising the agent.

4. To use pronouns which agree in person and number with their antecedents.

5. To use a colon before enumerations.

6. To use commas for punctuating :

   (*a*) Parenthetical expressions.

   (*b*) Expressions out of order.

   (*c*) Appositives.

   (*d*) Direct quotations.

   (*e*) The members of some compound sentences.

7. To capitalise proper adjectives, titles, and important words.

8. To use a hyphen in compound words and in dividing syllables.

9. To punctuate divided quotations properly.

10. To use the apostrophe to form plural possessives.

B. Business Letters

1. *Social Objective* : To write clear, concise, accurate, and complete order letters.

Enabling Objectives : To include all necessary information about quantities, brands, catalogue numbers, sizes, prices, shipping directions, and manner and amount of payment. To use infinitives as modifiers, for simplicity of statement (I.G.U. 14). To use tabular form when several articles are ordered. To use block or indented form consistently. To avoid abbreviations except in tabulated lists, and to put a period after each abbreviation used. To proof-read for errors.

2. *Social Objective* : To write pointed and definite letters of inquiry.

Enabling Objectives : To state the inquiry exactly. To organise clearly, putting first what is known, and then telling what is wanted. To gain brevity without brusqueness by omitting superfluous details and words. To learn to think clearly - to follow a logical or chronological order. To use verbal nouns (gerunds) for compactness of statement (I.G.U. 15). To use the perfect tense for indefinite past time (I.G.U. 18).

3. *Social Objective* : To write individual and tactful special requests.

   Enabling Objectives : To state the request briefly and specifically, with the reason for it. To ask rather than demand. To appeal, if possible, to the reader's self-interest. To write with directness and sincerity, so that the writer's individuality is impressed upon the reader. To tell the recipient in a clear and courteous way what he would probably ask in a personal interview. To use relative pronouns in the possessive (genitive) case and as objects of prepositions, for smoothness of expression (I.G.U. 12). To use participial phrases for vivid description or economical identification (I.G.U. 16).

4. *Social Objective* : To write pointed, clear, individual letters of inquiry of more difficulty than those in junior high school.

   Enabling Objectives : If there are several items, to arrange, them in such order and to ask the questions in such a way as to make the answer as easy as possible. To reveal the writer's interest in the request. To use the perfect tense for more exact indication of temporal relations (I.G.U. 18).

5. *Social Objective* : To write straight forward and effective letters of application.

   Enabling Objectives : To refer to the position advertised if the letter is an answer to an advertisement. To state briefly and honestly the applicant's age, qualifications, training, and experience, and possibly telephone number. To be neither boastful nor too modest. To list references with complete names and addresses. To use a definite first sentence and a vigourous last sentence. To use nouns in apposition for economy of expression (I.G.U. 20).

6. *Social Objective* : To write special request presenting more of a problem than those in the junior high school.

   Enabling Objectives : To be definite as to the purpose and importance of the request. To use transitional words, phrases, and sentences so that the relation between the items mentioned will be perfectly clear. To use subject clauses for conciseness (I.G.U. 19). To use the subjunctive to mark suppositions and wishes (I.G.U. 22).

7. *Social Objective* : To write explicit, courteous, and convincing claims and complaint letters.

   Enabling Objectives : To state all pertinent facts in chronological order or natural sequence. To enumerate facts if such form adds to clearness. To make a definite request. To assume that the company is glad to make the necessary adjustments. To use appositive clauses in sentences commenting upon ideas (I.G.U. 21). To use active verbs for vigour and passive verbs for reducing emphasis (I.G.U. 24).

8. *(Optional) Social Objective* : To write moving sales letters or display advertising.

   Enabling Objectives : To select arguments or qualities of the thing to be sold which will appeal to and convince the expected readers. To use specific, colourful diction. To stay within the truth. To gain emphasis by proper paragraphing. To stress one important idea, giving unity to the writing. To choose conjunctions which show accurately the relations between the sentence elements they connect (I.G.U. 25). To use some compound sentences without conjunctions.

9. *Social Objective* : To write condensed and accurate telegrams and night letters.

   Enabling Objectives : To give all necessary data - day, hour, place, names, situation, etc., that the recipient needs for understanding. To state necessary information in as brief form as clearness allows, omitting verbs, articles, and prepositions when they will be readily understood. To use "Stop" between sentences in a long message. To read the message looking for possible ambiguity.

Techniques Desirable in Writing Business Letters : A Summary

Social Techniques :

1. To be courteous and as brief as is consistent with perfect clarity.
2. To give definitely and specifically all information necessary to the recipient's understanding of the situation.
3. To state accurately quantities, prices, dates, names, addresses, and similar detailed information.
4. To express, where appropriate, one's individuality.
5. To be truthful in statements about one's self, and neither boastful nor over-modest.
6. To be especially courteous in making requests or complaints, assuming that the recipient of the letter will show equal courtesy.
7. To appeal, where appropriate and possible, to the self-interest of the recipient.
8. To select the important material and omit trivial details.
9. To organise the material on the basis of natural sequence, of logical or chronological order.

Language Techniques :

1. To employ occasionally, for simplicity, compactness, and smoothness, the following structural devices :

(*a*) Infinitives as modifiers.

(*b*) Verbal nouns (gerunds).

(*c*) Relative pronouns in the oblique constructions.

(*d*) Sub-junctive clauses.

(*e*) Appositive clauses.

(*f*) Participial phrases.

2. To employ, for precision, vividness, and economy, the following rhetorical devices :

(*a*) Specific, colourful words.

(*b*) Conjunctions and transitional words and phrases that will make relationships clear.

(*c*) Occasional compound sentences without conjunctions, punctuating with semi-colons.

(*d*) Active verbs for vigour and passive verbs for reducing emphasis.

(*e*) The perfect tense for indefinite past time.

(*f*) The past perfect tense for exact indication of time relations.

(*g*) Sub-junctive forms of the verb to mark suppositions or wishes.

3. To use tabular form consistently wherever such form would make for convenience.

4. To avoid abbreviations except in tabulated lists, and to put a period after each abbreviation used.

5. In composing telegrams, to omit whatever can be understood from the context, and to use "Stop" to indicate the end of sentences in long messages.

C. News Stories

1. ***Social Objective*** : To write an entertaining anecdote or incident for an interested group or for the school paper.

Enabling Objectives : To condense at the beginning of the story all essential information regarding time, place and situation. To write concisely, expanding the lead with illustrations and examples. To punctuate and to paragraph conversation correctly. To select the important points of the game, the circus, the trip, so that the group may share the experience. To end when the point is made. To give variety to sentence structure. To use adjective prepositional phrases for identification of effective description (I.G.U. 11). To increase smoothness and conciseness through the use of relative pronouns in the possessive (genitive) and objective (accusative) cases (I.G.U. 12).

2. *Social Objective* : To write an announcement for the school paper or for the bulletin board.

   Enabling Objectives : To gain clearness by direct sentences. To gain emphasis by means of brevity and arrangement. To avoid exaggeration and overstatement. To use infinitives as modifiers in order to secure conciseness (I.G.U. 14). To use the perfect tense for indefinite past time (I.G.U. 17).

3. *Social Objective* : To write an account of a sports event or other school function for the newspaper.

   Enabling Objectives : To obtain accurate and exact information and to report it objectively. To give the reader the impression that he is observing action by the use of varied sentence structure, concrete details and specific nouns. To gain variety by the use of different connectives instead of too many *and's* and *so's*. To write fitting headlines and lead. To reduce formality and gain speed by substituting participial phrases for adjective and even adverbial clauses (I.G.U. 16). To use modifiers, adjectives, adverbs, phrases, clauses, near the words they modify. To secure economy and exactness of expression by the use of verbal nouns (gerunds) (I.G.U. 15).

4. *Social Objective* : To write a news item including a report of an interview.

   Enabling Objectives : To choose the significant quality of the interview - personality, some particular opinion - to give form to a conversation upon a special question, omitting repetitions and insignificant remarks and treating what is significant adequately. To suggest the personality of the one interviewed through appropriate description. To record significant, definite observations. To use incidental quotation effectively. To secure clarity and brevity in the discussion of ideas by the use of subject clauses (I.G.U. 19). To secure terseness by the use of appositives (I.G.U. 20).

5. ***Social Objective*** : To write for the school papers an account of an assembly, a lecture, a play, or a concert.

Enabling Objectives : To use italics or quotation marks to indicate titles of books, plays, or musical compositions. To use simple paragraph organisation, limited to one idea with a "clincher" sentence. To use clear transitions from one paragraph to the next. To illustrate the main point concretely. To use appositive clauses in sentences commenting upon ideas (I.G.U. 21). To reduce subordinate ideas to subordinate clauses and keep parallel ideas in parallel form (I.G.U. 25).

6. ***Social Objective*** : To write a feature article for the school paper.

Enabling Objectives : To limit the subject. To assemble pertinent materials. To outline material according to a clearly developed original outline. To write in paragraphs corresponding to the topics in the outline. To use effective illustrations and comparisons. To gain variety by the use of noun, relative, and adverbial clauses. To combine into a compound sentence without conjunction two sentences so closely related that they should be one. To mark supposition or hope by the use of sub-junctive verbs (I.G.Us. 22 and 23). To use active verbs for vigour and passive verbs to minimise the doer. (I.G.U. 24).

Techniques Desirable in Writing News Stories : A Summary

Social Techniques :

1. To record only the important or significant events or facts, so that the reader's interest remains alert and does not become lost in trivial detail.
2. To obtain exact and accurate information and record it objectively.

3. To avoid exaggeration and over-statement.
4. To describe the personalities involved in the story where appropriate and where such description will add to the reader's interest.
5. To condense at the beginning of the story all essential information regarding time, place, and situation.
6. To choose a leading or significant fact or idea and build the story about it.
7. To make a clearly developed, original outline.
8. To develop this outline, expanding it by illustration, comparison, and example, and by concrete detail, and ending when the point is made.

Language Techniques :

1. To paragraph in correspondence with the topics.
2. To employ occasionally, for conciseness, smoothness, economy, and variety, and following structural devices:
   (*a*) Adjective prepositional phrases.
   (*b*) Relative pronouns in the oblique cases.
   (*c*) Infinitives as modifiers.
   (*d*) Gerunds.
   (*e*) Subject clauses.
   (*f*) Participial phrases in place of adjective adverbial clauses.
   (*g*) Subordinate clauses for subordinate ideas.
   (*h*) Parallel form for parallel ideas.
   (*i*) Compound sentences without conjunctions.
3. To employ occasionally, for conciseness and effectiveness, the following rhetorical devices :
   (*a*) Specific nouns.
   (*b*) Appositives.

(c) A variety of connective words.

(d) Active verbs for vigour and passive verbs to minimise the agent.

(e) The perfect tense to indicate indefinite past time.

(f) Sub-junctive verbs to mark supposition or hope.

(g) Clear transitional sentences.

4. To use modifiers near the words they modify.

5. To punctuate and paragraph conversation correctly.

6. To use italics or quotation marks to indicate the titles of books, plays, or musical compositions.

D. Reports

(Keeping records for one's self and for others; "relaying information"; digesting materials)

1. *Social Objective* : To keep accurate records in diary or journal form.

Enabling Objectives : To treat each incident separately. To write simply and naturally. To give personal comment on the recorded facts. To quote colourful words and expressions used by someone participating in the events. To write in complete and single sentences. To use a variety of connectives, not *and* alone. To collect material from books, to take notes, to cut, to develop themes based on such material. To improve ease by the use of participial and adjective prepositional phrases (I.G.Us. 11 and 16).

2. *Social Objective* : To record one's experiences and observations in such reports as those of laboratory experiments.

Enabling Objectives : To explain directly and clearly what was done and what happened. To arrange the information in this conventional order : (*a*) the problem to be solved, (*b*) the material used, (*c*) the procedure followed (arranged in chronological order), (*d*) the results, and (*e*) the conclusions drawn. To use diagrams, graphs, charts, maps, etc., to use helpful sub-heads. To use scientific terms precisely. To spell technical words correctly, developing the habit of looking up doubtful words. To develop each paragraph about a single idea. To use topic, transitional, and summarising sentences. To arrange material within a paragraph in logical order. To secure conciseness through the use of infinitive modifiers (I.G.U. 14). To increase smoothness and compactness by using relative pronouns in the possessive (genitive) and objective (accusative) cases (I.G.U. 12).

3. *Social Objective* : To summarise a single and simple discussion or speech.

Enabling Objectives : To grasp the objective (main purpose, thesis) of the discussion or speech. To grasp the plan of the whole - the number of supporting points and their relation to each other and to the main theme. To summarise the discussion or speech by following the plan of it in a condensed and simplified form. To use transitions and other links. To secure directness in discussing actions by using verbal nouns (gerunds and infinitives) as subjects (I.G.U. 13).

4. *Social Objective* : To record a meeting or musical.

Enabling Objectives : To discuss the most important events recorded. To summarise the effect of the whole meeting or musical. To describe otherwise as well as by adjectives, *e.g.*, to compare and give particular details, to quote and give examples. To increase exactness and ease by using verbal nouns as objects of verbs and especially of prepositions (I.G.U. 15). To express definite past tense by the past (imperfect) tense (I.G.U. 17).

5. *Social Objective* : To summarise as oral discussion.

Enabling Objectives : To grasp the objective (point) of the entire discussion and the contributing points made by each speaker, ignoring unimportant details. To arrange these in chronological order or, if this summary of the discussion be sharply limited, in some such simple order as *pro* and *con, agreed* and *disagreed, for* and *against*. To punctuate and paragraph conversation. To secure clearness and brevity in the discussion of ideas by the use of subject clauses (I.G.U. 19).

6. *Social Objective* : To write the report of a committee or of an officer.

   Enabling Objectives : To outline the activities, usually in chronological order, and to state conclusions drawn or recommendations made. To phrase correctly such special reports as resolutions. To write with as little verbiage as possible, elminating all unnecessary adjectives and adverbs. To express indefinite past time in the present perfect (perfect) tense (I.G.U. 18). To use active verbs for vigour and emphasis and passive verbs for variety or minimising the agent (I.G.U. 24).

7. *Social Objective* : To record minutes of a club meeting.

   Enabling Objectives : To follow the conventional form by giving in the third person a brief chronological summary of the activities and programme of the meeting. To record all business : (*a*) by giving in exact phrasing motions made, (*b*) by stating names of members presenting and seconding such motions, and (*c*) by stating disposal of the motions. To summarise discussions on motions or on business. To summarise papers, speeches, reports. To sign the minutes. To condense and reduce emphasis by using appositives in place of relative clauses (I.G.U. 20). To increase clearness and compactness in the discussion of ideas by the use of appositive clauses (I.G.U. 21).

8. *Social Objective* : To answer a discussion question in a letter or in an examination.

   Enabling Objectives : To state the theme or main point clearly and simply. To back this up by proof, by illustration, by quotation. To point out fallacies in arguments. To enumerate where that is effective. To mark suppositions and wishes by the use of sub-junctive verb forms (I.G.U. 22, 23).

9. ***Social Objective*** : To take notes on paragraphs, articles, chapters, or whole books read, for use in a report or thesis.

Enabling Objectives : To grasp the main point of the selection. To grasp the chief supporting points, ignoring minor detail. To recognise the commonest kinds of organizing plans, such as the "chain pattern", the "hand pattern", the "target pattern". To restate in words other than those of the original the ideas gained. To select pertinent quotations for exact reproduction and to copy them exactly. To take brief but adequate notes on cards, "punching the path" of the sections and giving complete and accurate reference. To organise and file material for reference. To head such notes by probable subject headings likely to be helpful in later use of the notes, using italics, capitals, colons, parentheses, and brackets according to the conventions. To express coordinate ideas in parallel form and subordinate ideas in appropriate subordinate clauses (I.G.U. 25).

10. ***Social Objective*** : To take notes on a lecture, a sermon, an address.

Enabling Objectives : To grasp the speaker's main point by watching for statements of it or for clues to it. To sense the plan by watching for some one of the commonest patterns. To appreciate emphasis as shown by position and length of points. To analyse the personality of the speaker by what he says, his organisation, his language and such mannerisms and characteristic as voice, walk, gestures, and facial expression. To recognise fallacious reasoning and to evaluate opinion.

11. ***Social Objective*** : To write a club paper, or informational article.

Enabling Objectives : To consider the audience or readers in order to meet their needs and interests by the facts used and by the method of presentation. To limit the subject sharply so that there will be few generalisations and many concrete details. To plan the supporting points in an easily followed and logical pattern. To keep the listener or reader conscious of this plan by frequent "sign posts" (transitional elements). To add to this plan, which is complete in itself, an introduction and a conclusion only when the occasion and the audience make them necessary. To develop each main part of the paper as a unit, making it as vivid and interesting as possible by concrete details, ample proof and illustration, and explanation. To sue variety in sentence length, especially as a means of emphasis.

12. *Social Objective* : To keep interesting diaries and journals.

Enabling Objectives : To begin as vigourously as possible, on the *in medias res* theory. To report observations and opinions. To evaluate them by comparing them with other observations and opinions.

Techniques Desirable in Writing Reports : A Summary

Social Techniques :

1. To meet the needs and interests of the reader or audience by the facts used and by the method of presenting them.
2. To detect fallacies and to evaluate opinions.
3. To analyse a speaker's personality.
4. To give personal comment on recorded points where appropriate.
5. To state directly and clearly, in laboratory reports or the minutes of meetings, what was done and what happened.
6. To become familiar with the commonest kinds of organising plans, so that they can be easily used and recognised.
7. To grasp the main point of the whole and of each part, ignoring unimportant details, and to state these points simply and clearly.
8. To take brief but adequate notes, extracting the pith of the article or speech and of each part thereof.
9. To limit the subject.

10. To arrange the material in logical, chronological, or other simple order, both as a whole and in each part.
11. To develop each main point as a unit, using discussion, concrete detail, illustration, proof, and explanation for effectiveness.
12. To begin and end vigourously, using formal introduction and conclusion only when the audience and the occasion require them.
13. To select pertinent and colourful quotations and reproduce them accurately.
14. To use diagrams, maps, charts, graphs etc., where appropriate.

Language Techniques :

1. To indicate transitions clearly by the use of topic, transitional, and summarising sentences.
2. To employ, for conciseness, smoothness, clarity, and emphasis, the following structural devices :
   (*a*) Participial and adjective prepositional phrases.
   (*b*) Relative pronouns in the oblique cases.
   (*c*) Subject clauses.
   (*d*) Appositive clauses.
   (*e*) Verbal nouns and infinitives as modifiers.
   (*f*) Verbal nouns as objects of verbs and prepositions.
   (*g*) Parallel form for coordinate ideas.
   (*h*) Subordinate clauses for subordinate ideas.
3. To employ for ease, variety, economy, and emphasis, the following rhetorical devices :
   (*a*) Appositives.
   (*b*) A variety of connectives.
   (*c*) Elimination of unnecessary adjectives and adverbs.

(*d*) Active verbs for vigour and passive verbs for minimizing the agent.

(*e*) The imperfect tense for definite past time.

(*f*) The perfect tense for indefinite past time.

(*g*) Sub-junctive verbs to mark supposition or hopes, or wishes.

(*h*) Variety in structure and length of sentences, especially with a view to emphasis.

4. To use technical and scientific terms precisely and to spell them correctly.

5. To punctuate and paragraph conversation.

6. To file notes an eye to convenience in future use, employing the conventional card system and the conventional punctuating devices.

7. To sign the minutes of meetings.

E. Opinions

(Senior High School Only)

1. *Social Objective* : To write an effective open letter to the school or village paper.

Enabling Objectives : To present the situation which prompts the open letter briefly and simply. To voice the protest or opinion with clarity and good humour. To organise logically. To present evidence which will prove the point. To give an example or illustration. To use clear connective clauses. To vary the composition by using complex sentences effectively. To clinch the argument by an effective closing sentence. To gain emphasis by placing important items or words first or last in the sentence of paragraph by putting important ideas in the shortest sentences, by using rhetorical questions, and by using similes and metaphors. To use the perfect and past perfect tenses for accuracy of temporal sequence (I.G.Us. 17 and 18). To increase flexibility of expression through varied use of verbal nouns (gerunds and infinitives) (I.G.Us. 13, 14 and 15).

2. *Social Objective* : To write logical, convincing editorials.

   Enabling Objectives : To choose from the news of the day those questions which suggest effective editorials. To clip and file helpful material on specified subjects. To compare conflicting ideas. To sum up ideas skillfully. To distinguish straight thinking from confused logic. To differentiate between opinion and facts. To offer conclusions that are warranted by the facts. To form opinions from first-hand observation and experiences. To choose vivid verbs and specific adjectives or to make keen comparisons. To use clear transitions. To secure directness by the use of the subject and appositive clauses (I.G.Us. 19 and 21). To use the dictionary habitually for spelling, pronunciation, meaning.

3. *Social Objective* : To write a book review for a club meeting or a newspaper.

   Enabling Objectives : To read with observation and some discrimination. To think definitely and clearly about the books read. To test the reality of the book with one's own experience. To support opinion by carefully selected evidence. To use brief quotations effectively. To write a single paragraph that interprets the book or summarises the main point. To write clearly and honestly a report that reflects the author's own opinion. To decide what facts will contribute most in giving the reader a true impression of the book. To analyse the novel from the point of view of the author, telling how he planned it, why he began where he did, what his climax is, how the conversation is used to promote the story, whether the author is chiefly interested in plot, setting, or character, whether his characters are individuals or representatives of groups, what his attitude toward life is - for example, decadent or healthily youthful. To mark doubt or supposition by the use of the subjunctive (I.G.Us. 22 and 23). To express coordinate ideas in parallel form and subordinate ideas in subordinate clauses (I.G.U. 25).

Techniques Desirable in Writing Opinions: A Summary

Social Techniques :

1. To voice opinions, arguments, and protests courteously, honestly, and clearly, and to support them by facts or other evidence, by examples, and by illustrations.
2. To choose those facts or items which will most interest the reader or contribute most to his understanding of the idea or situation.
3. To distinguish between right thinking and fallacious or confused reasoning.
4. To differentiate opinion and fact.
5. To interpret and summarise facts clearly.
6. To compare conflicting ideas.
7. To form opinions from first-hand observation and experience.
8. To think definitely and clearly about one's reading.
9. To analyse fiction from the point of view of the writer.
10. To organise logically.

Language Techniques :

1. To clinch as argument by an effective closing sentence.
2. To use clear transitional and connective terms or clauses.
3. To gain emphasis by placing the most important words first or last in the sentence or paragraph, and by putting the most important statement into the shortest sentence.
4. To employ, for flexibility, clarity, economy, and variety, the following structural devices :
   (*a*) Gerunds and infinitives in varied uses.
   (*b*) Subject and appositive clauses.
   (*c*) Complex sentences.
   (*d*) Parallel form for coordinate ideas.
   (*e*) Subordinate clauses for subordinate ideas.
5. To employ, for flexibility, emphasis, and variety, the following rhetorical devices :

(*a*) Rhetorical questions.

(*b*) Similes and metaphors.

(*c*) Vivid verbs and specific adjectives.

(*d*) Brief quotations.

(*e*) The perfect and past perfect tenses for accuracy of time sequence.

(*f*) Sub-junctives for indicating doubt or supposition.

17

Instrumental Grammar

The content and method of instruction in grammar should be determined by the purposes which grammar can serve. Because scientific investigations have failed to show the effectiveness of grammar in the elimination of usage errors, it is not here organised for that purpose. There is no scientific evidence of the value of grammar, which warrants its appearance as a prominent or even distinct feature of the course of study.

On the other hand; in the process of building better sentences and more coherent paragraphs pupils must manipulate the various elements of the sentence, and in the process they should gain concepts of those elements. If as these concepts emerge the teacher applies to them the appropriate grammatical terminology, the pupils acquire labels which will be very convenient in referring to these concepts on future occasions.

For example, in a second grade many of the pupils employ only the subject-predicate-object order of sentence arrangement, so that monotony results. The teacher presents a brief story, four or five simple sentences, all in this monotonous form, but some of them with time or place expressions at the end. For example :

> Freddy was four years old yesterday. Mama took him to the park in the morning. He played till noon in the sand pile. Mama got him his first sundae on the way home.

Then she suggests that this might sound better if some of the sentences were turned around, like this :

> Freddy was four years old yesterday. In the morning mama took him to the park. He played till noon in the sand pile. On the way home mama got him his first sundae.

She asks the pupils to point out the words that were moved. Then she offers, perhaps in context, other sentences, which have time or place expressions at the end, and asks the pupils to turn these around. Then she says that we call these expressions that tell when or where adverbs. She asks them to make some sentences with adverbs first. She will need to repeat this procedure, perhaps several times for many classes, before the pupils master this manipulation of the sentence, and on these occasions she simply calls the expressions to be moved adverbs.

Note that the pupils are not given any definitions, and do not make any for themselves. They are not required to use the grammatical terminology and are not formally tested on the recognition of adverbs. They simply learn by normal desirable manipulation of a sentence element, which the teacher calls by its proper name, exactly as they have developed the concepts and learned the words, *bell, school, truth*. No time at all has been spent on grammar as such. The pupils have not felt the strain, which attends the attempt to grasp the abstract generalisation which formal grammar would have presented. Such presentation of grammar is entirely informal, yet may be quite systematic. It is incidental to and instrumental in the improvement of sentences, but it is in no sense accidental or haphazard.

Grammar so taught is certain to be practical because it is learned not merely for use but in use. Moreover, *no time at all has been taken to teach it;* it is merely a by-product of other work that needs to be done.

The list of instrumental grammar units printed here is meant to be illustrative rather than prescriptive or exhaustive. An attempt has been made to choose the most useful ones, but no teacher or curriculum maker can go very far wrong in the choice of units if he insists upon teaching each *in* its application. The arrangement is based largely upon the Stormzand and O'Shea tables in *How Much English Grammar*, and especially for grades 2 and 3, upon the constructions employed in the Composition Standards (pupil composition) included in the current courses of study for the city of Chicago.

The reader is particularly cautioned against the assumption that because this grammar outline is presented separately any grammar is to be taught separately, even for later application. This outline might be omitted entirely without changing the curriculum in the least; it is printed here merely to demonstrate to the skeptical that the grammar is being taught - through use.

A. Instrumental Grammar Unit, Grades 2 - 6

1. *Primary Objective* : To reduce the tendency to speak and especially to write fragmentary sentences by acquiring the concept of the sentence as a group of words which makes sense.

Enabling Objectives : To distinguish between such (simple, but complete) sentences as, "The ice cream and cake were good", "I ate five big cookies", and such fragments as, "Every one of the boys", "Falling down stairs", "Ram into the house". To recognise the completeness of such simple commands as, "Come to me at once", and "Please take this note to Mr. Johnson." To see that all of a simple question is needed to make sense; *e.g.*, "Where are you going?" or "Have you seen my cap?" (The attention of the teacher is called to the fact that in conversation and to some extent in other forms of oral communication expressions, which would if standing alone be "sentence fragments" may serve the purpose of sentences. No definition of the term sentence is to be attempted; the teacher speaks of the complete statements, questions, and commands as sentences, and the children pick up this term as they do *blackboard* and *recess*. And most certainly there is to be no attempt to distinguish the three types of sentence - merely experience in recognising all three kinds as sentences.)

2. ***Primary Objective:*** To guard further against fragmentary sentences by extending the concept of the sentence.

Enabling Objectives : To feel the unity of such sentences as, "When I was five years old we moved into a new house" (with initial adverbial clause), and, "I am going home if you are going to play marbles" (with final adverbial clause). To feel the incompleteness of such expressions as these adverbial - clause fragments "When papa was a little boy," and, "If you had a pet rabbit", except when in conversation they may serve as responses.

3. *Primary Objective* : To reduce the tendency to speak and especially to write run-on sentences, whether with or without *and*, by sharpening the concept of the sentence as the expression of a single thought.

   Enabling Objectives : To feel the weakness of a whole paragraph (oral or written) strung together with *and's*. To feel the difference between such a pair of sentences as, "I was four years old. Paul was almost three", and the compound sentence, "I was four years old and Paul was almost three". To feel the difference between such proper compound sentences as, "Mother was very tired, and she went straight to bed" and such improper ones as "My dog's name is Spot and I have a kitten too". (The teacher will speak of good and bad "compound sentences" and the brighter children will imitate her.)

4. *Primary Objective* : To provide variety in sentences by learning to shift adverbs and adverbial phrases.

   Enabling Objectives : To see that such expressions as *today, at Christmas, here, in the country, at the bottom of the well,* placed at the beginning of a sentence, tell when or where the action goes on. To see that some are single words, which the teacher calls adverbs. To see that some, called adverbs phrases by the teacher, are two or more words.

5. *Primary Objective* : To secure speed and ease in narrative by combining sentences with the same subjects into sentences with compound predicates.

   Enabling Objectives : To recognise the common elements in pairs of sentences like *John fell down* and *John hurt his ankle*. To see that these words tell who or what did (does) or was (is). To hear the teacher call these elements subjects. To see that the rest of each sentence tells what the subject did (does) or was (is). To hear the teacher call these predicates.

6. ***Primary Objective :*** To secure sentence variety and paragraph coherence by learning to use initial adverbial clauses, especially those introduced by *when* and *if*.

   Enabling Objectives : To see that a group of words introduced by *when* may do the same work as an initial adverb, *e.g., When it was three o'clock* and *At three o'clock.* To see that these *when* expressions contain subjects and predicates and yet are not sentences (cf. I.G.U. 2). To see where in the sentences these *when* expressions end. To become accustomed to hearing these expressions called adverbial clauses. To see that initial *if* expressions are like the *when* clauses.

7. ***Primary Objective :*** To increase effectiveness and accuracy of expression by learning to use adverbial clauses in the predicate position.

   Enabling Objectives : To see that *When I saw a red light I stopped* and *I stopped when I saw a red light* are just the same and that *What I saw a red light* is used in the same way (adverbial clause, *cf.* I.G.U. 6). To see that *if* clauses may be moved in the same way. To see what expressions beginning with *after, before, until, while, since* (in time sense) also tell *when,* and are, if they have subjects and predicates, adverbial clauses. To see that *where* clauses are like *in the country* except that they have subject and predicate. To see that *unless* and *because* clauses are like the *if, where,* and *when* clauses.

8. ***Primary Objective :*** To increase the vividness and colour of statement by means of adverbs (modifiers of verbs) in the predicate position.

   Enabling Objectives : To see that *soon, yesterday,. then, afterwards,* and other time adverbs, may be put first or next to action or being word without changing the meaning. To recognise them in both positions as adverbs. (Initial adverbs of time were studied in I.G.U. 4). To see that other words, like *well, quickly, suddenly,* may tell how instead of where or when he did (does) or was (is) and to become accustomed to hearing them too called adverbs.

9. *Primary Objective* : To increase vividness and colour by increased and more accurate use of modifying adjectives.

Enabling Objectives : To see that *big* in *A big boy carried me across the street* tells *what kind of* and really changes the meaning of (modifiers) the word *boy*. To see that in *Mother gave me a big apple, big* modifies *apple*. To see that *other* in *Bring me the other book*, which *points out* or tells *which*, also changes the meaning of its noun. To become accustomed to the teacher's calling these describing and pointing out words adjectives, and to her saying that they "modify" their nouns.

10. *Primary Objective* : To improve ease and clarity of statement by employing simple relative clauses (with the relative as subject).

Enabling Objectives : To see that *fastest* in *The fastest runner was an Indian*, and *who ran fastest* in *The runner who ran fastest was an Indian* both modify runner. To see that *last* in *I could not see the last horse*, and *which stood at the end of the line* in *I could not see the horse which stood at the end of the line* do the same work in the sentence but that the latter is a clause instead of a single word. To see that *who* and *which* refer to *runner* and *horse*. The nouns the clauses modify. To become accustomed to the teacher's calling such words relative pronouns. (The examples offered by the teacher should include modifiers of both subject and object nouns, should include, *who, whom, that*, and *which* clauses, should include restrictive and non-restrictive clauses, but no distinctions should be attempted; the point is to give experience with many types of relative pronouns and relative clauses in order to make the concept broad).

B. Instrumental grammar Units Grades 7 - 12

11. *Primary Objective* : To use adjective prepositional phrases for effective description or identification.

Enabling Objectives : To see that in *a powerful team* and *a team with power, powerful* and *with power* both modify *team,* and are adjective expressions. To see that if one word (the preposition) of the phrase were dropped out the rest would not be related to the sentence. To call these relational words prepositions.

12. *Primary Objective* : To increase smoothness and decrease verbosity through the use of clauses introduced by relative pronouns in the possessive (genitive) and objective (accusative) cases, for smoothness and economy of expression.

Enabling Objectives : To see that in *The man who was captured by the bandits is my cousin* and *The man whom the bandits captured is my cousin,* the underlined clauses modify the same noun *man,* to which the pronouns *who* and *whom* refer. To see that the underlined clauses in *The man from whom the bandits took the watch is my cousin* and *The man whose watch the bandits took is my cousins* also *modify man.* To see that the preposition can be shifted to the end in such clauses, *e.g., The man whom the bandits took the watch* FROM *is my cousin.*

13. *Primary Objective* : To secure directness and force in discussing actions by using infinitives as sentence subjects.

Enabling Objectives : To see that in *Telling stories is easy for me, telling* is the subject. To see that *To tell* can be substituted for *telling* and be the subject of the sentence. To call these the verbal noun (gerund) and the infinitive. To see that both gerund and infinitive may take objects and be modified by adverbs.

14. *Primary Objective* : To secure conciseness by using infinitives as adjective and adverbial modifiers.

Enabling Objectives : To see that the underlined part of the sentences *The first man who signed the Declaration was John Hancock* and *The first man to sign the Declaration was John Hancock* are the same in function, but that the second is only an infinitive with object (or modifiers, or both). To see the underlined infinitives in *French is easy to read but hard to speak* as modifiers of the adjectives. To see that *to win* may be substituted for the underlined adverbial clause in *He will do anything honorable in order that he may win.*

15. ***Primary Objective*** : To increase exactness and ease by using verbal nouns as objects of verbs and prepositions.

Enabling Objectives : To see that the gerund in *Joan usually preferred walking home* is the object of the verb, and that the gerund in *Martin received a reward for returning the purse* is the object of the preposition. To see, from examples found in books, that the gerund may also be modified by a noun or pronoun in the possessive case. To see that such a possessive modifier always represents the person who does the act expressed by the gerund.

16. ***Primary Objective*** : To reduce formality by substituting participial phrases for adjective and even adverbial clauses.

Enabling Objectives : To see that *sitting on the bench* in *The man sitting on the bench is hungry* is the equivalent of the relative clause *who is sitting on the bench* and must modify *man*. To see that *sitting* is the principal word in the phrase. To see that *sitting* implies rather than states action. To see that such forms (participles) take objects and adverb modifiers, just as gerunds do. To see that these participial phrases may come before the nouns they modify, especially subjects, and take the place of adverbial clauses, *e.g.*, *John, realising his danger, dropped to the ground or, Realising his danger, John dropped to the ground* instead of, *Because he realised his danger, John dropped to the ground.*

17. ***Primary Objective*** : To use the past (imperfect) tense always and only to indicate definite past time.

Enabling Objectives : To see that in such sentences as *John ate his dinner hastily* and *Our family lived three months in Milton* the speaker always has in mind a definite, though possibly extended, past time, which he could name if he would. To recognise *was eating* as equivalent to *ate* but emphasising the action as in progress. To accept past tense as a term applicable to these verbs.

18. ***Primary Objective*** : To use the present perfect (perfect) tense always and only to indicate indefinite past time or action just completed.

Enabling Objectives : To see that *last year* (a definite past time) might appropriately be added to *I lived in Boston* but not to *I have lived in Boston.* To recognise that in saying *I have seen him somewhere* the speaker merely placed the act before the present. To recognise the feeling of action continuing right up to but not including the present in *I have eaten a big dinner* and still stronger in *I have been sitting here an hour.* To accept the term present perfect (perfect) as applicable to these *have* and *has* verbs.

19. ***Primary Objective*** : To increase clarity and brevity in the discussion of ideas by the use of noun clauses.

Enabling Objectives : To recognise that direct quotations after verbs of saying are objects of the verb. To see that clauses introduced by *that* after verbs of saying (indirect quotations) are objects. To remember that the object of a verb is always a noun or pronoun. To accept the term noun (substantive) clause for these expressions. To see that in *That you knew me surprised Jim, That you knew me* answers the questions, What surprised? And must be the subject. To see that this remains true when the sentence is rearranged to read. *It surprised Jim that you knew me.* To recognise advantage of introducing noun clauses with *that.*

20. ***Primary Objective*** : To use appositives as shorter and less emphatic substitutes for relative clauses.

Enabling Objectives : To see that such expressions as *my older brother* in *Have you ever seen John, my older brother?* stand for the same persons or things as the nouns that immediately precede them. To see that these expressions modify these nouns just as relative clauses like *who is my older brother* would. To see that each of these expressions consist of a noun (or, rarely, a pronoun) with its modifiers. To accept the designation *appositives* or nouns in *apposition.*

21. ***Primary Objective*** : To improve clarity in the discussion of ideas by the use of appositive noun clauses.

Enabling Objectives : To see that in *The idea that I should win never entered my mind* and *I never had any ideas that I should win, that I should win* modifies (by explaining) *idea*. To see that this group of words is a clause but that it is not a relative clause. To see that the clause really restates *idea*, just as appositive nouns repeat in other words the nouns they modify. To accept the term "noun clause in apposition" or "appositive clause" used by the teacher. To see that appositive clauses are usually attached to abstract nouns, *e.g., idea, thought, supposition, claim, fact, statement, doubt*.

22. ***Primary Objective*** : To mark suppositions and contrary to fact wishes by means of the sub-junctive mode.

Enabling Objectives : To see the difference in meaning between *Even if he is your friend* and *Even if he were your friend*. To see the same difference in such pairs as *If he still wants to go, it is impossible* and *If he still wanted to go, it is* (would be) *impossible*. To see that one of each pair of verbs has regular present form and that the other has the form of the past plural, but that both refer to present time. To learn that these contrary to fact verbs are called sub-junctives. To see the difference between *If he heard me, he did not answer* and *If he had heard me, he would not have answered*. To see that in these sentences *heard* and *had heard* both indicate past time but that the contrary to fact (sub-junctive) verb has the form of the past perfect.

23. ***Primary Objective*** : To reinforce the sub-junctive implication of the conditional clause with a sub-junctive in the conclusion.

Enabling Objectives : To see that *would have answered* in *If he had heard me, he would have answered* implies that he did not answer, and to apply the term subjunctive to it also. To see that the conclusions of contrary to fact present conditions usually have *would, could* or *should* verb phrases and the conclusions of contrary to fact past conditions usually have *would have, could have,* or *should have* verbs.

24. *Primary Objective* : To use the active voice habitually for vigour and the passive occasionally to minimise the action or the agent.

Enabling Objectives : To see that such pairs of sentences as *Henry, our youngest player, scored the winning run* and *The winning run was scored by Henry, our youngest player* express the same thought in almost the same words. To see that in *Henry scored* the subject, *Henry,* acts but that in *The run was scored* the subject *run* is passive, *i.e.,* does not act but is acted upon. To learn that the verb is said to be *active,* or *in the active voice,* when subject is active, and passive when the subject is passive. To see that a passive verb always consists of some form of *to be* and a (passive) participle.

25. *Primary Objective* : To express coordinate ideas in parallel form and subordinate ideas in subordinate clauses.

Enabling Objectives : To see that in *Our boys were light but they played hard,* there are two clauses neither of which modifies the other and that they are connected by *but.* To see that in *If you are busy or if you have company I will come again later* the two *if* clauses both modify *will come* and are connected by *or.* To see that any two clauses connected by *and, or,* or *but* are grammatically parallel or coordinate. To see that a clause introduced by any connective other than *and, but,* or *or* modifies part of another clause and is therefore of a lower order or subordinate. To call all these other connectives, except the relative pronouns, subordinate conjunctions.

18

Usage

I. Aims and Procedures of Corrective Teaching

The first essential in any programme of correct English in the schools is a clear recognition of differentiation or gradation of usage. There is a world of differences between the social implications of the sentence, "I seen them books yesterday" and those of the sentence, "I was told there was no chance of Mr. Smith being elected". The teacher must realise the usage varies from the grossly illiterate to the most precise of literary distinctions, that the line between permissible and non-permissible uses is by no means fixed, and that the correction of expressions accepted by a high percentage of linguistic experts is a sheer waste of time.

What Is Correct? - The consideration of what is "correct" in English usage seems not to have appeared much before the eighteenth century. Prior to that time the interest in language centered on vocabulary, on the coining and borrowing of words. But in the eighteenth century there grew up a number of theories of language, which influenced to some extent the usage of their own day and established a body of traditional rules, many of which survive to the present time. Some of these rules were linguistically sound; many were not.

Any approach to the problem of "correctness" today must be cognisant of the dual nature of language tradition. There is, on the one hand, the tradition of the living, spoken language, based upon the phenomena of actual usage; on the other, there survives the tradition of authority, based upon the classics of literature and the rules of grammarians. Upon the failure to recognise clearly this double source of authority hang many of the absurdities of textbooks and the perplexities of English teachers.

The determination of correctness in English Usage must rest upon these criteria :

1. Correct usage must find its authority in the living language of today.
2. It must recognise dialect and geographical variations.
3. It must judge the appropriateness of the expression to the purpose intended.
4. It must recognise social levels of speech.
5. It must take into account the historical development of the language.

With these criteria in mind the following rule of thumb is serviceable : Good English is that form of speech which is appropriate to the purpose of the speaker, true to the language as it is, and comfortable to speaker and listener. It is the product of custom, neither cramped by rule nor freed from all restraint; it is never fixed, but changes with the organic life of the language.

The Aim - In the teaching of correct usage the aim is habit formation, not knowledge of correct forms. "Until a language form is definitely established as a habit, it has not been taught." The study of grammar without application to writing and speaking leads merely to the knowledge of the correct form. This, however, is insufficient to ensure correct usage, which can be established only through practice.

Framing Language Habits - Habit formation is mainly a matter of repetition, practice, and experience with the act to be learned, but is achieved more economically when a person has clearly in mind what he is to learn and has a keen desire to form the habit.

To change language habits is among the most difficult of all the tasks we undertake in the name of education. The results gained are perhaps among the most expensive - when we consider the time spent and the gains in other phases of child development which might be accomplished in that same time. What does it profit (assuming success in developing the habits in a docile and faithful subject) if a person of twelve, seventeen, or twenty-two invariably says, "He beg*an*", "The pipe bu*rst*", and "He thr*ew* it swift*ly*", and yet has developed prejudices against "English" has been denied pupil experience that really trains in clear thinking and in effective expression, has little effectiveness in conversation, has very limited reading power and little interest in reading?

Therefore an essential in teaching correct English is, strangely enough, less emphasis on errors and more emphasis on interesting language activities. The elimination of errors has become an end in itself in to many classrooms. The pupil should be led to do interesting things with language, and to derive the satisfaction that comes from the applause of his teacher and classmates. When he sees that errors are hindrances to the success of his undertaking, when he realises that a certain standard of accuracy is demanded by his critical audience, he is in the best possible frame of mind for a vigourous and self-motivated attack on his own errors. The positive approach through worthwhile activities, which are interesting in themselves, will do more to break down the customary attitude of passive resistance than any amount of specific drill, no matter how badly needed.

All habits must be in the service of some purpose or goal or drive. The service that correct English usage can render is that of making one's speech and writing more intelligible, more forceful, and more acceptable to others. From infancy on up, the greatest drive toward improvement of language is that we shall be able to express ourselves more adequately to others and to understand what others are trying to express to us. With young people correct usage is largely a matter of acceptability. More than anything they wish to retain their standing as members of the group and must make their language conform to current group standards. The English teacher then has two problems : to create an attitude and atmosphere of willingness to accept standards of expression which society in general deems "correct" and to provide opportunity for the practice of these forms until they become agreeable, natural, and habitual.

The motivation of the breaking of bad speech and writing habits is therefore primarily a matter of classroom atmosphere. Boys and girls are rigid conformists and are ready to go to work if they realise that their deficiencies stamp them as outsiders and make them seem a little queer. Of a teacher who makes his pupils his allies a parent any truthfully say, "I sent my son to the school master but the fellows educated him".

Diagnostic, practice and mastery tests, which make goals visible, enable the pupil to measure his own progress, and make education a game in which a score is kept, help to arouse a desire to use correct English. A good slogan in corrective teaching is, "Every lesson a test, and every test a lesson". Dr. Symonds has experimental evidence to prove that test motivation is equal in teaching value to five sheer repetitions.

Attentive repetition is, of course, the indispensable factor in the mechanism of habit formation. A pupil must hear the correct form, say it, and write it under approximately normal conditions until their correct reaction is so strong that it is automatically used.

Thorndike, in recent work, has emphasised the importance of identifiability of material to be learned. Nothing, perhaps, is more important than to make clear to pupils exactly what it is that they shall learn. While we commonly believe that learning fails to take place mainly because of insufficient motivation, we underestimate the extent to which learning fails to take place because of lack of understanding of what is to be learned.

Experiments have shown that where the correct and incorrect forms are presented side by side illustration of model's clearly labelled "right" and "wrong", and with the critical words italicised or underlined in such a way as to make them stand out and hence come sharply to the focus of attention, the results show better learning than where merely the correct forms are presented without particular emphasis on the word or phrases whose usage is being corrected.

To focus the pupils' attention on a correct form, we should concentrate on one point at a time, always make clear what the critical point at issue is, and "make the clearing up of a specific error or difficulty an opportunity for producing a wider and deeper insight into the working principles of the language". The practice periods, whether the drill takes the form of dictation, filling blanks, error correction, error recognition, a game, oral practice, or a test, should be brief, frequent, and sharp.

Classroom Procedure - Because errors differ widely in persistency and in the difficulty of the principle involved, the classroom procedure in establishing correct language forms var es. Steps commonly included in a campaign against a serious, persistent error are : (*i*) Observation of the speech and writing of the pupils to find which pupils need drill; (*ii*) Pre-test to discover whether the pupils know what the correct usage is; (*iii*) Clear oral or printed explanation, based on examples, of the critical point at issue; (*iv*) Pupils' reading aloud of correct sentences to give abundant practice in speaking the forms to be learned; (*v*) Practice in error recognition, error, correction, blank filling, or crossing out the incorrect; (*vi*) Using the correct expression in original sentences or paragraph; (*vii*) Mastery test to measure achievement and ability to select invariably the correct forms. (*viii*) Follow-up to prevent exception and to insure habit formation. Obviously either this training should be individual, or pupils who have established the desired habit should be excused from the class practice. These exercises will at least sensitise the student to his own error. When such practice is accompanied by interest and zeal, when the practice is means for achieving some desired end, when a strong sense of personal satisfaction accompanies or follows the practice, learning and habit formation result.

Avoiding Exceptions - Exceptions - retard or prevent habit formation. Because the child continues to live in the same environment which has been responsible for his incorrect usage, he is likely to attempt to master two languages - one for general use and another to satisfy his English teacher. By a skillful teaching of conversation, however, we can help pupils to fuse their two languages into a natural, correct, vigourous, vivid speech and writing which is effective in the classroom, at home, and on the baseball field.

The Error Box is a help. When a pupil hears an incorrect pronunciation or sentence, he jots down on a piece of paper the error, the corrected form, and the name of the maker and the recorder, and slips the paper into the Error Box. Once a week the Error Box is opened and the errors discussed. Dr. O'Rourke's experiments indicate that a contest between the two halves of the class is a particularly effective device for error elimination. The contest is usually limited to the points in usage taught during the term or preceding terms. A side scores by reporting in a whole sentence an error made by a member of the other side and correcting the error, and is penalised for reporting a correct sentence as an error. A "Never Again" notebook list of a pupil's own errors also helps him to avoid exceptions.

The active cooperation of all the teachers of the school is essential if exceptions are to be reduced to a minimum. And an English teacher should cooperate with himself by holding his pupils absolutely responsible for correct forms, which have been thoroughly taught. Every effort should be made to see that wrong practice does not occur.

II. Correct Forms to be established

As the heading of this section indicates, attention should centre, not upon errors, but upon the correct forms.

The lists of Usage to be mastered which is presented here has been compiled in accordance with the following principles :

1. The more frequently a construction is used, the greater is the need to make the correct form of it habitual.
2. Corrective teaching should deal only with the points on, which pupils fall into real error. No time should be spent in teaching the use of the preferred one of two correct forms. (O'Rourke shows that many such forms cannot be taught successfully).
3. The more heinous or noticeable an error is, the more important is the establishment of its correct correlative.
4. A course of study can list only those Usage on which mistakes are made by *many* pupils. There will be many unpredictable faults of single individual's and these the teacher must ignore or try to correct according to their apparent seriousness and the individual pupil's freedom from more glaring faults.

The lists of Usage to be mastered are arranged by categories to make them convenient for use as desk check lists in surveying pupil's errors. This arrangement is not intended to suggest a grammatical attack in corrective work.

To attemp to eradicate all errors at the same time is grossly ineffective. Nowhere is the slogan, *Divide and conquer*, more applicable. The teacher who thinks of building the correct habits rather than of eliminating errors will realise the necessity of "one small point at a time". An order of attack is, therefore, suggested by the numerals following each item, at the right. The items are also relisted in this order.

A. Forms to be Mastered in Kindergarten - Grades 6

1. *Use of Irregular Verbs :*

(a) Past of *see, do come, go, run, become.* 3

(b) Perfect tense of *see, do come, go, run;* passive voice of *see, do run.* 4

(c) Past tense of *give, eat, know, take, bring, grow, throw.* 17

(d) Perfect and passive of *give, eat, know, take, bring, grow, throw.* 18

(e) Past of *say, sit, start, ask, help, teach, ring, sing, drink, lie, write.* 29

(f) Perfect participle of *sit, teach, ring, sing, drink, lie, write.* 30

(g) Past tense and perfect tense of *break, choose, freeze, speak, steal.* 43

(h) Past tense and perfect participle of *set, hurt, put, climb, sneak.* 37

2. *Verb Number :*

(a) You *were;* you *weren't;* he, she, it *isn't.* 6

(b) *I'm not;* we *were;* we *weren't.* they *were* they *weren't, weren't* they. 7

(c) I, we, you, they *haven't.* 8

(d) James and John *are, were, have, do.* 19

(e) Several of the boys, some of the men, *are, were, have, do.* 27

(f) Only *one* of the boys *is.* 26

3. *Use of Pronouns :*

(*a*) *You* (not *youse*): *himself* (not *hisself*): *themselves* (not *their selves*). 20

(*b*) My *father and I* (not *me and my father*) went to the store. 9

(*c*) Masculine, *he*: feminine, *she*; neuter, it. 10

(*d*) *Yours* (not *your*); *his* (not *hisen*); *hers* (not *hern*). 22

(*e*) *Who* for persons, *which* for all other objects. 28

4. *Use of Adverbs :*

(*a*) Sings *well*, told it *well*, reads poetry *well*. 21

(*b*) Writes *clearly*, runs *swiftly*, draws *beautifully*. 34

5. *Use of Adjectives :*

(*a*) *That* (not *that there*) tree; *this* (not *this here*) book. 14

(*b*) *A* boy, *a* house, *an* automobile, *an* interesting story, *an* egg. 32

(*c*) *Those* (not *them*) apples. 5

(*d*) Correct use of *worse* (not *worser*), *worst* (not *baddest*), *better* (not *gooder* or *more better*), *best* (not *goodest*). 23

(*e*) *More beautiful, most beautiful; cheaper, heavier, easiest*. 36

6. *Redundancies :*

(*a*) *John* (not *John, he*) went away; my *mother* (not *mother, she*) made me a cake. 15

(*b*) My *dog's* (not *dog, his*) tail wagged faster; my Uncle *Bob's* (not *Uncle Bob, his*) farm is near the city. 24

(*c*) Where does he live (not *live at*)? Where are they going (not *going to*)? 44

(*d*) He ought (not *had ought*) to pay for it; he ought not (not *hadn't ought*) to lie about it. 45

(e) John *hasn't any* pencil or John *has no pencil* (not John *hasn't no pencil*). 13

7. *Diction :*

(a) Please *let* (not *leave*) me pet the dog. Mother would not *let* (not *leave*) me go again. 11

(b) May *have* (not *of*) been: might *have* (May've, might've are quite correct in informal *speech*); (not *of*) come; would *have* (not *of*) gone; could, should, must *have*.

(c) *Take* (not *bring*) this to the office as you go. May I *take* this paper to Mr. Wilson? 31

(d) I visited *at* (not *by*) my cousin's home yesterday. 38

(e) Is your father *at* (not *to*) home? Were you *at* (not *to*) the circus? 39

(f) I got the candy *from* (not *off*, or *off of*) Arthur. 40

(g) My little brother wanted to go with *us* (not just *go with*). My little brother wanted to *go along*. Give me a sandwich to take *with me* (or *along*). 41

(g) Miss Jones *taught* (not *learned*) me that in the second grade. Miss Smith, won't you *teach* (not *learn*) me to use this index? 12

(h) The sun *rises* (not *raises*) every morning. It *rose* (not *raised*) at six this morning. Are my marks *rising* (not *raising*) any?

(i) The temperature has *risen* (not *raised*) ten degrees since nine o'clock. 35

8. *Sentence Unity :*

(a) To speak in complete sentences (except such elliptical sentences as we all naturally use in replying to questions) 1.

(b) To avoid stringy *and* sentences in speaking 16.

(c) To mark the ends of written sentences by periods or question marks. 2

(*d*) To avoid stringy *and* sentences in writing 33.

(*e*) To write no sentence fragments as sentences 42.

B. The order of attack in Kindergarten - Grades 6

Note: This arrangement is based primarily upon Dr. L. J. O'Rourke's Study : *Rebuilding the English Curriculum.*

1. Sentence unit *a*	16. Sentence unity *b*	31. Diction *c*
2. Sentence unity *c*	17. Irregular verbs *c*	32. Adjectives *b*
3. Irregular verbs *a*	18. Irregular verbs *d*	33. Sentence unity *d*
4. Irregular verbs *b*	19. Verb number *d*	34. Adverbs *b*
5. Adjectives *c*	20. Pronouns *a*	35. Diction *i*
6. Verb number *a*	21. Adverbs *a*	36. Adjectives *e*
7. Verb number *b*	22. Pronouns *d*	37. Irregular verb *h*
8. Verb number *c*	23. Adjectives *d*	38. Diction *d*
9. Pronouns *b*	24. Redundancies *b*	39. Diction *e*
10. Pronouns *c*	25. Diction *b*	40. Diction *f*
11. Diction *a*	26. Verb number *f*	41. Diction *g*
12. Diction *h*	27. Verb number *e*	42. Sentence unity *e*
13. Redundancies *e*	28. Pronouns *e*	43. Irregular verbs *g*
14. Adjectives *a*	29. Irregular verb *e*	44. Redundancies *c*
15. Redundancies *a*	30. Irregular verb *f*	45. Redundancies *d*

C. Forms to be Mastered in Gradess 7 - 12

The junior and senior high schools may well use some procedures not appropriate with younger pupils. Responsibility for doing corrective exercises should more and more be left to the individual pupil, who can check his own errors in written drills, and can get more help from explanations of principles involved.

Concerning written exercises and tests one experienced supervisor says to his teachers, "Furnish keys to exercises with notes on cases needing comment. Make the keys teach. Let the pupils mark and rate themselves by the keys. Don't collect pupils' work or rate it. Occasionally give pupils tests of achievement in the particular work each is doing. Do not let pupils see the tests in advance. Rate the tests yourself."

Graphs of progress and a high but reasonable standard of achievement make practice more effective. If each student keeps a graph of his marks in mastery tests, he knows exactly what progress he is making.

Because in the world of habit formation there is backsliding, we should watch for breaks in the habit connections and repair the damage by review. For that reason the secondary-school list includes in smaller type, without ordinal letters, the items that are also set down for grades 1 to 6. Obviously a pupil should work on correct forms he does not habitually use in his speech and writing, not on forms he has already mastered, and should progress at his own rate.

1. *Verb* :

I'm not; he *isn't*; it *isn't*; they *aren't*; I *haven't*; he *hasn't* (not "I ain't seen him today").

Let me come in. Please *let* me drive the car. Father *let* me have it. *Leave* it there.

May *have* seen (not "of"); might *have* seen; must *have* seen; could *have* seen; would *have* seen; should *have* known; couldn't *have* known.

(*a*) Correct spelling of contractions : *aren't*, *haven't*, *didn't*, *wasn't*, *doesn't*, *it's*, *can't*, etc. *You're* late. *Who's* captain of the team? 5

(*b*) *Ought* to go (not "had ought"); *ought* not to go. 8

(*c*) Use of *shall I* in questions, *Shall I* go with you? 9

(*d*) Correct use of *learn*, *teach; bring*, *take; rise*, *raise; tell*, *ask; lend*, *borrow*. 21

(*e*) Correct use of *lie*, *lay*, *sit*, *set; affect*, *effect; accept*, *except; loose*, *lose*. Mother is *lying* down. How long have you *sat* in the first row? Father *taught* me that trick. 32

(*f*) If I *had gone* (not "would have gone"); I wish I *had gone* (not "would have gone"); if he failed (not "would fail"); I wish we *had* a better baseball team (not "would have"). 52

Principal Parts

Principal parts of *do, run, see, go, come, become.* Use, for example, of *did, ran, saw, came, became, have done, had run, has seen, have gone, have come.*

(g) Principal parts of *break, choose, freeze, speak, steal, swear, tear, wear, begin, drink, ring, sing, sink, shrink, spring, swim.* Use, for example, of *began, sang, rang, is broken, is frozen, is torn, has rung.* 7

(h) Principal parts of *drive, ride, rise, strive, write, blow, fly, grow, know, throw, buy, eat, fall, get, give, take.* Use for example, of *gave, knew, threw, have driven, have eaten, have fallen, have given, have taken, have written, might have known.* 22

(i) Principal parts of *attack, beat, bring, burst, climb, drag, draw, drown, show, say, teach, lie, sit, set.* 33

Agreement with Subject

You *were*; you *weren't*; we *were*; we *weren't*; they *were*; they *weren't*; *were* you; *weren't* they.

(j) He *doesn't*, she *doesn't*; it *doesn't*. 1

(k) Agreement of the verb with the subject when the subject is after the verb. There *are* two. There *were* two. There *were* the books? On the bank *were* some water lilies. 3

Agreement of a verb with a compound subject joined by *and*. How *are* Gladys and jimmy? George and his sister *were* chosen.

Agreement of a verb with a subject followed by a phrase. One of his tonsils *is* diseased. The scenery in the Alps *is* beautiful.

(l) Agreement of a verb with a compound subject joined by *or* or *nor*. Neither John nor James *seems* to be in a hurry. 23

(m) Agreement of verb with *each, every, either, someone, somebody, anyone, anybody, everyone, everybody, no one, nobody, and a person.* Each of the girls *was* rewarded. 34

(*n*) Agreement of a verb with such a words as *news, mathematics, civics, measles*, or *two-third*. News *is* scarce. Measles *is* a contagious disease. 35

(*o*) Agreement of a verb with a relative pronoun. She is one of the girls who *are* organising a writer's club. 36

Tense

(*p*) The use of past tenses ending in *d* : *asked, helped, started, used, said.* I *asked* him yesterday (not "ask"). John *helped* to distribute the fruit. We *used* to live in Trenton. 10

(*q*) Avoidance of careless shifting of tenses. He looked at me and *said* (not "says"). 48

(*r*) The use of the past tense for past time. He *gave* it to me yesterday. He *came* along. He *ran* all the way. I *came* to America five years age (not "have come"). 49

(*s*) Use of the past perfect tense. I found him almost well, although he *had been* very sick. 50

(*t*) Use of the present perfect tense. *Have* you *bought* your tickets? 51

2. *Pronouns* :

Correct formation of pronouns : *your* (not "yourn"); *our* (not "are"); *himself* (not "hisself"); *themselves* (not "theirselves").

Avoidance of the double subject : my father said (not "my father he said"); Mary came (not "Mary she came"); Sherlock Holmes walked around.

(*a*) Avoidance of *what* when the antecedent is expressed. Here is the book *which* you asked for (not "what"). The boys *who* went had a good time (not "what"). 15

Placing a pronoun in the first person last in a series. *Dad and I* were playing ball (not "me and

Dad"). *He and I* did it (not "me and him" or "I and he").

(*b*) Correct spelling of these pronouns : *Ours, here, its, theirs, yours, whose.* Is that dog *yours?* 16

(*c*) Omission of useless pronouns. *Ivanhoe* tells of King Richard (not "in I vanhoe it"). 24

(*d*) Inserting I when it is the subject. *I* received your letter of March 14 (not "received your letter of March 14"). 26

Use of *who* for persons, *which* for animals and things, and *that* for persons, animals, and things. I saw a man *who* looked like my father (not "which").

Case

Personal pronoun as subject and predicate nominative. John and *I* are going to camp this summer. *We* girls went. It was *she*. It was *he*.

(*e*) Avoidance of *them* as the subject. *Those* are the ones I mean (not "them"). *Those* are mine (not "them"). 2

(*f*) Personal pronoun as object of a verb and of a preposition, especially in a compound object. Margaret invited you and *me*. No one but *him* knows the answer. 6

(*g*) Correct use of *who* and *whom*. I do not know *who* he is. *Who* do you think she is? *Who* do they think will be elected? 38

Reference

(*h*) Pronouns relating *to each, every, either, neither, anyone, anybody, everyone, someone, somebody, no one, nobody, one, many a,* and *a person*. Every girl did *her* best. Everyone did *his* work. Each runner put *his* foot on the line. A person can find what *he* looks for. 25

(*i*) Clear reference of pronouns. Mary said to her friend, "I am mistaken" (not "Mary told her friend that she was mistaken"). 37

3. *Adjectives* :

Avoidance of *them* modifying a noun : *those* books (not "them"); *those* chickens; *those* papers; *those* things.

Avoidance of "that there" and "this here". *That* boy is the one I mean (not "that there"). *This* desk is too low for me (not "this here").

Use of *a* and *an* : *an* apple; *an* airplane.

Correct use of such comparatives and superlatives as *worse* (not "worser"); *worst* (not "baddest"); *better* (not "more better" or "gooder"); *heavier; kinder; cheaper; more beautiful; easiest; laziest; most beautiful; most wonderful.*

(*a*) Use *of this, these; that, those.* I like *this* kind of apples but prefer *that* kind of grapes. 18

(*b*) Use of an adjective after a copulative verb. I feel *bad*. The substance of the speech was fairly *good.* The rose smells *sweet* .27

(*c*) Avoidance of such overworked words as *fine, funny, awfully, nice, great*, and of the slang use of *some* and *swell*; an *artistic* hat (not "some hat"); a *delicious* dinner (not "a swell dinner"). 39

(*d*) Correct use of *fewer* and *less* : *fever* horses; *less* wheat. 40

4. *Adverbs* :

Avoidance of the double negative : *haven't any* (not "ain't got none"); *didn't do anything* (not "didn't do nothing") *haven't either; haven't a book; doesn't know anything; haven't anything; isn't ever coming back; can't see anything; haven't any paper.*

Plays *well;* writes *well;* slept *well;* do it *well.*

(*a*) Spelling of *too* and *there*. *There* are six. I am *too* tired to go. 4

(*b*) Use of *almost* and *somewhat*. I *almost* always walk home from school (no "most"). He is *somewhat* better (not "some"). 28

(*c*) Use of an adverb to modify a verb, an adjective, or an adverb. I *surely* was glad to see my mother (not "sure"). He had a *really* good excuse (not "real"). The book is *very* entertaining (not "real"). He didn't speak *distinctly*. Everyone will be treated *fairly*. 29

(*d*) Avoidance of negative with *hardly*, *scarcely*, *only*. He *is* hardly old enough (not "isn't"). There *is* only one bank in the town (not "isn't"). He *has* hardly any friends (not "hasn't"). I *can* hardly hear you (not "can't"). 14

(*e*) Omission of useless words : *again* (not "once more again"); *add* (not "add up"); *end* (not "end up") *return* (not "return back"). 41

(*f*) That's *as far as* I went (not "all the farther"). 42

5. *Nouns* :

(*a*) Spelling of the possessive singular of nouns : the *sun's* shadow; *George's* book; a *day's* work; a *lady's* picture. 11

(*b*) Commonly used plurals of nouns : *churches*, *houses*, *women*. 17

(*c*) Spelling of plurals of nouns : *potatoes*, *flies*, *donkeys*, *calves*, *proofs*, *oxen feet*, *sheep*, *data*. 43

(*d*) The formation of the possessive plural : *boy's*, *men's*, *ladies'*, *monkeys'*. 44

(*e*) It is two *miles* to town (not "mile"). He is six *feet* tall (not "foot"). We have six *bushels* of apples (not "bushel"). 45

6. *Prepositions :*

(*a*) Off (not "off of"). I fell *off* the chair. He got *off* the car. 12

From, *off*. I bought the baseball *from* Arthur.

At, to. Is your father *at* home? Were you *at* the circus?

At, by. Stop *at* my house on your way home.

(*b*) *Into*, *in*. Harold jumped *into* the water to save the child. 19

(*c*) *In*, *at*. We enjoyed ourselves *at* the World Fair *in* Chicago. 20

Avoidance of useless prepositions. Where does she live (not "live at")? Where is he going (not "going to")? To whom did you give the knife? (Not "To whom did you give the knife to?").

(*d*) Use of *different from* (not "different than"). Stenography examinations are different *from* other examinations. 46

(*e*) Avoidance of *due to* as a preposition phrase. *Because of* the rain the game was called after the fifth inning (not "due to"). 47

7. *Conjunction :*

(*a*) Avoidance of *like* as a conjunction. Do *as* I say. He talks *as if* he were sick. 13

(*b*) Avoidance of "being that" as a conjunction. *As* he was the only music teacher in town, I invited him (not "being that"). 30

(*c*) Avoidance of overusing *so*, *and but* to join clauses. Nothing seemed to stop Jimmy and his partner. They won the second set 7 - 5 and had the lead in the third set (not "partner so they"). 31

(*d*) Avoidance of *where* and *how* in the sense of *that*. Did you read *that* Leo won the medal for the best-drilled cadet (not "where")? 53

8. *Sentence Sense* :

Avoidance of the half-sentence in speech and writing. He is a friend worth having. (Not "A friend worth having.") My second reason is that the prince was a barbarian. (Not "Second, because the prince was a barbarian.").

Avoidance of the comma blunder. Your letter came today. It was good to hear from you (not "today, it").

9. *Sentence Structure* :

(*a*) Observance of parallel structure. He taught piano, violin, and *voice* (not "vocal"). 54.

(*b*) Avoidance of a confusing or amusing dangling participle. While I was walking down the street, an automobile almost hit me. (Not "Walking down the street, an automobile almost hit me."). 55

(*c*) Placing modifiers so that the meaning will be clear. The general lost nearly a thousand men (not "nearly lost"). 56

(*d*) Using all necessary words. My sister graduated *from* high school last June. I have never seen *him* or spoken to him. 57

D. The Order of Attack in Grades 7 - 12

1.	Verb *j*	20.	Preposition *c*	39.	Adjective *c*
2.	Pronoun *e*	21.	Verb *d*	40.	Adjective *d*
3.	Verb *k*	22.	Verb *h*	41.	Adverb *e*
4.	Adverb *a*	23.	Verb *l*	42.	Adverb *f*
5.	Verb *a*	24.	Pronoun *c*	43.	Noun *c*
6.	Pronoun *f*	25.	Pronoun *h*	44.	Noun *d*
7.	Verb *g*	26.	Pronoun *d*	45.	Noun *e*
8.	Verb *b*	27.	Adjective *b*	46.	Preposition *d*
9.	Verb *c*	28.	Adverb *b*	47.	Preposition *e*

continued . . . .

10. Verb *p*	29. Adverb *c*	48. Verb *q*
11. Noun *a*	30. Conjunction *b*	49. Verb *r*
12. Preposition *a*	31. Conjunction *c*	50. Verb *s*
13. Conjunction a	32. Verb *e*	51. Verb *t*
14. Adverb *d*	33. Verb *i*	52. Verb *f*
15. Pronoun *a*	34. Verb *m*	53. Conjunction *d*
16. Pronoun *b*	35. Verb *n*	54. Sentence Sense *a*
17. Noun *b*	36. Verb *o*	55. Sentence Sense *b*
18. Adjective *a*	37. Pronoun *i*	56. Sentence Sense *c*
19. Preposition *b*	38. Pronoun *g*	57. Sentence Sense *d*

References

1. Some teachers will prefer to keep records of all the errors they hear, and after a time to compare the error lists of each child or of a whole class with the list in the course of study, in order to determine which to attack first. Others will prefer to keep on the desk a copy of the course-of-study list and to note opposite each usage the initials or number of the child making a mistake. The purpose of either procedure is to discover what error, if any, are general in the group and what the serious weaknesses of individual pupils are. Observation is indispensable for no tests yet in general use will reveal language *habits*.

2. In the elementary school, and especially in the primary grades, the explanation should be a minor feature or be omitted entirely. The dependence should be upon clear examples for imitation. Explanation is likely to be abstract and therefore of little use to the child, whose mind still thinks in concrete and specific terms.

3. Miss. Cutright has recently shown that in the elementary school a variety of drills is better than any one type, and that if correction of oral usage is to be attained a large part of the drills should be oral. Language games did not prove effective in her experiment.

19

Spelling

A good business house does not send out misspelled letters. Rarely does one find a misspelled word in a book, a magazine, or a first-class newspaper. In a social letter or letter or application an error in spelling is more surely discovered than any other error and is commonly considered a sign of carelessness or ignorance. In the business and social world, spelling, like grammatical correctness and the use of periods and capitals, is considered an index of a person's education. Hence in school, spelling should be thoroughly taught and a high standard of achievement in spelling should be required.

Class Spelling Lists

In selecting words for spelling lists and arranging them for study the following points should be considered :

1. The frequency of misspelling of the words, as indicated by :
   - *(a)* Study of pupils' papers in all subjects in local schools.
   - *(b)* Other Available Investigations, Such As Ashbaugh's *The Iowa Spelling Scales* (Public School Publishing Company); Lester's *Spelling Review* (John A. Lester, Pottstown, Pennsylvania); *Sixteen Spelling Scales* (Teachers College Of Columbia University); and Buckingham's *Extension of the Ayres Spelling Scale* (Public School Publishing Company).

2. The frequency of use of the words, as indicated by :
   - *(a)* Study of pupils' writing.
   - *(b)* Such investigations as Horn's *A Basic Writing Vocabulary* (University of Iowa); Thorndike's *Teacher's Word Book* (Teachers College of Columbia University); McKee's *The Vocabulary of Children's Themes* (University of Iowa); And Breeds' *How to Teach Spelling* (F. A. Owen Publishing Company).
3. The comprehension of the word by the pupils for whom the list is intended. (Although, as the committee of the National Society for the Study of Education sensibly says, "In curriculum making attention should be given to the interests, needs, and activities of both child life and adult society", spelling words ought to come within the pupil's writing vocabulary chiefly.)

A. Spelling in Grades 2 - 6

Classroom *Study of Spelling*

Investigations in the field of spelling have proved the necessity of close attention to the words to be mastered and the desirability of "multiple sense appeal", *i.e.*, the use of eye, ear, voice, and hand; in study. Successful methods of spelling study differ in the order in which they employ these sense appeals but rarely omit any of them. The words chosen are for the most part already familiar in revealing contexts before they are taught or assigned for study. In the primary grades spelling study must be conducted as a group exercise by the teacher; at the junior high school level most pupils should have adequate ideals of methods of such study and sufficient dependability to do their work individually. In the primary grades there are no trouble spots within the words, every letter needing careful attention, as Dr. Ernest Horn has shown. In the secondary school, on the other hand, C. H. Ward and others have shown that difficulty is pretty well localised - for example, in letters representing obscure sounds, in double letters, in syllables of words often mispronounced. All the modifications to suit the pupil's maturity do not change fundamentally the pattern of multiple sense appeal, with concentrated attention.

Three ways to motivate the study of spelling are : (*i*) Graphing each pupil's progress as indicated by his marks on tests; (*ii*) Dividing the class into two teams and posting on the blackboard each day during the tournament the number of words missed by each side; and (*iii*) Pitting two (or more) classes against each other. Such contests between teams or classes utilise both cooperation and competition. By a variety of activities spelling should be made a matter of personal pride.

In this spelling investigation in Philadelphia, Dr. Rice demonstrated years ago that drill, which does not hold the attention of pupils, is worse than a waste of time. If, however, a person is eager to learn to spell and derives satisfaction from improving his spelling, through attentive repetition automatic spelling control will be developed. A pupil who has a real desire to learn to spell has taken the first long step toward becoming a good speller.

In teaching spelling it is wise to concentrate on a few words at a time and aim at mastery, but also to review frequently the difficult common words. It should not be assumed that words once taught are fixed for life.

How to Learn to Spell a Word

In studying a word, a good procedure for a learner is, (*i*) to say each syllable distinctly and look at the syllable as he says it, (*ii*) with eyes closed to think how the word looks, (*iii*) to look at the word against to check his impression, (*iv*) to write the word and check with the book, and (*v*) to repeat twice the writing and checking. If on any one of these five trials he misspells the word, he should copy it in his spelling notebook for review. Finally he should write the group of words studied as a parent, brother, sister, or friend pronounces them for him.

Spelling in Written Work

Misspellings in unhurried written work are avoidable, and pupils should develop the habit of avoiding them. Fortunately mistakes are confined, according to investigators, almost exclusive to words about which the pupils feel some doubt. If when pupils write their first letters or other compositions in the primary grades they are encouraged to ask for the spelling of all words that trouble them, they will be started on the right path. Pride in legible, correct writing must be cultivated. After the pupils have learned to use the dictionary, they should be expected to check doubtful spelling by it. Server penalties for misspelling common words which have been studied will reduce spelling errors but will harmfully restrict the writing vocabulary unless classroom time is allowed for proof-reading and for looking up doubtful words.

Spelling in Grades 7 - 12

The greatest weakness in teaching spelling in the secondary school is probably an attempt to teach too many and too difficult words; the result is a failure to transfer correct spelling from the spelling lesson to the written work of the pupils in all subjects. Short lists absolutely mastered are worth more than long lists half learned. In other words, the major objective in the teaching of spelling in the high school is to train pupils to write correctly every time the common words which are commonly misspelled. A pupil is likely to find a complete list of words he misspells in his writing surprisingly short, perhaps not more than twenty-five words long probably not more than a hundred.

All high-school graduates should spell correctly all the words in the following list :

does	threw	stretch	preferred
know	two	toward	usually
off	whole	certain	ninety
there	whose	describe	quantity
too	writing	hoping	interesting
write	all right	led	athlete
asked	almost	library	prevent
buy	beginning	separate	captain

Continued . . . .

coming	children	speech	course
dropped	colour	whether	formerly
shining	forty	won't	athletics
stopped	its	wouldn't	sandwich
sure	loose	description	intramural
taking	lose	disappointed	studying
their	loving	finally	laboratory
quite	together	generally	choose
truly	until	government	don't
woman	across	grammar	losing
believe	business	similar	laid
busy	can't	necessary	quiet
through	women	principal	weather
written	fourth	probably	answered
break	minute	sincerely	didn't
different	piece	definite	doesn't
isn't	receive	divide	really
easily	lady's	occurred	
immediately	ninth		

Teaching and Testing

Secondary teachers should not depend solely on incidental instruction in spelling, but should include testing, teaching, and retesting. Skillful teaching helps pupils to master troublesome words.

If testing precedes teaching; each pupil's entire attention in studying the class list can then be focused on learning to spell correctly those words that he did not already know. This troublesome residue may vary from none, or a few words, on the part of the best spellers to comparatively long lists for the poorer spellers.

The original testing, if the teacher wishes, may be done out of class by "spelling partners" or by home dictation, each student keeping his individual error list. "Spelling partners" get the benefit of the double pronunciation of the words and the noting of their visual forms.

Most words missed in the pretest may be studied independently by the pupils, but a few of the "demons" must still be taught as class work from which those who did not miss the words are excused. This teaching should be concentrated on the hard spots, and should emphasise the right letters, without suggesting what others might be substituted.

20

Corrective Work in Reading

Three means are usually available for identifying pupils who are sufficiently retarded in reading to need corrective or remedial instruction :

1. When school systems keep sufficiently detailed records, pupils who are retarded in reading may be identified at the time of promotion. Pupils, who over a period of years have received consistently low academic marks in reading, and in other subjects dependent upon reading, are likely to need special help. If possible, interviews with teachers in preceding grades should be used to supplement the records.

2. Certain types of classroom behaviour are suggestive of difficulties in reading. For example, incomplete contributions indicate that a pupil grasps only a "part of the story". When behaviour suggesting reading deficiencies occurs frequently enough to interfere with a pupil's school progress he should become a subject for special study.

3. Standardised reading tests are the readiest means of identifying pupils who are handicapped by reading deficiencies. A series of tests administered to all pupils at the beginning of the school year assists in identifying those who are retarded in reading.

No single method of identifying retarded readers is entirely satisfactory; decisions should be based upon the combined results of the three methods mentioned above. In the case of inconsistent results further study and analysis are desirable.

After pupils who are in need of corrective and remedial instruction have been identified, their reading practices must be further analysed to determine the answers to three questions : (*i*) What is the exact character of each pupil's reading deficiencies? (*ii*) When did the deficiencies begin? (*iii*) What caused the deficiencies to begin? The extent to which an analysis should be carried will vary with individuals. The outline, which follows, is designed to include all the steps in a thorough analysis. The teacher may make use of only those parts of the outline, which are necessary in the study of each case.

Diagnosis of Reading Deficiencies

I. Careful analysis of records of school progress, observations of classroom behaviour, and performance on tests :

   A. Listing of the probable shortcomings as revealed by this evidence.

   B. Verification by additional tests and observations.

II. Enlargement of the examination to include additional phases of reading :

   A. Use of such additional standardised tests as appear to be necessary, *e.g.*, test (*i*) of oral reading, (*ii*) of rate, (*iii*) of comprehension, (*iv*) of rate of association.

   B. Informal observation of pupil's reading habits :

      (1) Character of expression in oral reading.

      (2) Eye-movements, regular or irregular in silent reading.

      (3) Lip or head movements, if any, during silent reading.

      (4) Pupil's ability to interpret materials in regular class work, as shown by, (*a*) his answers to thought questions, (*b*) his answers to factual questions, (*c*) his execution of

written or printed directions, (*d*) his formulation of titles for paragraphs, (*e*) his location of points by skimming.

III. Survey of all available contributing influences which may aid in determining the origin and cause of deficiencies :

(*a*) Mental ability; (*b*) Present health status; (*c*) Physical history; (*d*) Social history; (*e*) Family history; (*f*) Personality traits and interests.

Modifications of Teaching Procedures

Teachers sometimes think that corrective and remedial instruction require unusual methods with which they are unfamiliar. A few extreme types of reading disability may necessitate special methods, but most types respond to methods which any skillful teacher of reading would use in regular class instruction. The chief difference between corrective or remedial teaching and regular class teaching is in the diagnostic procedures, which enable the teacher to select instructional procedures suited to the needs of individuals.

Corrective Instruction in English Classes

In order to provide effective corrective instruction in classes it is desirable that pupils with similar deficiencies be grouped together. If segregation is impracticable or in convenient, several groups may be cared for in one class by means of differentiated instruction. The two units, which follow, are designed to suggest methods of differentiating instruction in English to overcome reading deficiencies.

Oral Reading : For Pupils Retarded in Fundamental Reading Habits

Primary Objective : To entertain other through effective oral reading.

Enabling Objectives : To develop ability to cope with new and unfamiliar words. To improve accuracy of word recognition. To improve expression in oral reading.

Activities : Preparation of selections or parts of selections to be read orally to class. Dramatisation of favourite parts. Oral reading of selections for entertainment of others.

Studying new and unfamiliar words by : aid of the dictionary; aid of diacritical marks; looking for familiar syllables; analysing words into prefixes, root words, and suffixes; using words in sentences. Discussing ways in which new words have been used at home and in other classes. Playing games involving the selection of root words, prefixes, and suffixes. Sight reading of selections not previously studied. Detecting errors in oral reading of other pupils.

Materials : Short stories, historical events, current events, poems, etc. Selected parts of longer selections which are used for class reading. Selections voluntarily suggested by pupils. Standardised oral reading tests.

Differentiation : Self-analysis as needed by individuals to determine character of errors. Studying errors revealed by individual tests. Practice to overcome individual deficiencies.

Appraisal of Growth : Do pupils demonstrate power to read effectively selections of greater difficulty? Are pupils gaining in power to cope with new and unfamiliar words? Do pupils challenge attention of other members of class when reading orally?

Silent Reading : For pupils Retarded Primarily in Power of Interpretation

Primary Objective : To improve power of interpretation in silent reading.

Enabling Objectives : To direct attention to content more effectively. To ascertain the exact thought of an author. To improve ability to interpret increasingly difficult materials.

Activities : Silent reading of short stories to be retold orally. Silent reading of paragraphs to select a title telling what the paragraph is about; to formulate a question answered by the paragraph; to select or organise the essential thought in the paragraph. Execution of written or printed directions. Finding answers to fact questions given before or after a selection is read. Organising the answers to questions that require reading of several sentences, paragraphs, or even pages. Outlining passages into essential thoughts and supporting details. Preparing a brief synopsis of the events in a story. Indicating the major divisions of entire selections.

Materials : A variety of reading materials graded in difficulty to suit pupil's attainments. Short stories, current events, informational material. Texts and references for subject other than English. Formal and informal practice exercises.

Differentiation : Each pupil will select materials suited to his level of attainment. Relatively long periods of silent reading to develop power of sustained application. Practice exercises to measure improvement. Frequent informal timed tests.

Appraisal of Growth : Are pupils gaining in power to ascertain the exact thought of an author? Do pupils gain in power to interpret materials of greater difficulty? Are pupils' scores on practice exercises improving?

Remedial Instruction for Seriously Retarded Readers

Since remedial instruction for seriously retarded readers must be adapted to the needs of individual's specific prescriptions cannot be given here. In all cases, careful diagnosis should precede training, and the teacher should make adjustment in instructional procedures as a more thorough understanding of a pupil's deficiencies is attained. The suggestions for remedial instruction which follow are so arranged as to indicate possible relations of remedial measures to deficiencies and causes and to show how to select remedial procedures on the basis of a careful individual diagnosis.

I. For pupils who fail to direct attention to content effectively :

Cause	*Remedy*
Overemphasis on oral reading in lower grades.	Silent reading to follow directions or to find answers to questions.
Poorly developed habits of sustained application.	Relatively easy and interesting content.
	Periods of silent reading followed by periods of discussion.
Lack of interest in material.	Periods of silent reading followed by

	periods of discussion in which pupil is led to participate. Material chosen to meet special interests. Material which will help solve some problem in which the pupil is interested. Questions and suggestions. Teacher's brief telling of the story before pupil reads it.
	Completion of story by pupil alone (following arousal of interest by reading part of story). Use of individual hobbies and special interests for motivation.

II. For pupils who do not give sufficient attention to detail.

Cause	*Remedy*
Habits of superficial reading.	Specific directions to centre interest on important points. Questions which direct attention to details.

III. For pupils who interpret inaccurately :

Cause	*Remedy*
Careless or ineffective reading habits.	Practice in reproducing content of short selections.
Insufficient motives for exactness in interpretation.	Practice in following printed or mimeographed directions for making or doing something which the pupil desires to do well. Direction of attention to faults in product due to inexactness in following directions. Rereading by pupils of parts of selections misinterpreted

IV. For pupils who are unable to interpret with facility materials ordinarily assigned to pupils of their grades :

Cause	*Remedy*
Meagre reading experience resulting from absence from school, illness or physical disability, lack of interest, etc.	Variety of interesting reading material of easy gradient.
Retarded mental development	Materials suited to pupil's ability

Poorly developed habits of recognition.	(See suggestions for improving habits of recognition given below).
Unexplained difficulties in the initial stages of learning to read.	(See references to reports of case studies dealing with special deficiencies for sources of suggestions).

V. For pupils who fail to relate reading materials to previous experience and to think independently :

Cause	*Remedy*
Lack of training in using reading as an aid to higher thought processes.	Thought-provoking questions asked either before or after passages are read.
	Relatively easy passages increasing in difficulty as pupil's ability improves.
	Guidance of pupil in the study of problems in subjects other than reading.
	Problems requiring the pupil to compare and contrast his own experience with that of which he is reading.

VI. For pupils with meagre meaning vocabulary :

Cause	*Remedy*
Limited experiential background or limited reading experience	Provide rich direct experiences through field trips, projects, experiments, etc.
	Stimulate wide reading of relatively simple and varied selections. Encourage use of dictionary when unfamiliar words are encountered. Assist pupil to derive word meanings independently by directing attention to content.

VII. For pupils exhibiting inability to cope with new or unfamiliar words :

Cause	*Remedy*
Lack of training in word recognition.	Divide words into syllables to assist pupil in recognizing familiar parts.
	Direct attention to phonetic elements which assist in word recognition.
	Compare unknown words with familiar words containing similar phonetic elements.
	Use words missed repeatedly in quick perception drills.
Lack of training in the use of the dictionary.	Emphasise practice in the use of the dictionary.

VIII. For pupils who are inaccurate in the recognition of familiar words :

Cause	*Remedy*
Eye defects which interfere with visual acuity.	Correction with glasses by competent specialist.
Careless habits of recognition.	Provide practice in careful reading of relatively easy material.

IX. For pupils whose oral reading is jerky and expressionless :

Cause	*Remedy*
Poorly developed habits of recognition.	(See suggestions above for training in recognition).
Failure to direct attention to content effectively.	(See suggestions above for directing attention to content).
Reading materials too difficult speech defects.	Use easier material.
	Provide corrective speech exercises.
	Consult specialist in speech training.
Poor breath control.	Provide training incorrect breathing.
Extreme timidity or self-consciousness while reading.	Set up audience situations which inspire confidence.

X. For pupils who have a narrow span of recognition :

Cause	*Remedy*
Overemphasis on oral reading in lower grades.	Provide practice in rapid silent reading of relatively easy material.
Overemphasis on word drill in lower grades.	Direct attention to thought units by passing pencil under them, as The boy saw the dog and ran away. Drill with flashcard exorcises using familiar phrases. Have pupil read silently as teacher reads aloud emphasizing phrasing.

XI. For pupils whose rate of reading is slow :

Cause	*Remedy*
Difficulties in interpretation.	(See suggestions above for improving comprehension and interpretation).
Poorly developed habits of recognition.	(See suggestion above for improving habits of recognition).
Slow learning in all subjects	Accelerate growth in reading ability by giving extra time to rapid reading.
Slow rate of associating idea and words	Provide timed exercises requiring the pupil to read as rapidly as he can interpret. Provide opportunity for much rapid reading of relatively easy material. Encourage voluntary practice of rapid reading.
Improper habits in the mechanics of reading such as excessive vocalization or excessive head movement.	Explain effects of improper habits and give suggestions for overcoming them.

XII. For pupils who have the habit of rapid superficial reading :

Cause	*Remedy*
Poorly developed habits of interpretation.	(See suggestions above for directing attention to content).
Overemphasis on speech of reading, sometimes resulting in desire to excel classmates in rate tests.	Use exercises for directing attention to content.

Evaluating the Effectiveness of Corrective and Remedial Instruction

Throughout the period devoted to corrective and remedial instruction it is desirable to check frequently the progress of pupils in order to determine the effectiveness of the instructional procedures and to assist in adjusting them to the needs of the pupils. The measures used for this purpose may include : (*i*) The teacher's observations of the reading practices of the pupils; (*ii*) Records of improvement on practice exercises; and (*iii*) Improvement in scores on standardised tests.

Definite records of improvement may be obtained by devoting a few minutes of each reading period to practise exercises which may be scored objectively. Such exercises may be prepared by the teacher or suitable practice materials may be purchased from publishing houses.

It is highly desirable, in evaluating the effectiveness of a programme of corrective or remedial teaching, to administer a battery of standardised reading tests not only at the beginning and at the end of the period of training but also some months after the training has been discontinued. This procedure will enable the teacher to estimate the amount and the permanence of improvement and will aid in identifying the pupils who need continued guidance in reading.

References

1. This chapter is prepared by James M. McCallister, Edith E. Shepherd, and Arthur E. Traxler.

2. *See* also :

   (*a*) Gates, Arthur I., *The Improvement of Reading : A Programme of Diagnostic and Remedial Methods* (New York, the MacMillan Co., 1927).

   (*b*) Gray, William S., with the cooperation of Delia Kibbe, Laura Lucas, and Lawrence W. Miller. *Remedial Cases in Reading : Their Diagnosis and Treatment*, Supplementary Educational Monographs, No. 22 (Chicago, Department of Education, Unviersity of Chicago, 1922).

   (*c*) Monroe, Marian, *Children Who Cannot Read 'Chicago'* University of Chicago Press, 1932.

3. See also :

   (*a*) Gates, Athur, I., *op. cit.*

   (*b*) Gray, William S., *op. cit.*

   (*c*) Monroe, Marian, *op. cit.*

4. McCallister, James M., "Character and Causes of Retardation in Reading among pupils of this *Seventh and Eighth Grade*". *English School Journal*, XXXI (September, 1931), pp. 44-45.

5. See also :

   (*a*) McCallister, James M. and Baker, Grace H., "Corrective Instruction in Reading in Seventh-Grade English Classes," *English Journal*, XXI (November, 1932), pp. 734-43.

   (*b*) Shepherd, Edith E., "Some Silent Reading Lessons in Junior High School English", *School Review*, XXIX (March, 1921), pp. 206-15.

   (*c*) Traxler, Arthur E., T*he Measurement and Improvement of Silent Reading at the Junior - High - School Level* (Chicago, University of Chicago Libraries, 1931).

6. See also :

   (*a*) McCallister, James M., "The Effectiveness of Remedial Instruction in Reading in the Junior High School", *School Review,* XXXIX (February 1931), pp. 97-111.

   (*b*) Miles, Dudley H., "Can the High School Pupil Improve His Reading Ability?" *Journal of Educational Research*, XIV (September 1926), pp. 88-98.

21

Corrective Work in Speech

The speech of an individual reflects his educational, social, physical, mental and emotional status. If his status in one or more of these respects is inferior to or greatly different from the norm of the group in which he moves, he becomes *ipso facto* a possible candidate for remedial speech.

The variations from the norm which are due to a different language environment or to bad speech habits may well be handled by the teacher with no special training in speech correction. Such a teacher, however, should be keenly aware of the futility, and indeed the positive danger, of tampering with many types of speech disorders, which are symptoms of a pathological mental or physical condition. Listed below are several types of speech disorders, which the teacher should refer to a specialist before attempting remedial work.

A. Serious Difficulties, Requiring Specialists

1. The rapid, indistinct, or stuttering speech of the very "nervous" child. This will often be associated with facial grimaces and tics.
2. Hoarseness.
3. The slow, monotonous and partly unintelligible speech of poorly coordinated or partly paralysed children.
4. Extremely delayed or retarded speech.
5. Any form of defective speech in the case of a "sickly", asthenic child. This includes children who have had many severe illnesses as infants or young children.

children suffering from heart disease or from rare, undiagnosed diseases.

B. Difficulties not Requiring Specialists

1. *Voice and its Use :*

(*a*) *Loudness* - Just loud enough for the occasion (not too weak and not too powerful).

(*b*) *Pitch* - An appropriate pitch for the age and physical state.

(*c*) *Quality* - A pleasant quality (not harsh, thin and strained but resonant and pleasant).

(*d*) *Rate and rhythm* - Avoidance of excessive rate and jerky phrasing.

(*e*) *Variety* - Change of pitch and loudness to suit the sense of what is said.

2. *Utterance and Enunciation :*

(*a*) Articulation clear-cut and intelligible (not mumbled)

(*b*) Phrase as unit (not word).

(*c*) *Weak forms* - Unstressed "a", "and", "have" (not A, AND, HAVE).

(*d*) *Sentence pattern* - Speaking according to sense (not sing-song).

3. *Consonants :*

(*a*) Ben's ball (not Pen's pall).

(*b*) not to be omitted - up (not uh).

(*c*) my mama (not by babba).

(*d*) ten (not then), beauty (not beautty).

(*e*) today (not todthay).

(*f*) nine (not dide).

(*g*) kite (not tite).

(*h*) go (not doe).

(*i*) going (not goin and not goingk and not goingg).

(*j*) fine (not pine and not vine).

(*k*) very (not fery and not wery).

(*l*) see (not thee and not she and not he).

(*m*) hilz (not hills), prezident (not president).

(*n*) chores (not shores and not kores).

(*o*) college (not collich), jump (not yump).

(*p*) little (not witto and not liddo).

(*q*) red (not wed and not yed), try (not twy).

(*r*) will (not vill).

(*s*) white (not wite).

(*t*) think (not tink and not fink and not sink).

(*u*) mother (not mudder and not muver and not muzzer).

4. *Vowels and Diphthongs :*

(*a*) "Short A" candy (not cendy), catch (not ketch), can (not kin).

(*b*) "OU" about (not abaut).

(*c*) "Long I" mine (not moin and not mahn).

(*d*) "OI" boil (not berl).

(*e*) "ER, UR, etc." personal (not poisonal), hurt (not hoit).

(*f*) "Short E" again (not agin), friend (not frand), pen (not pin).

(*g*) "Short U" come (not calm), just (not jist).

In dealing with pronunciation we must not forget that in the English language there is no one recognized authority, nor would strict uniformity be desirable if obtainable. Minor variations in sounds or stresses grow up through adaptations to different physical or mental environments. New Englanders, for instance, say *path*, while most other Americans say *path*. Midwesterners pronounce the *r* in *car* while many Virginians leave off the *r* and insert a *y*. *House* in the eastern South approximates *hoos*, elsewhere *hows*. While the London pronounciation runs together the last two syllables of such words as *necessary, library, dictionary,* American usage gives the *a* of the next-to-the-last syllable a secondary accent. Although until the new Webster, the dictionaries required that *address* (noun) be accented on the second syllable, custom is establishing *ad'dress*. In such cases as those cited above insistence by the espousers of one variant upon its adoption by everybody is absurd. Such differences are desirable. They indicate life. Dictionaries should be followed with a judicious ear turned toward the habits of speech of the cultured people of the section concerned. The same liberality, which is advocated in grammatical usage should be applied also to pronunciation.

22

The Place of Electives in the English Curriculum

Definition - Elective courses are semester units, usually of a specialised character, designed to be taken by students in addition to the required work in the subject. Sometimes, where the English requirement is stated in semester hours rather than in units of work, elective courses may be substituted for the regular work of one or more semesters. They carry the same number of recitation hours as the English work of the same semesters and require an equal amount of extra - class preparation.

The Need for Them - Individual differences of ability and of interest are now recognised everywhere - verbally, at least. When we speak of variation in ability we are usually thinking of differences in levels of ability, but we might equally well think of *different directions* in which ability may extend. The vast field of "English" is by no means homogeneous, and some pupils find certain corners of it much more profitable than others. Because of native differences in capacity, because of temperamental bent, because of acquired special interests, one pupil enjoys most, and profits most by, dramatics whereas his neighbour finds dramatics difficult and distasteful but grows almost visibly through experiences in journalism. Admitting that one man's meat may be another man's poison; the school should make some effort to provide each pupil with an appropriate intellectual diet.

Limitations - No more elective courses should be offered than the English staff of the school can make vital. Few instructors are capable of teaching well electives of more than one kind; *e.g.*, speech, and creative writing. The small schools is, therefore, wise to limit itself to a single elective, and certainly should not offer more than one elective at a time.

Pupils should complete successfully at least the work of the tenth grade before substituting any elective for a regular semester's work. Preferably the work of the eleventh grade also should be complete before election is permitted. Few pupils who wish to study English less than three and one-half years have a sufficiently strong interest in the work of any elective course to warrant their taking it. The requirement of a grade of eighty or eight-five in the work of the preceding semester, or a similar average in all English courses, is not unreasonable; but it should always be waivable when in the judgement of the instructor or the principal a special situation calls for such action.

Because of their nature, the electives suggested here should be substituted below the twelfth grade only for semester courses in composition. An exception might be made of creative writing, because, it, like literature, aims so largely at helping the pupils see people and life truly.

23

Electives Courses in Speech

Improvement in conversation should be the paramount aim of high-school courses in speech. To accomplish this, thinking, oral language, and control over meaningful bodily action and voice must be improved. Courses in Direct Address and Dramatics give opportunities for well-motivated speech training.

A. Direct Address

In order to give a student an understanding of the meaning of the term speech, this course might be opened with a discussion which would quite naturally lead to a consideration of the development of speech in the race and in the individual and the relation between the speech code and other codes. Speech may then be divided into its four elements : thought, language, voice, and action, and each student can easily be made to understand that proficiency in each is necessary to effective performance. An analysis of the voice and bodily action of each individual in order that a remedial plan for each student may be worked out should be a part of this introductory work.

Steps in preparing the short speech may be exemplified in speeches of introduction, presentation, and acceptance; in after-dinner speeches, and reports to clubs or committees. The study of the long speech should include speeches of eulogy, inauguration, lectures, and political speeches. Topics of current interest should be discussed briefly and at length.

In addition to worth-while subject-matter and a control of voice and body, the preparation and presentation of the foregoing will require a knowledge of oral language and of different audience attitudes. Differences between oral and written style should be emphasised, and models of speech composition may be studied to discover rules and principles. Pupils should be led to prepare their speeches by making outlines and then rehearsing alone, in order to avoid stilted language and to develop the power to think on their feet.

Speeches aimed at action, belief, entertainment, instruction, and impressiveness may be prepared for audiences with favourable, doubtful, and antagonistic attitudes.

Many of these speeches and discussions may be used in connection with training in parliamentary law, where the elementary principles of conducting a meeting are practised.

Radio speaking makes an interesting part of a course in direct address. Here the additional principles necessary for successful radio broadcasting may be brought out.

B. Interpretation and Acting

If the student has completed the course in Direct Address, it will be necessary only to recall individual difficulties in voice and action. Students who have not had these analyses will welcome suggestions for individual improvement.

Materials for oral interpretation may be selected from readings in literature courses. The characteristics of material, which reads well aloud, may be brought out. Selections, which would entertain friends of different ages and various tastes, may be chosen, as well as those appropriate to the class group. In all practice the purpose, the social motive, of the reading should be kept prominent.

After a choice has been made, selections should be given orally. Training in finding the meaning of the words and in discovering how an understanding of the author's life and experiences add to the meaning of the material should be carefully supervised. All literary and historical allusions should be considered. Students should be encouraged to relate personal experiences, which enrich meanings. They should understand effects of rhythm on meaning. A presentation will be clarified by a clear understanding of the characters speaking and those described, and by clear pictures of the setting and locale of various incidents.

When poems and stories are thoroughly understood the principles of effective voice and action should be applied to the oral presentation.

The second part of this course may be devoted to acting.

The criteria of worthwhile literature should be applied to plays. When plays have been selected, they should be analysed and interpreted in preparation for acting. The suggestions for finding the meaning of interpretative material will be helpful here.

When this has been accomplished, the attention should be turned to assimilation of thought and feeling. Training is given in building up a characterisation. Vicarious living will broaden human experience. Principles of visible action and voice should be applied to acting.

As a background for the acting there should be effective staging. Stage managers, property managers, stage carpenters, electricians, prompters, musicians, advertising managers, salesmen, ticket-takers, and ushers may be chosen from those members of the class whose interests lie in the various fields.

24

An Elective Course in Journalism

High school journalism, launched as an extra-curricular activity by some adventurous pioneers, has by its steady achievement during the last decade earned recognition as an integral and vital factor of the curriculum. A survey of high school publications today reveals six classes or types : newspapers, magazines, handbooks, annuals, anthologies, and publicity pamphlets. The preparation of handbooks and annuals is still carried on in most places as an extra-curricular activity, and the preparation of pamphlets has barely scratched the surface of its possibilities. On the other hand, news writing, advertising writing, magazine writing, and now creative writing are regular subjects of study, either in combination or separately. The elective here described centres about the weekly (rarely daily) newspaper, but a somewhat similar course may be based upon a monthly magazine. Creative writing is provided in a separate elective.

The high school news course presents a field of English expression parallelling life situations to an unusual degree, with ample room for adaptation to individual needs and differences. The news office furnishes a laboratory, the school newspaper a medium of expression, the students and the community an audience, school events and interests live subject-matter. Thus the newspaper enterprise comprises all the essential conditions of learning. The instructor makes learning faster and more certain by introducing information and principles of writing and editing at the time when the students realise their need. And the training goes beyond members of the newspaper staff, from cub reporter to editor, must exercise initiative, tact, accuracy, judgement, insight, and impartiality, as well as linguistic skills. Such a course deserves its increasing popularity.

Specific Objectives

The specific aims of journalism students and their instructors should include development of the following abilities :

A. *In Speech* :

1. To gather all essential data.
2. To ask clear, pertinent questions.
3. To obtain adequate groundwork for a clear statement of facts.
4. To appreciate good humour as a factor in human relationships.
5. To attain a more facile use of language in casual conversation and interview.
6. To eliminate gross errors in syntax, diction, and pronunciation.

B. *In Writing* :

1. To assemble and organise information according to the needs, interests, and demands of senior-high-school students and the members of the immediate community which the school serves.
2. To exercise the art of selection and evaluation in reporting what one has seen and heard.
3. To present clear, well-organised reports : *who, what, when, where,* and *why.*
4. To enjoy doing a variety of types of journalistic work : news stories, editorials, humour column, poems, short fiction, advertisements.
5. To express constructive student judgements and opinions.
6. To write courteous, effective letters of inquiry, information, publicity, announcement, solicitation, and orders.

Suggested Activities

A. Gathering News :

1. Observing special occasions.
2. Interviewing.
3. Attending lectures, plays, and concerts.
4. Reading books, magazines, other newspapers.

B. Writing for Publication :

1. News stories, with leads.
2. Literary and artistic news and criticism.
3. Editorials.
4. Features.
5. Columns.

C. Editing :

1. Making assignments to reporters.
2. Copy reading.
3. Writing headlines.
4. Preparing layouts.
5. Reading proof.
6. Condensing to fit space.

D. Managing the Business :

1. Campaigning for subscriptions.
2. Soliciting advertisements.
3. Buying the printing.
4. Keeping accounts.
5. Distributing the paper.
6. Arranging exchanges.
7. Maintaining editorial and business files.

E. Studying the Job :

1. Analysing and comparing metropolitan, community and scholastic papers.
2. Comparing news, editorial, feature, humour, and sports columns to discover content and style appropriate to each.
3. Comparing effective and weak examples from the same department to discover sources of strength in writing.
4. Securing hints from older practitioners, through lecturers, articles, and books about journalism or phases of it.
5. Evaluating the current issue of their own papers.

25

The Elective Course in Creative Writing

Pupils at various grade levels find a natural meeting ground in the elective class in creative writing. Certainly a few selected pupils from the ninth and tenth grades present no serious differences in ability to do original thinking and writing, and the stimulus of being with older classmen is especially valuable for gifted freshmen and sophomores.

The organisation of courses in creative writing may follow any one of a series of plans. (*i*) It may follow literary types : the short story, poetry, the article or essay, and the play. (*ii*) Its outline may be determined by special subjects or projects : the legends or history of the locality, region, or state, occasional literature such as the production of a pageant or play for school or community use, individual topics developed by the members of the class with the greatest possible freedom, reports on travels or excusions, extended autobiographies. (*iii*) The basis of its organisation may be correlation with other subjects or phases of school life : historic scenes, descriptions and social problems developed in stories, plays, and poems to comment on and interpret the pupil's views of the content and activities met in the work in extra-curricular activities, athletics, science, social studies, languages, music, and the arts; free translation of literature from other languages or creative writing in foreign language; illustration of the creative writing in graphic or industrial arts; dramatisation of a play in the drama class; individual or choric reading of poems in assembly. (*iv*) The course may deal imaginatively with social problems : unemployment, mass production of ideas and goods, social insurance, fascism, maintenance of world peace, equality of educational opportunity, or economic democracy.

Today all of these approaches are being used, either alone or, better, in various combinations. Whatever the plan, its success depends upon the thoroughness with which it is thought through and the readiness with which it is adapted to individual and group needs in each school and community. And however successful any programme may be, the work and the plan of the course must always be a cooperative pupil enterprise and will never be twice the same.

The activities of the classroom generally include much reading and discussion of stimulating literature selected from a world view and including ample contemporary American work, the constant reading (aloud and silently) of student writing produced by other students in the school or in other schools as well as within the class group, discussion of new plans and projects with chief emphasis on content rather than form, talks by local writers, actual writing by the students either alone or as a part of a group enterprise, and group and individual conferences. Cooperation with the staff of the literary magazine and the execution of some class project, such as the compiling by a committee of best writing of the semester or year in an attractive book for the school and town libraries, are valuable major activities. They can often be combined with a final assembly programme in which the creative work of the class is presented cooperatively by the authors and selected groups from the dramatics, speech, and music divisions of the school.

On the book shelf of every well-equipped creative writing class or club are the literary magazines of the school and the community, a wide list of exchanges from other schools, a constant flow of selected books from the libraries of town, school, and homes, and such volumes as :

Younger Poets	Nellie b. Sergent
Creative Youth	Hughes Mearns
Creative Power	Hughes Mearns
Singing Youth	Mabel Mountsier

The Hollow Reed	Mary J.J. Wrinn
Janitor's Boy and Other Poem	Nathalia Crane
A Backward Glance	Edith Wharton
Midwest Portraits	Harry Hanson
The Autobiography of Mark Twain	
My Thirty Year's War	Margaret Anderson
Saplings	Scholastic Publishing Company
The Way of The Makers	Marguerite Wilkinson
Off to Arcady (an anthology containing a section entitled "The Younger Choir")	Max. J. Herzberg
Songs of a Little Girl	Hilda Conkling
Anthologies of high schools	
Contemporary Poetry (excellent introduction)	Marguerite Wilkinson
Raw Material	Dorothy Canfield

Current magazines on the student level, including *Scholastic.*

The important principle throughout is to give each pupil in the group the opportunity to create freely out of his own experience and powers of expression, or to offer him the opportunity not to create, without reproach, since he may be storing up images from experience that he cannot yet translate into words.

All the pupils will be given some instruction in the craft of writing, but not at the price of deadening enjoyment or inhibiting the free flow of ideas. The knowledge of craft must sink out of consciousness before it will function in imaginative writing. Students do not learn to write by first mastering technique, but study of form can always be made a means of increased enjoyment in reading. No pupil should be asked to write a sonnet when he has nothing to say.

In building a class situation favourable to creative production, the faculty leader is in a key position; whenever possible he should be one of those to whom students go naturally with their writing. Quietly, unobtrusively, the must play an alert audience role. In casual meetings in the hall and club, in the street, and in private conference as well as in the classroom, without favouritism or sentimentality, an understanding gradually develops between him and his student writers. They are mutually interested in the serious business of creation. New ideas are mentioned casually, plans for developing stories and poems discussed, revisions tentatively suggested, encouragement given, and strategic places distinguished so that they may be made convincing. The scrawled sketch is always met with interest and acutely examined for the fresh phrase, the vibrating rhythm, and most of all for the significant idea and straight thinking. The high lights of his work are pointed out to the student as the germinal spots in his growth

Fully as important and inseparable from the guidance of the faculty leader is the regular meeting of the group. In this atmosphere of planned informality each writer is led to give the others his own honest emotion and thought; and to receive from them their comment and recognition. He is encouraged to overcome his individualism, to see himself in his social relationships, and out of his experience to find valuable social criticism for the rebuilding of our lives. In this age when the very existence of nations and the future of the major part of the peoples of the earth depends upon creative social thinking, and honest writer for any broad democratic audience will arrive at important conclusions. Suddenly in the midst of worth while reading and discussion the most reticent will have a significant word to say to those who are listening for the heart beat of new life. The way in which it is said will grow inevitably out of the group situation and the thought that is to be communicated. It is this consciousness of his own audience, which makes him "write not for himself but for that other self with whom the creative artist is always in mysterious correspondence."

Reference

1. Edith Wharton. *The Writing of Fiction*, p. 21.

26

An Elective Course in Grammar

This unit is designed to present systematic and logical grammar to those high school seniors who presumably will enjoy it and profit by it. This is not "practical" or "functional" grammar, not primarily "prescriptive" grammar; it is grammar as a body of classified knowledge about language.

I. Such a course might well begin with a historical survey, which would include :

(a) *The nature and function of language* - The theories concerning the origin of language; the language "families", especially the Indo-European; and the nature and field of grammar.

(b) *A brief historical treatment of English Grammar* - This should touch upon the highly inflected Old English, the breakdown of inflections in Middle English, the influence of Chaucer and the King James Bible, the "free grammar of Shakespeare; the grammar reformers of the eighteenth century.

(c) *The American language and grammar* - Differences between the American and the English usage; regional peculiarities; racial influences upon English language in America; survivals of older forms in isolated hill sections; the influence of the newspaper, the "talkies", and the radio upon the standardising of our language and grammar.

(d) *Current usage in English*—Recent and present changes in grammar : sub-junctive and future-tense forms; the "shall-will", "He *don't*" and "It is me" problems; the use of "flat" adverbs, etc.

(e) *Grammar curiosities* - "Fossil" expression (irregular verbs, old plural forms, etc.); elliptical expression (perhaps not "grammatical", but acceptable); expressions in which meaning, rather than grammar forms, controls; idioms.

II. The remainder of the course should be devoted to systematic and descriptive grammar :

(a) *The Sentence* - The completely structure and the elliptical or "truncated" sentence; kinds of sentence. Elements of the sentence : subject, predicate, complements, modifiers, independent elements; parts of sentence : words, phases, and clauses. The rhetoric of the sentence : use of long and short sentences, loose, periodic, and balanced sentences; sentence variety, sentence coherence.

(b) *Parts of speech* - Their nature and functions. "Properties :" declension of nouns and pronouns, conjugation of verbs, comparison in adjectives and adverbs. Verbals : participles, infinitives, gerunds, gerundives. The modes and tenses. The "relation" parts of speech : prepositions, conjunctions, conjunctive adverbs, relative pronouns.

(c) *Concord of parts of speech within the sentence* - Some adjectives with nouns, pronouns with antecedents, verbs with subjects.

The latter part of this course, while treating definitely of the "laws" and rules of formal grammar, should deal realistically with the subject, should present the facts. Grammar is but an attempt to codify the phenomena of language. Its rules are but statements of apparent tendencies and facts; and whenever the rules do not accord with the facts, the rules need to be restated or the exceptions noted. Thus, whether "It is me" is or is not allowable cannot be decided by reference to a grammar "rule" (which is only a generalisation made from supposedly observed facts) but by reference to present acceptable usage. In other words, this unit of grammar should deal with grammar in the scientific and sociological spirit as well as with grammar as logic.

Three methods of approach and study are suggested :

1. Students should be led to observe the facts of language as heard in speech and found in writing, and should make inductions and generalisations from the facts.
2. Comparisons and contrasts with other languages, which the students have learned, should be presented.
3. Books dealing with grammar from the historical, scientific, functional, and logical points of view should be made available to the students and used by them.